Reign of Henry III – 1216-72

London's first waterworks in Westminster

Birth of Geoffrey Chaucer

Henry VII's defeat of Richard III in the Battle of Bosworth Field

Henry VIII's reign begins

English Reformation

Dissolution of the Monasteries

Death of Henry VIII

Birth of W...

Defeat...

Death of...

Inigo Jones designed Covent Garden

Birth of Christopher Wren

12·6 — 1237 — 1343 — 485 — 1509 — 1529-36 — 1536-41 — 1547 — 1564 — 1570 — 1588 — 1603 — 1630 — 1632

1180 — 1200 — c 1200 — 1230 — 1236 — 1280 — 1290 — 1291 — 1338 — 1430 — 1441 — 1480 — 1514 — 1520 — 1530s — 1547 — 1577 — 1580 — 1583 — 1585 — 1587 — 1588 — 1597 — 1600 — 1609 — 1610 — 1612 — 1616 — 1619 — 1631

Completion of Moyse's Hall, Suffolk

Completion of Boothby Pagnell manor, Lincolnshire

Completion of Wilmington Priory, Sussex

Completion of Cressing Temple, Essex, Barley Barn

Completion of Winchester Hall

Completion of Cressing Temple, Essex, Wheat Barn

Completion of Old Soar Manor, Kent

Completion of Stokesay Castle, Shropshire

Penshurst Place, Kent, constructed

Completion of the Wealden house, Chiddingstone, Kent

Herstmonceux Castle, Sussex

Completion of Gainsborough Old Hall, Lincolnshire

Cardinal Wolsey begins constructing Hampton Court Palace, London

Completion of Layer Marney, Essex

Construction begins on Cowdray, Sussex

Completion of Nonsuch Palace, Surrey

Completion of Parham, Sussex

Completion of Longleat, Wiltshire

Completion of Holdenby, Northamptonshire

Completion of Theobalds, Hertfordshire

Completion of Burghley House, Lincolnshire

Completion of Wollaton Hall, Nottinghamshire

Completion of Hardwick Hall, Derbyshire

Completion of Doddington Hall, Lincolnshire

Completion of Pendean Farmhouse, Sussex

Completion of Audley End, Essex

Completion of Chastleton, Oxfordshire

Completion of Queen's House, Greenwich, London, designed by Inigo Jones

Completion of Banqueting House at Whitehall, London, designed by Inigo Jones

Completion of Kew Palace, London

1291 Stokesay Castle, Shropshire

1520 Layer Marney, Essex

1580 Longleat, Wiltshire

1631 Kew Palace, London

...ell manor, Lincolnshire

1338 Penshurst Place, Kent

1588 Wollaton Hall, Nottinghamshire

THE LIFE OF THE BRITISH HOME

THE LIFE OF THE BRITISH HOME

AN ARCHITECTURAL HISTORY

EDWARD DENISON & GUANG YU REN

A John Wiley and Sons, Ltd, Publication

ISBN 978-0-470-68333-0 (hb)
ISBN 978-1-119-94531-4 (ebk)
ISBN 978-1-119-94532-1 (ebk)
ISBN 978-1-119-94533-8 (ebk)
ISBN 978-1-118-31663-4 (ebk)

This edition first published 2012
© 2012 JohnWiley & Sons Ltd

REGISTERED OFFICE

JohnWiley & Sons Ltd, The Atrium, Southern Gate,
Chichester, West Sussex, PO19 8SQ, United Kingdom

For details of our global editorial offices, for customer services and for information about how to apply for permission to reuse the copyright material in this book please see our website at www.wiley.com.

Executive Commissioning Editor: Helen Castle
Project Editor: Miriam Swift
Assistant Editor: Calver Lezama
All photographs by Edward Denison unless stated otherwise in the Picture Credits
All hand-drawn illustrations and plans by GuangYu Ren

Cover design, page design and layouts by Emily Chicken
Printed in Italy by Printer Trento Srl

« Entrance to an Anglo-Saxon hall at
West Stow, showing the central hearth
and the chief's seat against the rear wall.

TO E AND G

ACKNOWLEDGEMENTS

Stories are brought to life by their characters. This story owes its greatest debt to the many passionate, generous and hospitable owners and managers of the sites that so enthusiastically opened their doors to this project. It has been a remarkable collaboration, bringing together a kaleidoscopic assortment of members from Britain's heritage industry. Above all, this book is a celebration of the historic places that are maintained and kept open to the public in the process of extending joy and knowledge to so many. If this story can play even a small part in supporting this endeavour, then we would consider it a success. The contact details of every site can be found at the back of the book (see page 302–3), but we would particularly like to thank the following people and places for their support: Gurminder Kenth at Aston Hall; Dominique Hérouard at the Musée de la Tapisserie de Bayeux; Lisa Hayes at Bignor Roman Villa; Jennie Organ at BioRegional and all those working for BedZED; Beverley Green at Brighton's Royal Pavilion and Museums; Philip Gompertz, Ruth Hudson and all the staff at Burghley House; Maureen Page and Dave Freeman at Butser Ancient Farm; Martin Crossley Evans, Neil Sapsworth and Tom Richardson at Clifton Hill House and the University of Bristol; Heather Ongley at Cowdray Heritage Trust; Essex County Council and Sheila Hennings at Cressing Temple; Elain Harwood and all those at English Heritage; Katherine Oakes and everyone at the Landmark Trust; Philip Davies and the staff at Fishbourne Roman Palace; Victoria Mason Hines at Gainsborough Old Hall; Liesl Barber and everyone at Hardwick Hall; Caroline Harber at the Bader International Study Centre at Herstmonceux Castle; Nicholas Charrington and the staff at Layer Marney; London Borough of Lambeth; Steve Mytton and those at Longleat; Jon Moore, Maz O'Brien and all the staff at Moor Park Golf Club; Norfolk Museums and Archaeology Service including Rebecca Barwick at Norwich Castle and Cathy Terry at Strangers' Hall; the residents of Albert Terrace, Norwich; all the staff and volunteers at Parham; all the staff at Penshurst Place and Gardens; Johanna Bennett and everyone at The Royal Academy of Arts; St Edmundsbury Borough Council at West Stow Anglo-Saxon Village, including Glynis Baxter, and particularly Mary Ellen Crothers for her professional insights; Emma Clarke-Bolton and the staff at Sarah Eastel Locations; Karen Wardley at Southampton City Council; Cathy Clark and all the staff at the superb Weald and Downland Open Air Museum; Hampshire County Council, Suzanne Philby, Gill Clements, Lisa Hole at Winchester Great Hall; the residents of Prince Consort Cottages, Windsor; and Jannette Warrener and all the staff at Wollaton Hall. It is our sincere regret that some important characters originally selected to be part of this story have had to be omitted due to the policies of off-site administrators. Beyond the characters that populate this story, there are so many other people that contributed to this project that it would be impossible to name them all in person, but their omission in no way diminishes our gratitude. Special thanks go to our parents for their unstinting support; Dr Ruth Brown for her invaluable editorial input; all the staff of the Rare Books Reading Room at the British Library; Margaret Richardson; Meg Cox for her suggestions and hospitality; Mark, Helen, Emily and Libby Higgins; Malcolm Cooper; Adrian Forty; Alan Powers; Historic Scotland; Alan for your gentle guidance; Emily Chicken for her excellent design; Abigail Grater for her dependable editorial hand and discerning eye; Julia Dawson for her expert proof-reading, all the staff at John Wiley & Sons, including Calver Lezama, Miriam Swift, Lorna Mein, and last, but by no means least, Helen Castle, for giving us the opportunity to write this book and for her patience, support and invaluable criticism, all of which went far beyond what can reasonably be expected.

CONTENTS

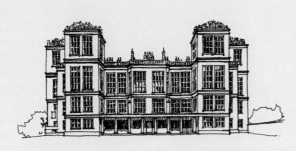
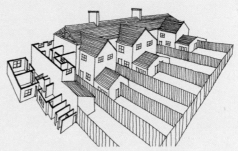

THE LIFE OF THE BRITISH HOME

INTRODUCTION

« The southwest elevation of Wollaton
Hall, Nottinghamshire, commissioned
by Sir Francis Willoughby and completed
in 1588.

… our dwelling houses in our life are only Inns, wherein
wee staie but for a time, but there we shal dwel as in our
proper & natural lodging unto the last day.

James Cleland, The Institution of a Young Noble Man,
Joseph Barnes, Oxford, 1607, p 130

Home – no other word possesses a meaning that is so indistinct
yet so universal. Defining our sense of place, home might be
anything from a physical structure – the rural dwelling of a
peasant farmer or the town house of an aristocratic lord – to an
elusive idea: the memory of a medieval hall or the pervasive pull
of rural retreat. This story about the British home is a journey
through the life of the physical structure and in particular its
plan; it is more about space than place – how the area defined
by the walls and covered by the roof evolved over the thousands
of years since humankind on this island off the coast of mainland
Europe ceased being nomadic and chose to settle. It explores
examples from the kaleidoscopic variety of types from the
earliest known dwellings to the 21st-century 'eco home'.

While the journey offers views of how we have styled, decorated
and filled our homes and the consequences of amassing these
homes to form villages, towns and cities, it is primarily an
exploration of the arrangement of space within the home and
how it evolved in response to our shifting needs and changing
conditions. It reveals the spaces that define home – the rooms
that we have created to help us pursue our private, social
and commercial interests over millennia and the fascinating
solutions that we came up with in seeking the seemingly
simple but ever elusive notions of comfort and convenience.

This story about the life of the British home charts its way
through the dominant types and trends of house planning. It
begins in the fourth millennium BC and ends at the dawn of
the third millennium AD. For guidance along the way, it gives
voice only to characters from each era and relies exclusively
on examples that are both still extant and publicly accessible,
with the exception of streetscapes and multiple-occupancy
housing, where many homes are gathered in a single building.
This deliberate proviso is designed to enable you, the reader,
to experience these remarkable homes beyond the printed page
by discovering them for yourself and finding out how these
individual sites fit into the wider landscape of our nation's
domestic history. From the earliest known settlements on the
remote Orkney Islands to some of the largest residential blocks
in Europe, almost every example illustrated in this journey
can be visited and most can be explored inside and out.

The journey does not claim or seek to be encyclopaedic by
attempting the impossible task of illustrating all types of home

from all periods, but looks instead for what shaped defining or dominant trends in home planning in each period and, in particular, originality, novelty and innovation. Consequently, the Stone Age roundhouse can claim equivalence with the medieval hall as much as the Tudor mansion shares the limelight with the Victorian apartment block, or the Georgian terrace with the Modernist villa. Examples of all these and many other types of home are illustrated throughout this journey, depicted either as photographs to reveal how they appear today or as diagrammatic plans and illustrations to explain how they appeared when they were built.

John Ruskin, the 19th-century writer and art critic, claimed 'there are but two strong conquerors of the forgetfulness of men, Poetry and Architecture'. If this is so, then the British home is either beneath architecture or a symptom of amnesia. Both, to some extent, are valid. The nation's spiritual homes, its cathedrals and churches, enjoy ample appreciation, and the former homes of the powerful and prosperous – the palaces, castles, and mansions – are resoundingly revered, leaving the more humble home comparatively and conspicuously overlooked. The homes of the wealthy few, though legendary, are significant on this journey for their role as pioneers that others emulated, but they were far from being the only examples and even further from being the most common. As William Morris, the designer, writer and admirer of Ruskin, said: 'they differ only in size from the little grey house[s] ... that form the mass of our architectural treasures, the houses that everyday people lived in'. On this journey it is not any single house but the wider idea of home that is given the spotlight, since home is what we all share in common, whether a peasant's cottage, tenant's flat, suburbanite's terrace, city-dweller's town house, aristocrat's apartment, lord's manor, or royal's palace.

STICKS AND STONES

THE ANCIENT ABODE FROM THE STONE AGE TO ROMAN INVASION

Home. There was, quite literally, no place like it until our ancestors switched from a nomadic life of hunting and gathering to a settled life of domesticity sustained by agriculture. During this transition, which took thousands of years, dwellings replaced mere shelters and their habitation heralded the home. In Britain, the origins of the home can be traced to the New Stone Age, or Neolithic period (*c* 6000–*c* 2500 BC), which began around the time that Britain finally became an island cast adrift from mainland Europe by the rising tide of Ice Age meltwater. The consequent development of the home on this island realm traverses nearly six thousand years of history: from isolated Stone Age dwellings built on Britain's periphery in the 4th millennium BC to the highest homes in Europe, built in the 3rd millennium AD, that tower over the nation's capital, one of the largest cities on earth. Launching us on this journey to explore the life of the British home are the earliest examples – the places and spaces in which our settled ancestors, whose forebears had only known how to roam, could call home.

The retreat of nomadism throughout the Neolithic Age and the emergence of permanent or semi-permanent settlements signalled not only the birth of the British home but also the pursuit of agriculture and the taming and organisation of the landscape during the Bronze Age (*c* 2500–*c* 700 BC). Agriculture, in turn, brought about important social and economic transformations in the Iron Age (*c* 800 BC–*c* AD 100). Throughout the thousands of years of early history that are parcelled into the fathomable portions of Stone, Bronze and Iron, the British home was born and flourished.

CELLULAR SETTLEMENTS

The perceived primitiveness of prehistoric dwellings in Britain belies their importance as the first manifestation of the home. The ancient inhabitants of this island were anything but incompetent at construction. Their concerted efforts to undertake ambitious building projects outside the domestic realm were immense and predate many early types of homes. Britain is peppered with hundreds of burial mounds and other sites devoted to rituals, such as Maes Howe in Orkney and, most famously, Stonehenge in Wiltshire, both of which were built in the 3rd millennium BC. The construction of these monumental sites required exceptional devotion to an ideological cause and an unprecedented level of social cohesion and organisation, whereas the emergence of the first settled homes on mainland Britain was consequent on something far more practical – the production of food.

The gradual process of human settlement and the development of agriculture began in remote areas of Britain where there was less competition for resources. Britain's first farmsteads were established at the very limits of the British Isles, on the Orkney and Shetland Islands, where the first known permanent dwellings were built. In this bleak setting and battered for thousands of years by some of the most hostile weather on earth, stands the Knap of Howar, a domestic structure that is not only the oldest home in Britain, but also the oldest standing building in Northern Europe. Dating from the mid-4th millennium BC, this conjoined farmstead predates the earliest Egyptian pyramid by one millennium.

Like the pyramids, the Knap of Howar was built from stone and therefore has survived virtually intact while other structures built from perishable materials that predominate throughout much of the British Isles have long since vanished. Ghostly shadows of postholes on aerial photographs are all that remain of the largest known Neolithic dwelling in Britain – the huge 24-metre-long and 12-metre-wide rectangular wooden structure built at Balbridie (Aberdeenshire). Consequently, the Knap of Howar and other Neolithic sites on the Orkney and Shetland Islands represent a historical treasure trove – a virtual time machine that reveals to those living in the 3rd millennium AD the layout of rooms, formulation of space and even the type and function of furniture of those living in the 4th millennium BC.

Other similarly enlightening homes can be found nearby, including the slightly later dwellings at Skara Brae. Built in the late 4th millennium BC and inhabited until the mid-3rd millennium BC, Skara Brae was not the home of a nuclear family but a sprawling residence for up to fifty people with sufficient numbers of dwellings to form a settlement – one of the first settled farming communities in Britain.

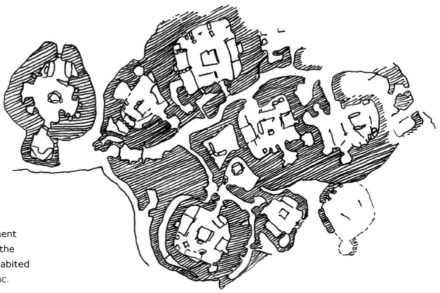

> The plan of the entire settlement at Skara Brae, Orkney, built in the late 4th millennium BC and inhabited until the mid-3rd millennium BC.

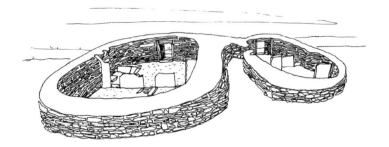

The inhabitants of Skara Brae and Knap of Howar were subsistence farmers who settled much earlier than their contemporaries in southern Britain. Their diet consisted mainly of wheat, barley, beef, mutton, pork, fish and various crustaceans, which they kept fresh and even farmed in stone tanks, supplemented by rare delicacies such as birds' eggs, whale, seal, boar and deer. They also traded pottery and other simple artefacts, such as tools, clothing and jewellery, with other communities in the region.

In both cases, the homes were stone structures dug partially into the ground and interconnected by doorways but without windows. Walls were sunken into middens that surrounded and insulated the buildings, while providing an element of support. The passageways that connected each dwelling were covered in large flat stones, and a drainage system in the floor that carried waste water away from the site could even have been one of the earliest forms of a sanitary domestic lavatory in Britain. The British home would have to wait another five thousand years before accepting a permanent place for this convenience. Roofs were made from a variety of perishable materials including driftwood, whalebone, earth, seaweed and hides, and the floors were laid with flagstones, creating a basic but cosy interior.

Although Skara Brae comprised eight family dwellings compared with two spaces at Knap of Howar, both were arranged in a cellular fashion, where separate living spaces were conjoined by doorways or passages. The two spaces at Knap of Howar are oblong in plan, one being a living space and the other a workshop. Thin upright flagstones divided the living space into two roughly equal parts, one of which contained a hearth and was used for food preparation. The workshop was similarly partitioned into three separate spaces. At Skara Brae the earliest dwellings were roughly circular with beds and dressers recessed into the walls. Later structures were more rectangular with round corners and their beds protruded from the walls into the living space. Not all the structures were for living in – one appears to have been a workshop.

Each of the living spaces at Skara Brae was defined by a cruciform layout. At the centre, physically and symbolically, was the hearth, providing light, warmth, a means of cooking and even a spiritual significance. If a dwelling was ever reconstructed, which many were, the hearth, which invariably was orientated on a southeast/northwest axis, remained unaltered. Orientated in this way the four sides of the building, marked by an entrance adjacent to a dresser and two beds opposite one another around the central hearth, corresponded to the four principal temporal moments of the year – midwinter sunrise and sunset and midsummer sunrise and sunset. The entrance was always aligned slightly off-centre to the right of the central axis, its stone door being lockable from the inside using a pole that fitted into holes in the door jambs. Behind the door was a stone box for storage that also had the function of directing people into the right-hand portion of the space, suggesting that the left-hand side might have been more private. The bed to the left of the hearth was always slightly smaller than that on the right, indicating that it was reserved for the female. On the wall adjacent to the entrance was a stone dresser, whose role is unknown but given its prominent location it must have surpassed mere storage.

Towards the end of the Neolithic Age, the dwellings at Skara Brae declined, replaced by smaller yet similarly cellular structures. These were the forebears of the roundhouse. The transition can be seen at Jarlshof, on the Shetland Islands, where the remains of over four millennia of domestic development that ended in the 1600s AD with the construction of a house by James V's grandson, Earl Patrick Stewart, can be observed. The earliest settlements at Jarlshof were overlaid by generations of settlers throughout the Bronze and Iron Ages. These settlers created a tradition of building roundhouses lasting centuries, which ended with the wheelhouse in the era that followed the Roman invasion of Britain. The wheelhouse gains its name from the radiating stone piers extending approximately halfway to the centre of the space that resemble the spokes of a wheel and supported the walls and roof. Although wheelhouses were a complex form of stone roundhouse, their partially sunken features meant that they possessed none of the perpendicular grandeur of the roundhouse.

From the middle of the 2nd millennium BC, the increasing tendency towards long-term settlement resulted in land division and the gradual proliferation of permanent homes. During the last centuries of the Bronze Age, from 1300 BC to 800 BC, land in much of Britain became more strictly controlled. Linear boundaries and field systems were established. Homesteads were constructed and occupied on a semi-permanent basis. Economically, agricultural production was shifting from self-sufficiency to surplus. By the Iron Age, at a time when Ancient Greece was in its prime and the Roman Empire was in its infancy, these processes had caused a significant increase in the density and permanence of settlements across Britain. Iron Age settlements, once they were established, tended to stay in use.

‹ View of the Knap of Howar, Orkney, built in the mid-4th millennium BC, showing the internal configuration of the two spaces.

⌄ The internal configuration of a dwelling at Skara Brae, Orkney. Note the covered bed (right), central hearth with meat curing above, cupboard behind and thatched roof.

In an era marked by significant rises in population, with millions of extra mouths to feed, agricultural production and intensity had to increase. A cycle of productive reciprocity emerged that propelled Iron Age Britain into a period of rapid development. For example, the introduction of iron into the ploughshare improved its effectiveness and played an important role in agricultural intensification, which helped to satisfy a growing population increasingly engaged with the extraction and processing of raw materials. This in turn improved standards of living and revolutionised established technologies such as the cartwheel or ploughshare. During the Iron Age, Britain experienced a proto-industrial revolution that sustained levels of population and development that would not be experienced again until the late-Anglo-Saxon period.

Agricultural surpluses and improved manufacturing techniques boosted regional trade, which led to the accumulation of wealth and power. As more and more people settled in larger and larger groups, tribes were established. Social hierarchies in and between tribes became more complex as interaction with other groups led to trade and warfare. Defence, something that had not concerned the inhabitants of Knap of Howar or Skara Brae, became a vital consideration in domestic planning.

The major changes taking place in Iron Age Britain played a significant role in the transition from a cellular collection of family settlements to the individual disconnected roundhouse in a larger community. This transition can be seen in the Orkney Islands at Bu, Pierowall and Quanterness, where some of the earliest stone-walled roundhouses in Britain were built. These early types evolved into complex roundhouses that were first built on Orkney around 500 BC before appearing on the mainland and western islands of Scotland. Complex roundhouses were larger and more sophisticated in their construction than their simpler antecedents and became the first British homes to possess intramural stores, stairs and galleries. However, despite the changes on the outside and in their method of construction, the interior of the roundhouse altered little from the dwellings in earlier cellular settlements. Both are approximately circular with a central hearth around which cooking, eating, socialising and sleeping took place in often different spaces separated by partition walls of stone or wooden screens.

Domestic structures throughout much of mainland Europe at this time were dominated by larger rectangular houses. The roundhouses that proliferated along the Atlantic coast were the exception to this rule. In Britain, the reverse was true – the roundhouse was the rule and the dominant dwelling type for over two thousand years. The roundhouses on the Shetland Islands are the northernmost examples of a tradition of Atlantic roundhouses that extended as far south as Portugal during the

Iron Age. Furthermore, here on Britain's northern periphery evolved a distinctive and complex version of the roundhouse that reached its apogee in the broch, a tall dry-stone tower whose retrospective appellation in the 9th century AD from the Viking word *borg* meaning 'fort' belies its true domestic function and its ancestry in the lineage of the roundhouse.

THE BROCH

The broch is a building type that is unsurpassed in Britain, even to this day, for its sophisticated use of dry-stone walling and internal arrangements. These Iron Age skyscrapers were built from approximately 200 BC to AD 200 and appeared predominantly throughout north and west Scotland. More than mere defensive forts, brochs were domestic structures of a scale and complexity hitherto unknown in Britain. The best extant examples include the partial remains at Dun Carloway (Lewis, 9.2 metres high), Clickhimin (Shetland, 5 metres), Dun Dornaigil (Sutherland, 6.7 metres), and Duns Troddan and Telve (Glenelg, 7.6 metres and 10 metres), but the most complete and largest of all is the 13-metre-high broch at Mousa (Shetland).

The broch's common characteristic is its tower-like structure composed of a massive double-skinned wall containing storage rooms and internal wooden galleries, and topped with a conical roof. Accommodating animals and humans under one roof as well as the various functional requirements of the home, the broch was a prehistoric version of the mixed-use high-rise in 21st-century cities – a residence, a place of work and a place of leisure.

Entrance into the broch was through a low passage up to seven metres long that penetrated the two layers of thick dry-stone wall. A wooden door halfway along this passage would have provided secure access and prevented draughts from reaching the inner

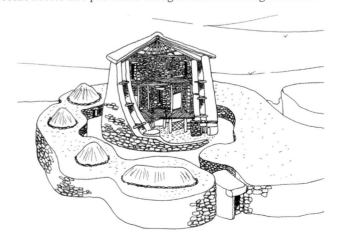

> A cut-away illustration of a broch showing possible internal arrangements including animal stables on the ground floor, raised first floor and mezzanine level, and cavity walls. The surrounding settlements would have been a later development.

chamber. Towards the end of the passage was a small room or pair of rooms that might have controlled access not only into the broch but also into the intramural staircases that led to the upper floor. They might also have been a form of prehistoric coat cupboard where visitors could leave their heavy fur clothing before entering the snug interior. The broch's windowless double skin acted like double glazing by creating an intermediate void between the freezing weather outside and the warm air inside, heated not only by the hearth but also by the livestock that lived on the ground floor. The dry-stone cavity wall also protected the structure from the driving rain that could easily penetrate one layer of dry-stone walling and prevented damp from reaching the inner chamber. The intramural gallery extended all the way down to the ground level in some brochs, while in others it terminated at the first-floor level that stood on a base of solid stone containing storage spaces. Storage was also a likely function of the intramural gallery, much like the ancient stone-lined souterrains. Another feature of this cavity was that, as the wall rose, its width decreased. The internal staircase therefore sometimes only served the first floor, as the narrowing void did not allow human access above this level. For access to any higher level or to the roof it would have been necessary to use a stair or ladder within the chamber.

Internally the size and arrangement of brochs varied considerably. Some were up to 10 metres in diameter. Some had their principal floors on the ground level, while the inhabitants of others occupied the first floor and reserved the ground floor for animals. Upper floors were made of wood laid on rafters that were supported on wooden posts in the ground and rested on or were suspended from stone scarcements in the wall. Long structural timbers did not exist in areas where brochs were constructed, so these ledges allowed the rafters to be much shorter than the width of the void and would be placed off centre to create partial floors, like a form of mezzanine.

The centre of the space was occupied by a hearth, where it was either situated in the middle of the ground floor or placed on a bed of stone or sand on the wooden upper floors. Raising the hearth on a bed of non-flammable material was also common practice in boggy or lake-based dwellings, such as crannogs or the swamp dwellings at Glastonbury and nearby Meare (Somerset) that were built on raised wooden floors. The smoke from the hearth would have been used to cure meats hung across the central chamber and, as with all early dwellings, it would fumigate the thatch roof as it permeated it, preventing infestations and damage from feasting birds. No ventilation hole was necessary in the roof as this would have had the undesirable effect of drawing up sparks from the hearth which would have set light to the thatch. The weight of the roof was supported structurally on the inner wall with the eaves extending beyond the outer wall to ensure the cavity remained watertight.

All brochs were circular in plan – the circle provides the strongest and most structurally sound base for a tower. Mousa, the only broch to survive to its full height, has a plan that is almost a perfect circle, though its walls in relation to the internal space (which is comparatively small in diameter) are thicker than any other roundhouse-type structure in Britain and therefore more capable of supporting the considerable load of a tall stone tower. The skills required to construct the dry-stone tower at Mousa are superior to most other roundhouse-type dwellings and therefore suggest the acme of a vernacular building tradition.

Later brochs in the north rather than in the west of Scotland tended to cease being isolated structures and instead stood among a group of smaller dry-stone dwellings. These formed a village-like settlement that was defensively encircled by an outer wall and ditches beyond: the early physical evidence of a shift from age-old passive communities to an increasingly volatile and violent society. Up to twenty of these broch settlements have been discovered, the most extensive and complex being Gurness in Orkney, which, by the 1st century BC, was large enough to accommodate thirty to forty families. Entrance into the settlement was gained via a gatehouse which provided access into the passageways that led directly to the broch and indirectly to the separate dwellings. Each dwelling differed in size and in some settlements had a little yard where smaller livestock, such as pigs, sheep and chickens, could roam. In plan, these supplementary settlements around the base of the broch recalled the cellular settlements on Orkney from three thousand years earlier, and their interior arrangements, unlike the broch itself, possessed similarly standardised fixtures and fittings.

THE ROUNDHOUSE

The broch's construction was so exceptional that until recently it was believed to have been imported by rich, powerful and conquering elites rather than to represent the most complex manifestation of the local roundhouse and the most skilled example of domestic construction in Britain up to the end of the Iron Age. Elsewhere in Britain, roundhouses might not have been so spectacular, but they could be every bit as sophisticated. Despite regional variations in size and construction, Bronze and Iron Age roundhouses throughout southern, western and northwestern Britain possessed a number of common characteristics that link them to the Atlantic roundhouse tradition. In theory, the roundhouse comprised two parts – a cylindrical wall beneath a conical roof – but variations on this theme would have been caused by all sorts of other factors, such as availability of materials, local building techniques, and climate. The evidence that exists of wooden roundhouses sheds light only on the most substantial structures that would have been the homes of the most prestigious, powerful, or largest families.

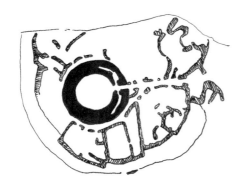

∧ The plan of a broch showing the thickness of the walls in comparison with outlying dwellings.

≫ A collection of different-sized Iron Age roundhouses reconstructed at Butser Ancient Farm, Hampshire.

> The interior of a regularly sized roundhouse at Butser Ancient Farm, Hampshire, with an inner ring of load-bearing posts and non-load-bearing walls.

∨ Illustration showing the different elements of a typical roundhouse.

The homes of the vast majority of the population, as occurs throughout history, surrender to neglect or vanish beneath subsequent layers of development, leaving no trace behind them. Therefore, while the roundhouse often attained an exceptionally high degree of sophistication in both wood and stone, most of the population lived in considerably more humble and probably even pitiable dwellings throughout the Bronze and Iron Ages.

Bronze Age roundhouses were less complicated and less structurally regular than their Iron Age successors, but the principal factor determining the form of this building type remained consistent and concerned the practical matter of how to support the roof. With some roundhouses reaching 20 metres in diameter, a conical roof of wooden rafters and wet thatch pitched at the minimum angle of about 45 degrees necessary to provide rainwater run-off could easily weigh in excess of 10 tons. Raising this roof structure above the ground safely and securely was a problem that taxed the minds of Bronze and Iron Age builders and led to a variety of extraordinary solutions. The case of the Atlantic roundhouse of northern Britain, whether complex or simple, has already demonstrated how a broad outer wall of stone negated the problem of bearing a heavy roof structure. The same was true in southwest Britain, where stone was also the predominant and most practical building material, but in areas

The internal roof structure of a large roundhouse at Butser Ancient Farm, Hampshire, which would have weighed in excess of 10 tons. Note the ring-beams of bound sticks tying the different lengths of rafters together as they rise to the apex of the roof. Only seven rafters actually reach the top.

where wood was the principal material used in the construction of houses, the solution impacted on the internal configuration of the home and the domestic functions performed in that space.

The smallest and simplest roundhouse type was a circular structure less than roughly seven metres in diameter – anything larger than this and the sheer weight of the roof bearing down on the walls would demand an alternative solution to an exterior load-bearing wall of stakes infilled with mud-rendered woven wattle screens. The interior of these smaller dwellings would have been open-plan, with a central hearth around which the family would cook and eat, while the periphery of the circle would be reserved for sleeping. Indeed, the 6th-century BC Cretan philosopher Epimenides described the family as 'those warmed at the same hearth'. As the building increased in size, the stakes or small posts were insufficient for carrying the roof.

More substantial posts were needed and these were fashioned from small or young tree trunks. These load-bearing posts were arranged in a circle and, depending on the diameter of roundhouse, they either formed the principal components of the external wall or they were freestanding columns inside a larger space. In the latter case, the external walls would be non-load-bearing panels of woven wattle and daub between stakes driven

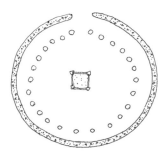

∧ The interior of a small and lightweight roundhouse at Butser Ancient Farm, Hampshire, similar to those built in Glastonbury, Somerset. Note the load-bearing walls and absence of an inner ring of supporting posts.

∨ The plan of a typical roundhouse showing the inner ring of supporting posts and central hearth.

lightly into the ground and secured under the rafters of the roof, forming a weatherproof curtain wall. All load-bearing posts were dug into the ground at their base, and their tops attached to the roof at a horizontal ring of smaller wooden sticks which formed a ring-beam that also secured and strengthened the rafters as they converged towards the apex of the roof.

Roundhouses grew to exceptionally large proportions during the Iron Age, the grandest, boasting monumental porticoed entrances, appearing in the West Country. It was common for these structures to have a diameter of over 15 metres, providing an internal floor area of nearly 180 square metres. These dwellings would have risen to over 10 metres high. With so much internal roof space it is likely that mezzanine or secondary floors were incorporated into the largest roundhouses, with the ground floor being used for livestock and the upper floors used for human habitation, much like some of the brochs.

Internally, these large roundhouses were not simple open-plan dwellings with a central hearth. At Bu, the early-Iron Age stone-walled complex roundhouse in the Orkney Islands, large up-ended flagstones acted as partition walls and divided the 10-metre-diameter interior into a series of smaller spaces that could be accessed by movable doorways of wood or woven

∧ A monumental roundhouse at Butser
Ancient Farm, Hampshire, modelled
on the excavations at Little
Woodbury, Wiltshire.

branches. Humans occupied the centre and part of the periphery of the circular space, which contained the hearth and areas for sleeping, cooking, food storage and entertaining, while animals occupied the rest of the periphery. In later complex roundhouses in northern Britain the stone walls were several metres thick and contained the intramural storage spaces and stairs that were a feature of broch construction and hint at secondary floors. In the wooden roundhouses of central and southern Britain, the internal configuration is harder to determine since partitioning, if it existed, was made of perishable materials such as wattle and daub or hide screens. Nevertheless, certain salient features such as a central hearth, accommodation of livestock, and some form of porch or entrance did recur, and the essential functions of domestic life – storing, preparing and eating food, entertaining and sleeping – were always accommodated.

HILLFORTS AND *OPPIDA*

The roundhouse was the most common type of home in Iron Age Britain and was invariably an element of a larger collection of dwellings that formed a settlement. As the Iron Age progressed, there was a growing tendency, especially in southern and central Britain, towards a more established nuclear

∧ The interior of a large roundhouse
modelled on the excavations at
Little Woodbury, Wiltshire.

form of an unenclosed settlement. Increasing trading links
with Continental Europe brought about new opportunities and
threats. In response to the changing conditions that characterised
the rapid development throughout the Iron Age, roundhouse
settlements tended to be sited within protective areas such as
enclosed homesteads or more substantial hillforts. Emerging in
the 7th century BC as Britain began to experience widespread
socio-economic change, hillforts were built on prominent
geological sites encircled by ramparts of wood, as at Danebury
in Hampshire, or stone, in the case of Chalbury in Dorset. Most
comprised small agricultural communities engaged in basic
domestic activities, but increasingly these activities extended
far beyond the settlement boundaries, demonstrating the major
restructuring of the landscape and the increasing complexity
of Iron Age society, especially in southern Britain. Developing
at the expense of other settlements, hillforts attracted more and
more inhabitants, becoming centres of power and wealth and
assuming a spiritual and commercial significance. Ritualistic
sites and large subterranean grain silos were often a feature of
hillforts, making them important local or even regional centres
of religion and trade and essential focal points for the safe
storage of the fruits of increasing agricultural productivity.

Towards the later stages of the Iron Age, the prominent hillfort was abandoned in favour of a larger and more formal settlement: the *oppidum*. Over a hundred years before the Roman invasion, Julius Caesar visited Britain twice, in 55 and 54 BC. Observing the large Celtic Iron Age hillforts and their clustered settlements encircled by wooden fences and defensive ramparts, he described them as *oppida*, likening them to those he had seen in Gaul. *Oppida* were the earliest manifestation of towns and not only unique to Britain but also the predominant settlement type across much of mainland Europe, including what is now Spain, France, Belgium and Germany.

Although *oppida* were also defensive settlements containing many roundhouses and other communal structures and amenities, they were often sited near river crossings, such as Dyke Hills (Oxfordshire), Salmonsbury (Gloucestershire), Wheathampstead (Hertfordshire) and Winchester. They also occurred on major land routes in southeastern Britain, suggesting a greater interest in trade than in conflict and a strengthening of ties with mainland Europe, particularly with the Atlantic trade route that entered Britain through the Solent. Extending over several square miles, these settlements were more diffuse than the concentrated urban models of Greece or Rome. Rectilinear street patterns and buildings, and an evident public realm and public institutions hinted at the first signs of urbanisation in Britain. Following the introduction of coins from Gaul in the early-2nd century BC, some British *oppida* even began minting their own currencies, which bore the name of the settlement, such as Calle (Calleva – today's Silchester, Hampshire), Camulo (Camulodunum – modern Colchester) and Ver (Verulamium – now St Albans).

The transformations associated with Iron Age Britain were not isolated occurrences confined to the British Isles, but were inescapably bound to events taking place in Europe. With the Roman Empire on Britain's doorstep following Julius Caesar's conquest of Gaul in the mid-1st century BC, Britain became increasingly drawn into a vast commercial sphere of influence extending as far south as Africa and as far east as the Baltic. Although the formal Roman conquest of Britain did not start until AD 43, it was already well under way in the 1st century BC where the tribes of southeast Britain were enjoying new-found wealth and prosperity as a result of their proximity to their new neighbours across the channel. As the Roman influence on British society in the century before Claudius's invasion intensified, it had an increasingly significant impact on the domestic realm, as the British home stood on the brink of the most significant changes it had ever faced.

ROMAN HOMES AND THE NEWFANGLED RECTANGLE

ROMAN BRITAIN AD 43–410

The Roman occupation of Britain is often viewed as an anomaly. Entirely novel and often revolutionary building methods, social customs and administrative practices are seen to have accompanied Emperor Claudius's arrival in AD 43 and just as quickly disappeared over four hundred years later with the Romans' official departure in AD 410. The Roman Empire is often portrayed as a blip in British history – an unwelcome visitation by an outsider on a reluctant host and one of only two successful invasions of this island in the last two millennia. However, the lasting impact of the Romans' influence upon Britain's subsequent urban and rural development challenges this overly simplistic portrayal. The extensive road network they laid, the urban street patterns they planned, and the sophisticated buildings and unprecedentedly comfortable homes they erected might not have been maintained by the Saxons, but they left an indelible mark on the landscape that can still be seen clearly to this day, and in their wider Empire they set a standard that every subsequent epoch tried to emulate.

Far from being an anomaly, the Roman era represents a strong thread in Britain's rich historical tapestry, providing many links between its Celtic predecessor and its Saxon successor. The foundations of many sophisticated Roman settlements, which continued to develop long after Roman withdrawal, were laid on Britain's largest *oppida*. The Celtic *oppidum* at Oram's Arbour, for example, became Venta Belgarum under Roman rule, which evolved into Winchester, the Saxon capital of Wessex. For the British home and its aggregation in urban settlements, Roman influence in Britain is less a story about an aberration than one about continuation.

URBANISATION

The original characteristics of the British home during Roman occupation are inescapably bound to urbanisation. In Iron Age Britain, the population had lived almost entirely off the land, with Celtic *oppida* representing the origins of large settlement in Britain, but the Romans accelerated this growth, elevating it to a process of urbanisation throughout the country. In doing so, they introduced to Britain the idea of what the Greek philosopher Aristotle referred to as the *polis*. Possessing administrative, legislative and commercial functions, a *polis* was, for Aristotle, the 'finished fabric of society reaching, as near as may be, the bound of perfectness'. Anyone outside the *polis* was either above or below humanity. Invoking Homer's famous words and underscoring the bond between the home and civilisation, Aristotle describes this piteous outsider as 'clanless, lawless and hearthless'.

For the Romans, this image of incivility could have been an apt description of the British. The peripheral province of Britannia was regarded as something of a cultural backwater inhabited by a boorish populace. The Roman historian, Lucius Cassius Dio Cocceianus, used Queen Boudicca, seen by many as the ultimate Briton, as an example of her country's crudity, citing her disgust with Romanised Britons and her disparaging description of Romans as 'men who bathe in hot water, eat prepared delicacies, drink unmixed wine, anoint themselves with myrrh, lie on soft couches and sleep with boys for bedfellows – boys past their prime at that'.

Romans viewed civilisation and urbanisation as two sides of the same coin. Gnaeus Julius Agricola (AD 40–93), the Governor of Britannia from AD 78 to 85, used urbanisation as a way of gaining favour with the locals and strengthening Roman rule. By Romanising the local population and instilling Roman values and customs in native Britons, Agricola established an urban class. His efforts, though successful, were promoted further by his son-in-law, the renowned Roman historian Caius Cornelius Tacitus. In his book devoted to his father-in-law, Tacitus praises Agricola for taming Britain's barbarian tribes, 'reconciling them to quiet and tranquillity' through the building of 'temples, courts of justice, and dwelling-houses'. Once his regime had instilled Latin and Roman habits in the British nobility, 'the toga was everywhere to be seen', despite its unsuitability to the British climate. Agricola's methods also stimulated an insatiable appetite among Britain's elites for Roman comforts – 'those luxuries which stimulate vice; porticos, and baths, and the sumptuous banquets'. Eyeing this emulation critically, Tacitus mocked the British for believing they were now civilised when 'in reality, it constituted a feature of their slavery'.

Whether civilised or slaves, Romanised Britons inhabited very different homes from their more primitive, but nevertheless free, forebears. Whereas before Roman occupation the British home was chiefly characterised by the roundhouse, the thriving Roman town extended the size, type and function of the home. With a rising population that exceeded 3 million by AD 400, Roman Britain accommodated a wider range of inhabitants with different occupations and domestic needs than ever before. The most renowned and novel home in Roman Britain was the villa – the ultimate expression of personal status and civilised domesticity, as well as a hub of commercialised agricultural enterprises linking town and country. Villas were therefore located in the country, but within easy reach of towns where their produce was sold. Powerful and wealthy villa owners enjoyed a dual residence, tending either to their political duties in the town or their commercial business in the countryside.

In the towns, urban elites, soldiers and imperial administrators enjoyed the comforts offered by Roman life and constructed a standard of home that had hitherto not been seen on British soil.

Bricks, drains, hot water, trussed and tiled roofs and mosaic floors were unprecedented novelties. Even the homes of urban artisans represented a very different space to that of the Celtic farmer. Rather than sharing their homes with livestock, the artisans shared their homes with proto-industrial machinery housed in integral workshops resembling an early form of cottage industry that remained a feature of some British homes up until the 19th century. The increasing production of a wider variety of artefacts and a monetised economy extending far beyond Britain's shores greased the wheels of commerce that ran more freely on the newly laid roads connecting trading centres across the country and ports, whence produce was shipped to mainland Europe and beyond.

Urbanisation in Roman Britain, as occurred throughout the Roman Empire, was also an important measure of cultural sophistication. The status of different towns was strictly hierarchical. At the base of this proto-urban pecking order was the *vicus* (eg Dorchester-on-Thames), the smallest type of self-governing settlement. *Vici* were particularly abundant on the periphery of the Empire, such as in northern England around military garrisons along Hadrian's Wall. Unplanned and informal in their layout, they resembled a Roman version of what would, by the late-medieval period, be described as a village – an informal, small and self-sufficient settlement composed of a collection of farmsteads.

Next on the hierarchy was the tribal *civitas*. Sixteen in all, these were the most numerous type of settlement in Roman Britain. *Civitates* were self-governing civil and administrative centres in former tribal areas and invariably a regional hub of commerce and culture. Whether they had pre-Roman origins, like Winchester and Canterbury, or they were founded by the Romans, like Wroxeter and Cirencester, their development depended on some form of military fortification. Responsibility for the provision and maintenance of the public realm rested with the locally elected councillors, or *decuriones*. These were

∧ Mosaic sequence depicting a gladiatorial
fight on the floor of the dining room at
Bignor Roman Villa, West Sussex.

wealthy nobles and town residents who had to personally
finance the construction and maintenance of public buildings,
recouping costs through locally administered taxes. Towards
the end of the Roman period, *civitates* were predominantly
residential settlements, some even becoming the largest towns
in Roman Britain with populations of up to 15,000.

The next level of settlement type was the *municipium*, but Britain
only ever had one of these: Verulamium, now St Albans. Above
municipia and representing the primary Roman settlement
type was the *colonia*, established by imperial charter for Roman
citizens and war veterans. Roman Britain possessed four *coloniae*.
The first was Colchester, or Camulodunum, which, prior to the
Roman invasion, had been a base of Britain's most powerful
tribe and site of a large *oppidum*. Colchester was Emperor
Claudius's first and primary strategic objective when launching his
invasion in AD 43. It was here that Claudius witnessed Britain's
official capitulation; six years later its status was elevated from
a garrison to a *colonia* – Britain's first urban civilisation and the
capital of the new Roman province of Britannia. Colchester was
furnished with lavish public and private buildings, including
magnificent houses, theatres, temples, an early Christian church,
and the only known Roman circus in Britain. It was here too that
the Romans planned Britain's first rectilinear street layouts and
used stone and mortar to construct extravagant buildings whose
magnificence would have dumbfounded the native population.

The second British *colonia* was Lincoln, or Lindum, followed
by Gloucester, or Glevum, and, over a century later, York, or
Eburacum. The great anomaly among major Roman settlements
in Britain was London, or Londinium. Growing rapidly from
nothing but fields before the Roman invasion, London became
one of the most important urban settlements in Roman Britain
and the pre-eminent commercial centre. Although London
officially was neither a *civitas*, nor a *municipium*, nor a *colonia*,
it bore an overwhelming influence and has had an unparalleled
impact on the life of the British home ever since.

THE ROMANO-BRITISH TOWN HOUSE

The difference between homes in Iron Age *oppida* and those in the countryside was not in their form but in their number. In Roman Britain, no such lack of distinction existed. The homes in large settlements under Roman occupation were altogether more civilised constructions than the worst type of fetid hovels belonging to subsistence farmers scattered throughout rural Britain and far beyond the influence of these emerging towns. The Roman town house and its exemplary rural counterpart, the villa, represent the foremost examples of originality in the life of the British home under Roman rule.

Throughout the Roman period, most Britons lived in simple huts that altered little from their Iron Age predecessors. These would invariably be round or oval in plan and, depending on the region, would be built of wood, wattle and daub, or dry stone, with a roof of thatch or turf and a floor of rammed earth or wood. Internally the space was open except for a pillar supporting the roof. Larger dwellings would have required more pillars to support the roof, in the manner of Celtic roundhouses. No partitioning defined the different daily functions such as cooking, eating and sleeping, though life revolved, quite literally, around the central hearth.

Any ambition among aspirational peasants in Roman Britain for better domestic conditions would have been revealed in the appearance of straighter walls that indicated an inclination towards rectilinearity. In domestic planning, the transition from pre-Roman to Roman Britain was marked by the quiet shift from the circular to the rectangular plan. The Roman invasion might have precipitated many changes in Britain, but for the Iron Age farmer one of the most basic was their acquaintance with the corner of a building.

Britain's adoption of rectangular homes, as were the norm on mainland Europe, was actually under way before the Roman invasion, which, just as occurred with urbanisation, merely hastened the process. Nobody knows for certain what caused the shift from circular to rectangular homes. Most people continued living in small and invariably modest dwellings that, if they retained their circular form, did so for good reason. Compared with the rectangle, the circular plan has many benefits. It is more robust, as corners are always points of structural weakness. It is more weatherproof, especially in resisting high winds that are a feature of the Atlantic coastal region. And the most spatially efficient plan is the circle, since it requires less building material to produce the equivalent internal floor area. Nevertheless, despite these advantages the rectangle prevailed and the roundhouse retreated into obscurity.

Perhaps the rectangular plan better suited a growing population with shifting social and economic habits. The changes that characterised late-Iron Age Britain put pressure on established communities, and the roundhouse with its circular plan was particularly awkward to extend or modify. Conversely, if the inhabitants of a rectangular home outgrew its four walls or needed to add extra spaces for the purpose of creating, for example, an artisan's workshop, they could replace one wall and extend it outward with comparative ease instead of building an entirely new structure. Following the Roman invasion, any inclination towards rectangular homes could be attributed to Romanising pretensions among Britain's aspiring population. This spirit of emulation reached a cultural high-water mark in the late 3rd and early 4th centuries that was not experienced again for a further millennium.

If rectilinearity was a novel concept to the rural farmer, the Roman town in Britain would have presented a profoundly alien landscape. With streets laid out in a grid system of perpendicularly arranged thoroughfares on to which rectangular buildings fronted, and with formal public spaces laid out as squares containing grandiose civic architecture, the Romano-British town was, quite literally, from another world. Often located on sites of former military forts and with street patterns deriving from earlier military settlements, Romano-British towns were not as densely populated as towns in many other parts of the Empire. Many possessed *area*, which was vacant land inside the city walls, as well as *territorium*, which was similarly vacant land, but cultivated.

Within these protective walls, an emerging class of artisans and economically autonomous merchants and powerbrokers enjoyed a degree of prosperity hitherto not experienced in Britain. A variety of small industries flourished, such as glass-making, weaving, earthenware production, metalworking and tanning, making the settlements virtually self-sufficient economically. A wide range of buildings, or *aedes*, were constructed to accommodate these new activities as well as novel housing types to live in or to rent to tenants.

Aedes were Roman town houses, comprising a row of two or three interconnected rooms constructed in wood and clay and roofed in thatch or tiles. Positioned perpendicularly to the street so as to maximise street frontages, the lines of rectangular buildings created narrow alleyways between buildings. Many town houses provided a combination of residential and commercial use, where the ground floor contained shops or stalls that opened out on to the street and could be covered by an awning. Artisans sold their wares from wooden stalls either on the street or behind a large opening in the wall that formed a miniature veranda, while also working in workshops to the rear of the building. At night everything could be packed away and shuttered up. Accommodation was shared with the working areas or could be located separately upstairs if the building had more than one storey.

High densities of closely packed and highly flammable buildings exacerbated the risk of major fires, which occurred with relative frequency in towns such as London and Colchester. Urban conflagrations provided the stimulus for progressive changes to building methods and regulations. Stone became a more common construction material and buildings were spaced further apart. A height limit for buildings of 18 metres was imposed by Emperor Nero in AD 64 following the great fire of Rome, reduced from 21 metres which Emperor Augustus had imposed over half a century earlier.

As Romano-British towns evolved, so too did the homes within them. As the needs of inhabitants outgrew the simple rectangle and more rooms were required, the economy of scale caused the plan to develop into a winged or courtyard configuration with an external corridor providing access to the rooms. Such buildings would have been among the largest category of urban homes, or *domus*, which were owned by the very wealthiest urban elites.

Most city-dwellers lived in small, simple houses of the winged or courtyard variety. When urban densities prohibited further outward sprawl, the only way to develop was upwards, giving rise to the apartment building, or *insula*. As a word meaning 'island', *insula* was also used to describe a city block. These multistorey high-density homes constructed by commercial landlords rarely, if ever, occurred in Britain's relatively low-density towns, but rose to eight or nine storeys in the largest imperial cities such as Rome. One of the tallest known buildings erected by the Romans in Britain was the three-storey tower at Stonea Grange in Cambridgeshire, but this was a public rather than a domestic building. Offering comparatively cheap rents that descended as the building ascended, the speculative nature of the large, often unsound, and hazardous *insulae* caused them to be ridiculed by the poet and satirist Decimus Junius Juvenalis (Juvenal, AD 65–140), who wrote in *The Evils of the Big City*:

> Here we live in a city which is supported by rickety props;
> that's how the landlord's agent stops it falling ... 'sleep
> easy!' he says, when the ruin is poised to collapse ... your
> third floor is already smoking; the last to burn is the man
> who is screened from the rain by nothing except the tiles,
> where eggs are laid by gentle doves.

THE ROMANO-BRITISH VILLA

It is tempting to assume that the Roman villa with its hot baths, glass windows, sumptuous decorations and central heating swiftly usurped Britain's humble, ancient and annular dwelling in a process of civilisation that swept the British Isles from the 1st century onwards, but such temptations should be resisted, for

Roman villas constituted a tiny minority of Britain's domestic building stock. It is their remarkable sophistication rather than their number that makes them stand out in the history of the British home.

Villas were agricultural institutions owned by wealthy landlords, who amassed their fortunes from rents and dues paid by their workers and tenants and by the income derived from the surplus their estate was obliged to produce. This surplus was sold at market in the nearby town, where other essential supplies and specialised items could be obtained. Such a vital connection between the town and country had never occurred before, and after the Roman withdrawal it did not occur again in Britain until the emergence of the great country houses of the 16th century, whose owners, like their Roman predecessors, enjoyed great wealth and power while experiencing the best of urban and rural living with extravagant residences in both places.

As a structure, the Romano-British villa was eminently varied. As a building type it extended the length and breadth of the Roman Empire – from Northumbria to Sudan and from the Atlantic Ocean to the Black Sea. Even the Romans seldom used the term 'villa' to describe the type of building with which the title is commonly associated, preferring instead *aedificium*, meaning 'building'. The Roman scholar and writer, Marcus Terentius Varro (116–27 BC), exploited the nebulousness of the word 'villa' when using it as the focus of debate between two characters in one of his stories. Noting that a building's location outside a city did not make it a villa and that there was no difference between the simple farm and a luxurious villa, the protagonists concluded that 'any estate was a villa from which profits from pasturage were drawn, whatever the source'. The essential characteristic of a villa then, irrespective of its physical make-up, was its agricultural function.

Unlike the Celtic farmstead which was entirely self-sufficient and separate from the town, the Romano-British villa's dependence on the town caused it to be located on or within easy access to major roads. Despite being built for military purposes, Roman roads subsequently played an important role in assisting trade, and many inns or *mansiones* were built along them. The siting of villas depended not only on good roads but also on good agricultural land – particularly for the growing of cereals – and a source of running water. Occasionally villas were also sited near to proto-industrial activities, such as stone quarries around Bath and Bristol, metal mines, or potteries as occurred at Water Newton (Durobrivae) in Cambridgeshire where the famous Castor ware was manufactured.

Collectively, the typical villa with its surrounding agricultural land, *ager*, was known as *fundus*. Used to denote any form of elementary unit, *fundus*, the home and the soil, constituted the basis of an ideal life in Roman times. The word was also used in reference only to land by the poet Quintus Horatius Flaccus (Horace, 65–8 BC) when he made his case for a healthy body and mind and argued against the amassing of wealth: '*domus et fundus*' or 'house and farm'.

Villas and their adjoining estates would be owned by wealthy landlords who either lived on the site with their families or managed the estate *in absentia* through a resident bailiff. In Britain, ownership of the villa estate was more commonly held by Romano-Britons than Romans, who would have retired to Rome after their tenure in the province. Villa estates provided employment and a means of living for the many families of freemen, tenant farmers (*coloni*), landless peasants and slaves who farmed the estate. The land, all of which was now under imperial jurisdiction, was divided into strips approximately 100 metres long, unlike the early Celtic fields that were arranged in squares. These had started to change and become more productive since improved methods of ploughing had been introduced from the Belgae tribes who arrived in Britain from northern Gaul (now Belgium). Rents were payable to the landlord either in labour, produce or money. Over time, the production of an agricultural surplus on villa estates cultivated a form of rural aristocracy.

The physical character of villas reflected Britain's social fabric in the early Roman period. Both were comparatively simple; the villa comprising a basic rectangular wooden-frame structure infilled with wattle and daub, covered with a thatched roof and accommodating a basic family unit with a small number of labourers or slaves housed either inside the main building or in outhouses shared with the animals. The physical influence of early Romano-British villas, particularly those in southeast Britain, developed not from the heart of the Roman Empire, but from the Low Countries. The home in Roman Britain and its development throughout the half-millennium of Roman

> A typical Romano-British corridor villa made of a combination of stone, wood and plaster, reconstructed at Butser Ancient Farm, Hampshire.

∧ One of the rooms inside a typical corridor villa at Butser Ancient Farm, Hampshire.

occupation therefore remained quite distinct from the Roman archetype. Masonry was used only very rarely in Britain in the 1st century AD, and although the use of stone increased, especially in the foundations of more substantial dwellings, and clay tiles or slate replaced thatch as villa construction proliferated following the swift growth of Romano-British towns from the late 1st century AD, the typical Mediterranean villa type with its internal courtyard was a model very rarely seen in Britain.

The original rectangular domestic unit comprising a row of individual rooms, such as at Park Street in St Albans, Ditchley in Oxfordshire and Lockleys in Hertfordshire, was imported from Northern Europe and was distinct from the typical Roman model that was planned around a large single room or hall, as occurred at Kingsweston in Bristol. Nevertheless, the acceptance and rapid proliferation of the villa type demonstrated a willingness among Britons to become Romanised in a process that paralleled the Celtic roundhouse's evolving rectilinearity. Resistance to Roman occupation and Romanisation exemplified by Boudicca's Iceni tribe in East Anglia may have had something to do with the relative paucity of villas in this part of Britain, but such defiance was uncommon, and when all freemen in Britain became citizens of Rome in AD 212 following Caracalla's *Constitutio Antoniniana*, Britain's Romanisation was entrenched further.

Villas can therefore be found throughout much of England, with the highest concentrations in the south.

Within a generation of the Roman invasion, the number of early villas in southeast England proved Britain's consent to a fundamentally new and different way of life that would lead to its complete integration with the social and economic institutions of the Roman Empire. This process of assimilation effected dramatic changes to the plan and layout of the home, as well as the social functions within it. Humans, animals and agricultural produce were increasingly housed separately. At first the animals and produce were removed to detached buildings, but later divisions occurred among the different people within the home as social hierarchies caused the partitioning of landlord's and workers' accommodation. Comfort, a feature of the home that we take for granted and that had not previously existed, became an important consideration in the planning of the modern Roman home of the 2nd century AD. Modern amenities and furnishings such as underfloor heating, running water, drainage, mosaics, paintings, glass windows and colourfully painted plastered walls were all elements of a trend towards comfort that reached ostentation in the largest and wealthiest homes.

As the Romano-British villa evolved and expanded along with the changes to the family structure, the villa acquired wings and a corridor that provided independent access to the growing number of rooms (eg at Lockleys, Park Street, Brixworth (Northamptonshire) and Hambledon (Hampshire)). Corridors could be arranged internally or externally, in the form of a wooden veranda. With wings at either end of the main body of the house, the basic plan became symmetrical with the entrance located centrally within the overall scheme. It is likely that these wings were occasionally constructed in the form of towers rising to two or even three storeys. A hall would often be sited directly inside the entrance, but no two villas were the same, despite the basic symmetrical H-shaped plan remaining the

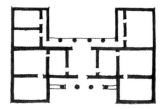

∧ The plan of a typical Romano-British winged corridor villa showing possible configuration of individual rooms.

＞ An illustration of a typical Romano-British winged corridor villa.

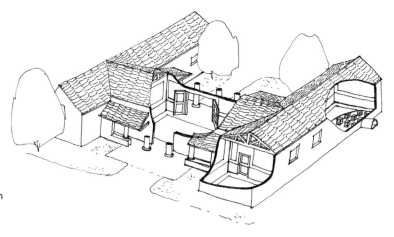

∧ The remains of the Roman bathhouse at Bignor, West Sussex.

pre-eminent type up until the 4th century. The first Romano-British villa known to have been built complete with wings rather than evolving from a rectangular form was 'Building B' in Oxfordshire, constructed in the late 1st century AD.

No preference had yet emerged for the internal configuration of rooms and the location of different functions within the villa, such as cooking, eating, sleeping, bathing and entertaining. Meals, prepared on stone hearths in integral kitchens, were eaten from low-standing tables by guests reclining on low couches or straw cushions warmed by the underfloor heating. The Roman system of central heating made sleeping on cushions on the floor or low wooden beds a nocturnal experience with a comfort hitherto not experienced by Britons.

Bathing was another uniquely Roman practice that introduced to Britain unprecedented standards of hygiene which, after the Roman withdrawal, were not achieved again for over a millennium. Bathing was easily accommodated into existing villa compounds by extending the wings or building bathhouses separated from the main villa. Wood- or charcoal-fired hypocausts providing underfloor and cavity-wall heating for the villa could be altered to meet the requirements of the various rooms of a bathhouse.

Bathing in a Roman villa was not simply a case of a quick bath: it was an elaborate procedure. The process began with disrobing in the *apodyterium* before a cold plunge in the *frigidarium*. A rubbing down and oiling in the warm *tepidarium* followed, preceding a rise in temperature with a hot bathe in the *caldarium* and a steaming in the *sudatorium* before a return to the *frigidarium* for the final nerve-shattering cold plunge. The bathhouse, like many domestic refinements afforded by the Romano-British villa, was a privilege enjoyed only in the country, as water sources in the towns were insufficient for domestic use. City-dwellers used instead the communal Roman baths which in Britain reached their apogee in the city that earned its name from this shared activity – Bath.

The wealthy villa owner wishing to expand their residence beyond the winged type tended, rather than extend the wings, to link their ends with an additional structure, creating an internal courtyard, as at Gadebridge Park or Dicket Mead in Hertfordshire. An evolution of this kind was the most common way in which courtyard villas in Britain materialised. Bignor in West Sussex, North Leigh in Oxfordshire and Chedworth in Gloucestershire were among the most developed examples of this building type in Roman Britain, which reached its zenith in the late 3rd and early 4th centuries. At Bignor, the first dwelling structure was a simple wooden hut that burned down and was replaced by a stone building. Over time this evolved into one of the largest villa complexes in Britain, with over fifty rooms arranged around a central courtyard and all luxuriously decorated with fine mosaics and underfloor heating even in the dining room.

Rarely were courtyard villas the result of an individual set-piece design. Only in the very largest and most opulent examples, such as the palace at Fishbourne in West Sussex, was an entire courtyard structure planned and built from scratch. These were afforded only by the wealthiest and most powerful families who would have had imperial connections beyond the province of Britannia. The owner of the palace at Fishbourne was the compliant British King Cogidubnus of the Regni tribe, whose capital was at nearby Chichester. Fishbourne is the earliest example of Britain's encounter with the novel art of architecture in the domestic realm, where, as so often occurred throughout history, it never matched the public buildings erected during the same period.

A dwelling type that was distinct from the courtyard or corridor-type villa and which might have evolved from the separate barn-like structures on the larger estates was the aisled house, characterised by a single rectangular room with two rows of pillars supporting a large trussed roof. Sometimes these appeared to be structures subordinate to larger villas, like at Empingham

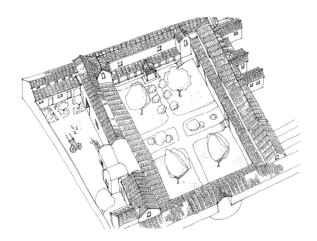

The collapsed floor of the heated dining room in the Roman villa at Bignor, West Sussex, revealing the hypocaust beneath.

An illustration of a large Romano-British courtyard villa based on the excavations at Bignor, West Sussex.

in Rutland, Mansfield Woodhouse in Nottinghamshire or Winterton in Lincolnshire. Elsewhere they were independent villas, as at Denton, Ancaster, Barholm and Wilsthorpe, all in Lincolnshire. The basic structure resembled the basilica and although it is thought to be a hybrid of the villa, its relatively free plan made it a flexible space suited to domestic and agricultural uses independently or combined, accommodating the landlord, bailiff, workers, produce, livestock and even farm machinery such as corn-drying kilns.

The high point of villa building in Britain, like the designs themselves, did not correspond to that in the rest of the Empire, nor did it correspond to the situation facing Romano-British towns. As conflict plagued much of Central and Western Europe in the 3rd century, Britain's physical isolation not only afforded it a degree of immunity but also brought about increased wealth from the rising cost of foodstuffs owing to a drop in production throughout Europe. Britain's prosperity at this time was almost unique in the Roman Empire and consequently attracted landowners from the Continent seeking to escape the troubles there. After a period of relative decline throughout the 2nd and 3rd centuries during which many villas deteriorated or were abandoned, Britain's remaining wealthy landlords got wealthier still and spent their new-found riches on larger homes furnished with even more luxurious fittings. The laying of mosaics, that most conspicuous and enduring sign of aspiration in the domestic realm that until now had been far more common in town houses and public buildings, increased throughout the late 3rd and early 4th centuries, as did their size and sophistication. The largest ever found in Britain was at a villa in Woodchester in Gloucestershire, which used over 1.5 million pieces in its depiction of Orpheus. Having been the exception rather than the rule, domestic mosaics depicting all manner of popular scenes from hunting to mythology became *de rigueur* among Britain's super-rich.

DECLINE

The prolonged wars and frontier campaigns that were weakening the Roman Empire finally caught up with the relatively isolated province of Britannia. Falling revenues from decreasing production and the resulting burden on the public purse caused taxes to rise. The powerful councillors on whose wealth the maintenance of civic life in Romano-British towns depended were exposed to the increasingly crippling financial demands from the state while suffering diminishing returns from the local populace. These elite and once coveted social positions could now lead to personal ruin and became actively avoided. Those who could, retreated from the waning towns to live out their years in the countryside in the quietude of villa life or left Britain altogether and returned to safer havens within the shrinking Empire. Commercial decline was reflected in the silting up of the major ports at London and York, and in the demise of a cash economy. The main mint in London stopped continuous production in AD 325, many years after the closure of the mints at Colchester and Wroxeter.

Sensing Rome's downfall, regional tribes intensified their attacks on British soil. Raids by Saxon armies increased from the mid-4th century, by which time Romano-British towns were in a permanent state of decline. The full retreat of Roman forces was inevitable and the final word came from Emperor Honorius. In response to pleas from the Britons to normalise ties with Rome in AD 410, he instructed them to 'look to their own defences'. Britain was on its own.

The decline of the Roman Empire had been long and slow, and, with Germanic tribes led by Attila the Hun threatening Rome itself in the mid-5th century, Honorius's chilling instruction had little bearing on the inevitable train of events that eventually terminated any further Roman influence in Britain; it merely officialised the end. By AD 420 the tribal leader Vortigern had assumed the role of sovereign ruler of Britain and invited Hengist and Horsa to settle in Britain and help him in his struggle against the encroaching Picts and Scots. His plan backfired when Hengist and Horsa mutinied and cemented Anglo-Saxon dominance.

The life of the villa owner became unsustainable. The economic system on which villas relied had disintegrated. Roads that connected the villa with the town fell into ruin as the engineering skills required to maintain them no longer existed. Even self-sufficiency became fanciful, as raids from hungry peasants or barbarian tribesmen made life on these isolated farmsteads a risky business. Many villa owners retired with their families to the relative safety of the towns despite the obvious deterioration there too, leaving their villas in the hands of former labourers or to decay.

The Saxon cleric and historian, Gildas, in *The Ruin of Britain* provides one of the lengthiest accounts of Britain's transition from Roman to Anglo-Saxon rule:

> All the major towns were laid low by the repeated battering of enemy rams; laid low, too, all the inhabitants – church leaders, priests and people alike, as the swords glinted all around and the flames crackled. It was a sad sight. In the middle of the squares the foundation-stones of high walls and towers that had been torn from their lofty base, holy altars, fragments of corpses, covered (as it were) with a purple crust of congealed blood, looked as though they had been mixed up in some dreadful wine-press. There was no burial to be had except in the ruins of houses or the bellies of beasts and birds.

Writing less than one century after the events, Gildas provides the closest account of Britain during the early Anglo-Saxon period, but his version is an elaborated story. The mass slaughter that was supposed to have drenched Britain in blood probably did not happen. Just as occurs in any transition of power by military means, there was bloodshed, but it was not in the apocalyptic form that Gildas describes. Evidence of population, economic and urban decline indicates a much longer and slower demise.

When compared with other historical periods, what the Romans achieved in domestic planning and design, albeit only enjoyed by a tiny proportion of the population, was remarkable. The Romans had elevated the status of the home to unprecedented heights. Its physical and conceptual construction employed the art of architecture for the very first time; a role, as with glass windows, that would not appear again until the late medieval period. Indeed, when one considers other elements of the domestic realm, such as the innovation of central heating or the flush lavatory, such comforts were not commonly enjoyed in Britain until even later, in the 20th century. For the home, the descent that accompanied Roman withdrawal was sometimes literal as well as metaphorical, as domestic buildings in Britain regressed a thousand years, often becoming circular sunken hovels before rising again in the form of the medieval hall.

‹ A mosaic at Fishbourne Roman Palace, West Sussex.

› Fishbourne Palace, West Sussex, as it would have looked like in the 1st century AD.

WOODEN WALLS AND FLEDGLING HALLS

ANGLO-SAXON AND VIKING BRITAIN
c AD 410–1066

« The interior of an Anglo-Saxon hall at West Stow, showing the hearth and the chief's seat at the farthest end from the entrance.

After centuries of strengthening social organisation marked by improving economic conditions, better communication and increasing urbanisation, the Roman withdrawal from Britain foreshadowed fragmentation and disorder. Instability and the pervasive threat of conflict undermined the cohesion that had existed under Roman occupation. Eager to fill the vacuum created by the collapse of the Roman state were disparate tribal groups without centralised social or political structures. Their power base, like the Celts long before them, but unlike their Roman predecessors, was bonded to the land rather than the town or city. For the home, this transformation in the way of life in Britain was immersed in the countryside where the home assumed a central role in the domestic, social and political life of smaller clan-based communities. Out of this transition and after centuries of slow development emerged a multifunctional space that was to dominate the home for the next thousand years and which still survives, at least in name, today: the hall.

The hall was a unique space and a focus not only of the home, but also of medieval society. Roman society had been highly centralised and relied on public institutions and spaces in urban centres, such as temples, basilicas, forums and markets that were distinct from the private realm of the home. In the medieval era the hall was a space in which home and public life converged – a theatre wherein life's affairs were played out – a place of public administration, a venue for social revelry, and a place of privacy.

TRIBAL BRITAIN

In the early 5th century, Britain was an irresistible prize eyed eagerly by potential predators. From the west came the Scotti, from the north came the Picts, and from the east came the Angles, Saxons, Jutes and Franks. For centuries these neighbouring tribes had been on the receiving end of assaults and slave raids by Roman armies, but the tables were turning. Wealth was buried in the ground as populations were steadily displaced or, worse still, stolen into slavery – the most famous victim of which was a boy named Patrick, the 16-year-old son of a Roman official who lived on the banks of the River Severn, who was taken from his family home to Ireland where he would later become the patron saint.

These incursions were the opening salvo in what would be over half a millennium of tribal rule in Britain dominated by the Angles and the Saxons, whose combined titles came to be synonymous with England and whose peoples came to refer to themselves as *Angli*, or *English*. Under the Angles and Saxons, Britain was divided into seven major tribal regions – the Anglo-Saxon heptarchy: East Anglia was populated by the Angles; the Mercian kingdom dominated the Midlands; the combined kingdoms of Deira and Bernicia occupied Northumbria; Wessex was home to the West Saxons; in Sussex were the South Saxons; in Essex were the East Saxons; and in the southeast corner of Britain was the wealthy and powerful kingdom of Kent.

Accompanying the arrival of Germanic tribes in Britain was a Germanic way of life that prized the bucolic over the urban. Single-roomed Germanic dwellings of thatch and wood stood in stark contrast to the multi-roomed Roman corridor or courtyard villas with their tiled roofs and stone walls. 'It is well known,' remarked the Roman historian, Tacitus, in his book *Germania*, 'that the nations of Germany have no cities ... They do not even tolerate closely contiguous dwellings.' Instead, the 'rude masses without ornament or attractiveness' were created by Germanic tribes who were 'wont to dig out subterranean caves, and pile on them great heaps of dung, as a shelter from winter and as a receptacle for the year's produce'. Although Tacitus's remarks were by this time nearly half a millennium old, there is no reason to suppose that the subject of his observations was not the model from which the sunken-featured timber structure, formerly known as the *Grubenhaus*, emerged to form the basis of the Anglo-Saxon home in Britain over the succeeding three centuries and, in turn, became the antecedent of the medieval hall.

In the 5th century the last remnants of Roman life gave way to a new era of Anglo-Saxon cultural ascendancy. The collapse of slavery and a return to the land built the foundations of the peasant agricultural system that supported Anglo-Saxon society. The basic element in this system was the family unit living on its farmstead. For towns and cities, which had been in decline for years, their fate during the first half of the century was abandonment and few were repopulated until the end of the century or even later. The 6th-century historian, Gildas, in *The Ruin of Britain* wistfully observed: 'the cities of our land are not populated even now as they once were; right to the present they are deserted, in ruins and unkempt'. For immigrants arriving in Britain, familiar only with building in perishable materials such as wood, wattle and mud, the bewildering splendour of former Roman stone structures was the subject of legend, as the Anglo-Saxon poem, *The Ruin*, conveys lugubriously:

> Wondrous is this masonry, shattered by the Fates. The
> buildings raised by giants are crumbling. The owners and
> builders are perished and gone ... There were splendid
> palaces, and many halls with water flowing through
> them; a wealth of gables towered aloft. Many were the
> banqueting halls, full of the joys of life – until all was
> shattered by mighty Fate.

Ruin was not only the subject of wistful musings by Anglo-Saxon writers; it was a popular literary theme for those whose

∧ The sunken-featured building showing the interior and sunken pit under the wooden floor.

survival was threatened by the Anglo-Saxons and the change they brought about. In different parts of Britain and at different times throughout the Anglo-Saxon period, instability reigned. The home, more than ever, became a place of refuge. The destruction of the home and in particular its hearth was a common metaphor for society's wider decline. In *An Elegy of the Death of Urien of Rheged* the 6th-century Welsh poet, Llywarch Hen (Llywarch the Old), used the despoliation of the hearth to amplify the sense of grief and loss at a vanished civilisation: 'Is not this hearth, where goats now feed? Here chatt'ring tongues, with noisy speed, Once talk'd around the yellow mead.' Llywarch's poem was written for his cousin, the former Cymric hero, King Urien, of the Kingdom of North Rheged in Cumbria, and depicts a vivid picture of a bygone age characterised by chivalry, hospitality and feasting enjoyed by Urien and his faithful band of warriors:

> Is not this hearth where emmets crawl?
> Here blazed the torch upon the wall,
> Around the crowded banquet-hall.
>
> Is not this hearth, where swine have plough'd?
> Here once bold warriors' tongues were loud,
> As mead-cups pass'd among the crowd.
>
> Is not this hearth, where scrapes the hen?
> No want was here among the men
> Of brave Owen and Urien.

Although Llywarch's poem was written in the 6th century for his fallen cousin, the use of the hearth and hall signifies their sanctity in the domestic context. As essential features of the home, they would reach their peak long after the demise of the Anglo-Saxons and would remain central facets of the British dwelling up to the 16th century.

THE RECTANGULAR HOME

The hall that the Anglo-Saxons brought with them from mainland Europe, unlike the hearth, was novel to Britain. Although it was similar to the earlier roundhouse in serving the functions of the home by providing a single space accommodating the family unit, it was dissimilar in supporting various other functions of a more complex society than its Iron Age predecessor as well as, not insignificantly, being rectangular. More than a home, the hall had both a private and public function, providing a place of work, business and entertainment. The steady evolution of the hall was one defining characteristic of the Anglo-Saxon period in Britain, which began with the wholesale importation of the humble rectangular wooden dwelling over a sunken pit and concluded with the great royal halls of Yeavering in Northumberland, Cheddar in Somerset, Cowdery's Down in Hampshire, and Northampton in Northamptonshire.

The defining dwelling type of the early Anglo-Saxon period, particularly from the 5th to the 7th centuries AD, was the sunken-featured building. The main characteristic of this type of structure was the 30-centimetre- to 1-metre-deep pit beneath a suspended wooden floor, which helped to mitigate damp by allowing air to circulate and extended the life of the building to between thirty and forty years. Sunken-featured buildings were typically rectangular in plan, their length being approximately twice their width. Sizes ranged from the diminutive (2 metres by 1 metre) to the capacious (up to and even beyond 10 metres long). The roof was supported on wooden posts set into the base of the pit. The number of posts depended on the size of the structure. Smaller structures had one post at either end supporting the gable, while larger structures would have had up to six forming a frame with wooden trusses inside the roof. At ground level, a floor of wooden planks was laid across and often beyond the pit walls, to meet the walls of the building. Regional variations were considerable, but exterior walls were invariably made from evenly spaced small timber posts infilled with screens of wattle and daub, or staves laid side by side and the gaps between them filled with mud or clay, or radially split planks that, if constructed well, required no infilling. Another function of the pit, especially in the deeper varieties, was the storage of non-perishables, where the subterranean void created a form of early undercroft or cellar, echoing the pit silos of Celtic hillforts which were sealed with clay to form an aerobic environment in which food could be stored.

Another contemporaneous Anglo-Saxon dwelling, similar to the sunken-featured building in scale and form, dispensed with the pit. Instead, the roof was supported by load-bearing posts embedded in trenches or post-holes. Screens of wattle and daub or planks of wood filled the spaces between the posts to create external walls. In bigger and more prestigious structures, such as royal households, the walls would have been fabricated entirely from tongue-and-grooved wood rendered with daub and the supporting posts braced with buttressing.

Curiously, while both the sunken-featured building and the post-hole structures derived from European origins, Anglo-Saxon Britain had no aisled structures, which were common in Europe and had even appeared in Britain in pre-Roman times, such as the Neolithic hall at Balbridie in Aberdeenshire. Both forms of Anglo-Saxon dwelling in Britain, whether in a rural or later urban context, relied on timber construction, which was a consistent feature of non-religious Anglo-Saxon building.

∨ The interior of an Anglo-Saxon family dwelling at West Stow Anglo-Saxon Village, Bury St Edmunds, Suffolk, showing the supporting posts set into post-holes beneath the raised timber floor.

» Collection of reconstructed Anglo-Saxon dwellings at West Stow Anglo-Saxon Village.

Timber was so essential in the building process that it formed the root of the Anglo-Saxon verb 'to build', *timbrian*, and was the most consistent feature of Anglo-Saxon building in Britain from their arrival up to the Norman Conquest in 1066, along with the thatched roof that covered these buildings, the ubiquity of which is revealed in the German word for roof, *Dach*.

Internally, Anglo-Saxon homes whether of the sunken-featured type or post-built type varied little, irrespective of size or location. The inner area was rarely formally subdivided; family and guests shared the interior space. A hearth formed the social and domestic focal point, around which the family and guests would eat, drink and be entertained. People would sleep on hides or straw-filled mattresses on the floor or in bordered areas in the corner of the house.

As communities grew and society became more complex, the concept of the rural village emerged from the 8th century, comprising a larger dwelling similar to a hall and owned by the wealthy and landed *eoldermen* or *thegns* with contiguous smaller domestic structures or bowers occupied by the families of lesser-ranking *ceorls* (freemen) and farmers. Other buildings, that might have included a church, accommodated different functions, such as workshops for the weaving of textiles or manufacture of pottery, for example, or for the storage of foodstuffs.

Consequently, the Anglo-Saxon home, rather than being a single structure in the manner of earlier roundhouses or Romano-British villas and town houses, often comprised more than one building, with a main hall surrounded by outlying and detached structures. Tacitus hinted at this in writing about the German way of life, suggesting, with veiled disdain, that 'every person surrounds his dwelling with an open space, either as a precaution against the disasters of fire, or because they do not know how to build'. Belittling the constructional acumen of these barbarian tribes was expected of a Roman who, in describing their domestic habits, claimed that the bravest and most warlike among them did nothing while 'surrendering the management of the household, of the home, and of the land, to the women, the old men, and all the weakest members of the family'. A woman's role was to ensure the smooth running of the household, by cooking, baking, brewing and weaving, and her rights were by no means ignored in a society that was relatively egalitarian when compared with the succeeding Norman culture. The men, however, according to Tacitus, were 'so fond of idleness [and] so averse to peace'.

Increasingly, the rural Anglo-Saxon timber home with its roof of thatch or mud amassed in greater concentrations as life in Anglo-Saxon Britain became more settled and ordered. Unlike in Roman Britain, this tendency towards early forms of urbanisation had little impact on the physical character of the Anglo-Saxon home, which remained fundamentally unchanged; only the size and number of structures varied to accommodate the needs of the family or the wider community.

The catalyst for the first permanent, settled, non-rural Anglo-Saxon communities in Britain was religion. Christianity had been a feature of late Roman Britain, but the supremacy of paganism led to Rome sending the Benedictine monk, Augustine, on a mission to convert Britain to Christianity in AD 597. To do this he first had to convert the Kentish King, Æthelberht. Kent's proximity to Europe and its strong links to Jutish and Frankish royalty made it the richest, the most powerful and the most culturally advanced region of Britain, elevating its king to the position of overlord of Britain, or Bretwalda. According to the Anglo-Saxon historian, Bede, King Æthelberht offered Augustine 'a dwelling place at Canterbury' and, invoking Classical parlance, described Canterbury as the 'Metropolis of all his dominions'. Having been abandoned since the mid-5th century, Canterbury was the ecclesiastical centre of Britain by the 7th century. Augustine became the first Archbishop of Canterbury and his fellow monks set about building the town's first cathedral, assuring Canterbury's revival. By the mid-7th century, it had a thriving merchant and artisan community and was even minting its own currency, which turned out the Anglo-Saxon coins, the *thrymsas* and, later, the silver *sceattas*. With its royal, ecclesiastic and commercial functions, Canterbury emerged as the first major Anglo-Saxon settlement in Britain and the first example of the sustained repopulation of a former Roman town.

WICS, BURHS AND VIKINGS

Canterbury's ascendancy began at the start of a period of relative peace lasting from the 6th to the 9th century that transformed the social and physical landscape of Anglo-Saxon Britain. With peace came prosperity. A steady rise in commercial activity combined with greater ties with Europe helped to create a demand for British produce and goods, particularly luxury artefacts, textiles and art. At key intersections in this expanding commercial network emerged embryonic marketplaces – the beginnings of an entirely new settlement type and the first of Anglo-Saxon origin. Situated near to repopulated former Romano-British towns, such as Canterbury, London and York, these new settlements emerged from the late 7th century and were denoted by their suffix 'wic'.

These mercantile settlements were undefended and often had a grid system of streets with groups of buildings densely arranged and serving a mixture of domestic, industrial and commercial functions. Among the first wics were Wessex's Hamwic, from which the later county of Hampshire takes its name; London's

Outside the major towns, the home in Viking Britain differed little from its Anglo-Saxon equivalent. Availability of materials and regional variations in construction practices inevitably produced exceptions to an otherwise remarkably consistent standard in domestic building. On the limestone steps of the Pennines, for example, Viking farmers built rectangular timber-framed structures up to 19 metres long that stood on limestone bases and were enclosed by dry-stone walls up to 3 metres thick. Unlike many Viking and Anglo-Saxon homes, these farmhouses were divided into two equal parts by a partition wall. A central hearth in one half indicates a domestic space separated from a storage or workspace in the other.

THE EMBRYONIC HALL

As building techniques improved during the 9th and 10th centuries AD, the home in Anglo-Saxon Britain grew in size and sophistication. This was an age in which, as Asser asserts, King Alfred encouraged people to 'build houses, majestic and rich beyond all custom of his predecessors, after his own new designs'. While the commoner continued to live in what the 10th-century monk, Lantfred, described in the context of Winchester as 'his cottage of dingy thatch' (*tugurium obsolete deserens tegetis*), the home of the nobility entered an entirely new phase that anticipated the rise of the great medieval halls. The simple arrangement of timber posts that rose from the sunken-featured building was replaced by a self-supporting timber frame dug into trenches or post-holes that formed the walls of larger hall-like structures. Stone, not employed in domestic construction since Roman times, started to be used, though only by the wealthy. King Alfred used stone and so too did King Harold, whose two-storey stone house is portrayed in the Bayeux Tapestry. The use of stone was one of the most conspicuous changes to occur to the late Anglo-Saxon hall. Stone was commonly used in the construction of churches and monasteries, but while Christianity played a crucial role in the development of Anglo-Saxon culture, its impact on the home remained limited. The method of construction used in most late-Anglo-Saxon halls relied on

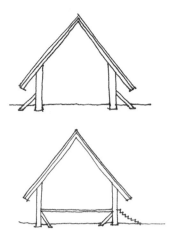

^ Top: Section through the hall at Yeavering, Northumberland, showing the method of supporting the timber frame.

Above: Section through Cheddar Hall, Somerset, showing an alternative method of supporting the timber frame.

‹ The two-storey stone house or palace of King Harold portrayed in the Bayeux Tapestry.

wood and was a precursor to the timber-framed building – a structure that did not rely on earth-fast foundations or gravity for its strength.

The more Anglo-Saxon carpenters honed their skills, the larger these timber structures became. Some were up to 30 metres long and 10 metres wide with adjacent entrances in the longest sides and a central hearth. The roofs covering buildings of this size imposed massive outward stresses on the supporting walls, which were countered by angled posts placed externally against the upright posts in the walls, forming a series of buttresses along the outside of the wall. Such advanced construction is exemplified by the huge buildings at Yeavering, the centre of the Anglo-Saxon Kingdom of Northumbria. In some instances, such as at Cheddar Hall in Somerset, these angled posts were placed internally and concealed beneath a floor of wooden boards. Most Anglo-Saxon buildings, however large, remained only one storey high. The hazards of constructing any higher than this are revealed in the *Anglo-Saxon Chronicle*, which reports a calamitous incident in AD 978 in which 'all the foremost councillors of the English race fell down from an upper floor at Calne [a royal manor in Wiltshire], but the holy archbishop Dunstan alone was left standing up on a beam; and some were very injured there, and some did not escape it with their life'.

The process of constructing large late-Anglo-Saxon timber halls is explained by the monk, Byrhtferth, who, in describing preparations for Easter celebrations in the early 11th century, writes: 'We first of all survey the site of the house, and also hew the timber into shape, and neatly fit together the sills, and lay down the beams, and fasten the rafters to the roof, and support it with buttresses, and afterwards delightfully adorn the house.' King Alfred provides a similarly instructive account in his *Version of St Augustine's Soliloquies*, where he recounts his expedition into the forest to gather the necessary resources to build a decent home. 'In each tree I saw something that I needed at home,' he wrote contentedly; 'it is no wonder that one should labour in timber-work, both in the gathering and also in the building.' The forest provided everything – cross-beams, bow-timbers and bolt-timbers, staves and stud shafts, and even helves for the tools. Having gathered the timber and 'fair twigs, so that he may wind many a neat wall, and erect many a rare house and build a fair enclosure', King Alfred believed the common man could 'therein dwell in joy and comfort both winter and summer'.

These descriptions provide valuable insights into the construction of Anglo-Saxon homes for which no physical evidence remains. Relying on wooden posts set into the ground, few houses lasted much longer than a generation. To understand their internal arrangements or their range of functions, Anglo-Saxon literature illuminates an otherwise obscure perception of the home's central feature, the hall. The building of a mighty hall, named Heorot, initiates the famous myth of *Beowulf*: 'for space and state the elder time ne'er boasted'. Inside Heorot were a roaring hearth, ale-benches, twisted ale cups, a dais, embroidered tapestries, all enjoyed by the king's feasting friends and companions, whose raucous revelry roused the wretched villain Grendel.

The description of Heorot, though the subject of legend, paints a vivid picture of the hall in late-Anglo-Saxon Britain. Socially halls were places of almost constant carousing and feasting, as well as places of business and privacy. Women and children slept in detached bowers, while the lord slept in the hall with his guests around the hearth. Furniture was sparse. Guests sat on benches and ate from temporary trestle tables covered with a cloth that, in the most opulent cases, would be furnished with imported cutlery and glasses or horn 'tumblers' for drinking. So highly prized were these items that they would have been bequeathed in wills. The only chair in the hall would have belonged to the host and would have been placed centrally at the end of the hall. Walls would have been painted in bright colours or bedecked with woven tapestries. In the centre of the hall there was always the hearth.

The hazards of having a roaring fire inside a wooden structure with a thatched roof were obvious, as the renowned scholar and monk, Bede (AD 672–735), described in an account of a domestic conflagration in *The Ecclesiastical History of the English People*:

> They sitting long at supper and drinking hard, with a great fire in the middle of the room, it hapned that the sparks flying up, the top of the house, which was made of wattles and thatch'd, was presently in a flame; which the guests spying on a sudden, they ran out in fright, without being able to put a stop to the fire, or save the house. The same being burnt down.'

Other characteristics of the Anglo-Saxon hall can be gleaned from Bede's work. In writing about King Edwin of Northumbria's conversion to Christianity by Saint Paulinus in AD 627, the hall is portrayed by Bede through the words of one of the King's advisors. He describes the fleeting life of man in this volatile age by using the analogy of a sparrow flying swiftly through the hall in winter, glimpsed only for a moment in the light and warmth before it flies out into the hostile night. Bede conjures an image of a large hall open to the elements, wherein the king sits to eat with his commanders and ministers in front of a roaring hearth. While the size, appearance and fabric of the hall may have changed over time, Bede's image of the hall is one that endured for centuries.

The Anglo-Saxons had taken time to develop their domestic environment and a permanent urban culture in Britain. Carpentry and construction techniques, along with urban development, were reaching their apogee just as the political landscape was about to confront the most fundamental change since the arrival of the Romans one millennium earlier. By the time of the Norman invasion in 1066 there were more than 100 towns in Britain accommodating approximately 10 per cent of a population of 2 million; almost twice as many towns as had existed during the Roman period when the population was approaching 4 million. During the same period the home had lost much of the sophistication it had acquired during the Romano-British period, before steadily regaining some of the comfort and conveniences associated with a more organised and prosperous society throughout the Anglo-Saxon age that laid the foundation of the medieval hall. However, the Anglo-Saxon proclivity for timber meant that within a century of the Norman Conquest there was virtually no trace of the Anglo-Saxon home, and Britain's once extensive woodland had been reduced to the sparsest in Europe, covering little over 10 per cent of the land.

In the 11th century, the Anglo-Saxon age of chivalry and the regal timber halls in which such noble customs were performed were consigned to history. Anglo-Saxon literature offers a glimpse of this demise through the eyes of a dispossessed and disoriented knight in the anonymously authored tale, *The Wanderer*:

> [H]e dreams that he is greeting and kissing his liege-lord, and laying his hands and head on his knee – just as he used to do when he enjoyed the bounty of the throne in days of old ... The bulwarks are dismantled, the banqueting halls are ruinous; their rulers lie bereft of joy and all their proud chivalry has fallen by the wall.

Written in the late 10th century, it unintentionally prophesies the events that were to unfold in the next century, when the Normans arrived.

THE HEARTH AND HALL

MEDIEVAL BRITAIN 1066–1485

In 1066 the illegitimate son of the Duke of Normandy, William the Bastard, conquers England. At no time since the Roman invasion of AD 43, nor perhaps at any time since, had a single event caused such wholesale change in Britain or, for that matter, in the re-branding of a man. William the Conqueror's defeat of King Harold at the Battle of Hastings touched every aspect of life in Britain, affecting its language, its customs and its laws. The new and more formal system that William imposed on Britain, which came to define life throughout the rest of the medieval period, revolved around the fief – a heritable unit of land that was leased by a lord to others of lower rank in return for different services. From 'fief' evolved the term 'feudalism', which has since become synonymous with the period.

One facet of daily life that remained comparatively constant amid the sweeping changes that engulfed Britain from the late 11th century was the home, and the one attribute of the home that epitomised this constancy was the hall. Having emerged in the late-Anglo-Saxon period, the hall dominated domestic planning up until the late 15th century, when the victory of Henry VII (1457–1509), 'the Gangster', over Richard III at Bosworth Field presaged the Tudor age.

Although the hall was a ubiquitous and essential feature of the home in medieval Europe, it varied from region to region and throughout time, altering in size, material, construction, orientation, scale and position within a building or settlement. Britain was no exception. The Anglo-Saxons brought the hall to Britain and had refined its form and function so that by the Norman Conquest it fully reflected the recent commensurateness of the family structure and household in Britain. By the 11th century, the social structure of a royal family, although larger and more complex than that of a peasant family, was essentially the same. Polygamy had given way to the nuclear family unit sanctified by marriage. For the home, this consistency reverberated through the hall, which appeared in all dwellings to a greater or lesser extent, whether a royal palace in extensive private grounds such as at Westminster (see page 76–7) or Winchester (see pages 76–8), a lord's castle like that at Norwich (see page 69–70), a knight's residence at the heart of a fief as at Old Soar in Kent (see page 82–3) or Moyse's Hall in Suffolk (see page 73–5), or a peasant's homestead.

Throughout the mid- to late medieval period, just as had occurred during the Anglo-Saxon era, the hall enjoyed a function beyond mere domesticity. It was as much a stage for public arbitration, where community matters were resolved by nobles, as it was an ostentatious venue for the lord or vassal to flaunt and fortify his position by bestowing generous hospitality or providing security. Such essential functions and inevitable physical variations persisted throughout the Norman and late medieval periods. Even as the life and customs of 15th- and

16th-century Britain proved increasingly incompatible with this large room that dominated the central portion of most homes, it endured – fuelled by the persistent hunger for status among medieval nobility. The history of the home throughout the medieval era is therefore a story characterised less by a variety of building types than by the variance in a single type.

MEDIEVAL SOCIETY

The Anglo-Saxon society that the Normans inherited was comparatively equal and fair. Domestically, the same rules applied to the uppermost tier of society as they did to the lowermost. Christianity had a growing influence upon daily rituals and social customs, such as marriage, which had become monogamous and consensual. Land was protected by heredity, whether owned by nobility or worked by a serf. Although these established customs were shaken to their core by the Normans, they helped to form the basis of the society that emerged from this tumultuous period so that, by the 12th century, the essential elements of medieval society were falling into place and could be defined by three broad categories, or orders: those who *prayed*, those who *fought*, and those who *worked*.

Those who prayed were the clergy. Highly revered in medieval Britain, their ranks included wealthy and powerful bishops who presided over ordained priests tending their village congregations and monks in their monastic community, all of whom were subject to their own legal and social obligations. The home for members of the clergy ranged from the bishops' palaces with their great halls and courtyard settings to the communal living of the monks' dormitory.

Those who fought were the nobility, embodied by the knight. Initially just a mounted soldier in shining armour, by the 12th century the knight was a person of power and considerable status who served his lord in return for a secure home on his estate. The lord, in turn, served the king by providing him with a loyal army drawn from his estate, as there were no permanent armies in the modern sense until much later. Service, not blood, was the currency of royal sanction and it defined nobility. The noble's home epitomised medieval society and embodied the status of its owner. The lord's manor, such as that at Stokesay Castle in Shropshire, was usually the largest and most ostentatious. It accommodated the entire household, including his family, permanent staff and retainers. Other smaller manors on his estate would be home to his knights. Dominating the plan of these high-ranking homes was the hall.

Those who worked or, more accurately, laboured, were the numerous ranks of peasants who tilled the land. Increasingly, labourers also included those engaged in other forms of manual work, such as millers, blacksmiths, tanners, bakers, cobblers, carpenters and other artisans. The home of the peasant was a humble affair, inconsistent in form, customarily small and utilitarian, but always a grade above the serf, whose pitiably low position in medieval society was matched by their domestic *cotes* of mud and thatch.

The three orders, despite some exceptions – royalty, bandits, merchants, woodsmen, tradesmen – encapsulate an elaborate social structure, wherein classes had not yet emerged and wealth, though important, was not the primary factor in determining social organisation. The strongest thread in the social fabric of medieval Britain was status. Measured not by affluence but by the elusive and fragile quality of power, status was determined by one's associations and obligations to a higher authority. These obligations affected everyone beneath the king and demanded, in return for use of the land, the provision of labour, both on the land and in military service, as well as food and other produce, such as military clothing and weaponry. It became a complex system of reciprocity where the king granted land to his lords in return for their loyalty and soldiers. The lord leased parcels of land, or fiefs, to his knights in return for their military service and loyalty, and the knights served their lord in return for the wealth they derived from the fief. This wealth was generated by the serfs, who worked the land in return for protection from the knights and the lord.

The serfs, although at the bottom of the medieval pecking order, were not entirely condemned to a life of drudgery. Their right to use the land was hereditary and could not be removed either from the serf by the knight or from the knight by the lord, unless either had violated their obligations to their superior. Social mobility, both upwards and downwards, was also possible, through exemplary service or military valour. Although the system appeared to be defined by obvious hierarchical lines of authority, the power structure was not strictly vertical, like a pyramid. It was characterised more by a complex web of social and political relations between competing people of constantly shifting statuses. These relations wound their way to the pre-eminent and absolute authority of the king or queen, to whom everyone ultimately owed something.

Having emerged around the time of the Norman Conquest, the three orders survived for almost half a millennium. The only threat to their distinction came from another group that grew in size and authority throughout the medieval period and whose primary occupation was trade. England's population around the time of Harold's defeat was approximately 2 million, but by the 14th century it had risen to over 7 million before being decimated by the Black Death of 1348. Rising wealth and population fuelled trade as the towns and larger settlements grew, becoming the strongholds of the emerging merchant classes, whose homes were defined by a burgeoning urbanity and flourished on their dense plots.

THE NORMAN TRANSITION

Prayers, fighters and labourers inhabited very different domestic structures in post-Conquest Britain. The clergy's homes in their ecclesiastical setting were as different from the lordly manor as they both were from the labourer's rural abode, but the centrality of the hall throughout remained consistent. Originality in the medieval home occurred much less in the plan than in the detail.

In the decades following the Conquest, the plan of the British home remained much as it had done in the decades leading up to it – it comprised a hall, which was simply a room, with the possible addition of a small private chamber. Britain's new rulers were preoccupied not with enhancing the domestic realm, but with consolidating their authority. Strengthening their grip on power, the Normans stripped former Anglo-Saxon elites of their wealth, influence and land. They built a network of military fortifications, known as motte-and-baileys, throughout the newly conquered kingdom. The Anglo-Norman chronicler, Orderic Vitalis (1075–*c* 1142), described the role of these defensive structures in his *Historia Ecclesiastica*, explaining that William 'appointed strong men from his Norman forces as guardians of the castles, and distributed rich fiefs that induced men to endure toil and danger to defend them'. The process that Vitalis observed was the start of the golden age of the castle.

Private castles were a quintessential product of the Norman's militaristic society. Where the tribal structure of Anglo-Saxon Britain produced fortified communities, the Norman system of military tenure governed by regional lords produced private fortifications ranging from diminutive isolated towers, or keeps, with their square plan encircled by a moat or defensive earthworks, to fully fledged castles comprising a number of buildings within a compound surrounded by an impregnable perimeter wall. However, early-Norman castles were not homes, though they nevertheless all contained halls. Rather than being places of domesticity, their primary function was as a military installation vital to the consolidation, maintenance and projection of an individual's power and his obligation to the crown, and they would not be surrendered even on pain of death. When remarking on a baron's 'deep-seated' feelings towards his lord, the Anglo-Norman chronicler, Jordan Fantosme, claimed 'they will not surrender their castles no matter what harm may come'. Some of these, such as Norwich Castle or the Tower of London, were magnificent stone structures, unprecedented in scale and grandeur both from the outside and within.

∧ The Norman castle at Norwich.

> The interior of Norwich Castle (1067–1121)
which once housed the Great Hall.

From the late 11th century, private castles were built on strategic sites all over the country, as well as in major towns. In settlements such as Lincoln, Chester and York, the building of these costly fortifications by William's loyal lords caused the destruction of large numbers of former Anglo-Saxon dwellings in and around these once fortified communities. The construction of castles required royal consent, but in the early 12th century, during The Anarchy that occurred over the question of royal succession following the death of Henry I in 1135, many rebel nobles built them without the king's blessing. Known as 'adulterine castles', these were then systematically destroyed during the late reign of King Stephen (*c* 1096–1154) and throughout the reign of his successor, Henry II (1133–89), as they sought to reassert royal authority. By the end of the 12th century, few adulterine castles remained standing.

Nevertheless, officially sanctioned castles and localised defensive towers, such as the peel towers of northern England, continued to be built all over Britain and particularly in the Scottish Marches and the Welsh borders up until the 15th century, by which time the nature of warfare was shifting and the proliferation of gunpowder finally rendered all but the most substantial stone fortifications impotent. The chief object of the magnificent turreted towers that appeared across the British landscape thereafter was pretence, not defence.

THE MEDIEVAL HOME

The home in medieval Britain could neither be defined by a family unit nor by a house. To understand the social and physical structure of the medieval home, one has to envision an extended household surrounding a familial core served by a large staff who worked for the family on a permanent basis and sometimes over generations, together with part-time retainers. This army of staff, which served the lord and his family faithfully at home, also followed him wherever he went, whether on business or into battle. This private workforce that was needed to ensure the sound operation of the household carried out their duties and led their very un-private lives around an assortment of supplementary buildings and structures, including detached chambers, kitchens, larders, stores, brewhouses and all manner of accommodation for livestock, such as horse stables, cowsheds, pigsties, sheep pens, henhouses and dovecotes. *The Calendar of Liberate Rolls* compiled under Henry III even documents an elephant house at the Tower of London that Henry had ordered the Sheriff of London to build 'without delay' in 1255. No matter how numerous or bizarre these peripheral structures surrounding the medieval household were, at the heart was always the hall.

The lord's manor epitomised the medieval household and was aptly described, albeit in its very late stages, by the clergyman, William Harrison (1534–93), in his *Description of England*:

> [T]he mansion houses of our countrie townes and villages are builded in such sort generallie, as that they have neither dairie, stable, nor bruehouse annexed unto them under the same roofe (as in manie places beyond the sea [& some of the north parts of our countrie,]) but all separate from the first, and one of them from an other.

The manor house was the nucleus of the lord's estate and the residence of the lord's household. Official obligations, such as to the king's court or in military campaigns, meant that the lord was often away from his principal home. He might also spend parts of the year either in other manor houses on his estate, on neighbouring estates, or, especially in the late-medieval period, in an urban residence. Peasants or serfs residing on the manor were the lord's tenants and lived in rural villages or hamlets. These settlements were typically clusters of meagre dwellings of wood, or perhaps stone, and thatch, each within their own small plot of arable land, or toft, with a church and sometimes a smaller manor house, all surrounded by more extensive agricultural land and woodland beyond. It was from this communal rural setting that the village descended and from here that the medieval term home derived, reminding us of the consonance between community and family in defining our sense of place that was originally not constrained by the walls of a house.

The house of most tenants invariably comprised a single or double room occasionally accompanied by other structures, such as stores, latrines or brewhouses. The dark, damp and malodorous internal space was used for most of the domestic functions of two or, very rarely, three generations. These conditions and the high rates of infant mortality meant that life expectancy for the typical inhabitants of these medieval homes would have rarely exceeded 30. Daily life concentrated around the central hearth over which, unlike in the manor houses, cooking was conducted on trivets. The case in Bedfordshire's Coroners' Rolls where a one-year-old girl, Alice le Bercher, from the village of Cople died on 30 November 1273 from burns caused by a pot of boiling water falling on her, illustrates how dangerous this arrangement was and how frequent injuries or even fatalities were among members of the crowded household.

Tenants of the manor ranged in social standing from lowly serfs to free peasants who worked the land and were bound by various forms of obligation and payment to their vassal or lord. Such obligations ranged from regular provision of labour to payments in kind throughout the year. Everything they possessed in life, even their invariably humble houses, was the property of the lord, who could raze their homes and relocate their village if he so wished, and which often occurred. The 15th-century lord of Herstmonceux manor in East Sussex, Sir Roger Fiennes, uprooted the entire settlement of Herstmonceux because it interfered with his hunting ground. Fiennes was Treasurer to Henry VI and had accompanied his father, Henry V, to the Battle of Agincourt in 1415. In 1441 he built a large home on the manor and called it Herstmonceux Castle (see pages 119–21). The name of Herstmonceux originated with the fusion of the 12th-century owners of the land, the de Herst family, and the 13th-century owners, the Monceux family.

The conventional forms of bondage that characterised medieval society in Britain eventually gave way to more formal arrangements of indenture and contributed to a rapid and often unsustainable increase in household sizes by the end of the medieval period. From as few as ten people in a small manorial household to fifty in the household of a knight in post-Conquest Britain, the number of dependants in the households of the most powerful lords could exceed two hundred by the 15th century.

EARLY NORMAN HALLS

The general rule in medieval domestic planning was that there was no rule. The internal configuration of the hall, although infinitely varied, was characterised by almost austere simplicity, whether in a royal household or a diminutive manor of a minor noble. Halls were either rectangular or parallelogrammatic in plan and always possessed a central hearth around which members of the household slept, ate, entertained, did business and undertook matters of public interest.

In early-Norman Britain up to the 13th century, halls were often raised on semi-submerged undercrofts or lower floors, and were known as 'upper halls', as at Boothby Pagnell in Lincolnshire and Moyse's Hall in Suffolk. Upper halls were characteristic of contemporary French domestic planning. They were depicted in an account by the 12th-century French poet, Chrétien de Troyes, in his version of the Anglo-Saxon legend of Perceval's search for the Holy Grail, the knight being taken by his hosts 'up the stairs and into the main hall, which was lovely'. In post-Conquest Britain, however, they were unsuited to the comparatively rudimentary timber structures. Reliant on stone, at least on the ground floor, they were thus confined as a building type to the wealthiest households. Where no direct access was made internally between the two levels, an external wooden staircase provided access to the upper floor.

The hall's elevation also afforded a degree of protection in unsettled times, performing a function similar to that of the

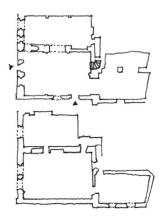

↑ The ground- and first-floor plans of
Moyse's Hall (c 1180), Bury St Edmunds.

〉 Moyse's Hall (c 1180), Bury St Edmunds,
Suffolk, one of the few surviving Norman
domestic structures built of stone in
Britain. The building comprises two
parts each with a gabled roof: a private
chamber (left) above a storage area on
the ground floor; and the main hall (right)
above an undercroft which was likely to
have had a commercial function.

castle keep. However, placing a hall on an upper level had the
socially undesirable effect of obscuring its view from the ground
and thus diminishing its status. Such understatement proved
unpopular in Britain and contributed to its demise. In its place
rose the open hall. Situated on the ground floor, these great
open halls of medieval Britain gained their name from being
open to the roof. More than in France or anywhere else on
the Continent, the open hall in Britain assumed an unrivalled
prominence and reverence in domestic life throughout the
rest of the medieval period.

In both upper and open halls, an attached room sometimes
served as a bedchamber or a venue for conducting private
business. In the most affluent cases, an annexed chapel was
also built and usually located close to the upper end of the
hall, sometimes with direct access leading from the hall and
sometimes detached, as occurred at the castle of St Briavels in
Gloucestershire, where, according to the *Calendar of Liberate
Rolls*, Henry III ordered 'a chapel of wood with posts to be
constructed before the door of the king's chamber'. The chapel
was used for both secular and non-secular purposes and became
an essential feature of a royal or noble household, the material
contents of which would accompany the head of the household
wherever they went, carried on horseback by dozens of staff
in a vast train that could be on the road for weeks at a time.

The development of the Norman hall was ultimately constrained
by the limited skill of the medieval carpenter, whose responsibility
it was to construct the walls and, most significantly, the roofs
of these growing structures. Halls remained relatively small
and seldom more than 7 metres wide because the distance
between adjacent walls was determined by the maximum length
of available structural roof timbers. Surpassing this distance
required carpenters either to innovate or to support the roof on
pillars of stone or wood. The latter solution had been used in
Anglo-Saxon times and created arcades along the length of the
hall that supported the hull-like roof. The interiors of arcaded
halls were similar to churches, where the aisles defined the
nave, so it is no coincidence that the English word 'nave'
derives from the Latin word *navis*, meaning ship, nor that
the German word *Schiff* means both nave and ship.

The posts supporting an aisle were a short-term solution
and were an undesirable yet unavoidable obstruction that
undermined the efficient functioning of the post-Conquest
hall. One of the few remaining examples from the period is
the stone-pillared Great Hall at Winchester, commissioned by
Henry III in 1222 and constructed by the master stonemason,
Elias of Dereham, between then and 1236. Its beautifully
crafted marble columns stand, albeit at a slight angle owing
to the outward pressure of subsequent roofs, to this day.

Although they never completely disappeared, aisled halls declined in the 13th century as a result of innovations in roof construction. The revolutionary tie beam and collar beam permitted, for the first time ever, the effective bridging of a distance greater than the length of a single timber independent of pillars. By the late 14th century, the ability of the medieval master carpenter to roof a space without intermediate support reached its peak with the re-roofing of the 20-metre-wide Westminster Hall, commissioned by Richard II, which was among the earliest and certainly most extravagant demonstrations of the new hammerbeam roof.

The improved skills of the medieval carpenter, which enabled these large unsupported roofs and a reduction in the cost of timber construction, reinstated timber as the pre-eminent material for domestic buildings at a time when stone was being used almost ubiquitously in the construction of religious buildings and causing Britain's cathedrals to reach new heights. The growth in the size of domestic halls caused older and smaller structures to be either replaced or adapted. Where these were made of stone, the cost of adaptation or extension was considerable. Consequently, many stone houses from the 12th and early 13th centuries were dismantled down to their undercrofts or to the lower part of their ground-floor walls and reconstructed in timber. The original structure provided a solid foundation or continuous sill supporting the timber structure above. The age of the great timber-framed halls had arrived.

∨ The aisled Great Hall at Winchester, commissioned by Henry III and built between 1222 and 1236. The massive pillars made from Exeter marble have been supporting a roof for nearly eight hundred years and can be seen to be leaning outwards under the pressure.

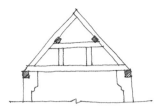

∧ The tie beam and collar beam (depicted here connected with queen struts) were innovations in roofing that allowed wider spans to be bridged without the use of pillars, thus superseding the aisled hall.

∨ The hammerbeam allowed for exceptionally large unsupported roofs, among the largest of which was Westminster Hall in London, commissioned by Richard II in 1393.

Homes in Britain had up to this point generally been in poor physical condition. William Harrison described them as 'slightlie set up with a few posts & many radels [hurdles]'. Coroners' records attest to the flimsiness of the common person's home and provide a grim roll call of those who lost their lives as a result. On 14 June 1273, a young girl named Agnes Abbotsley died in the Cambridgeshire village of Eaton Socon after being crushed by the collapsed wall of an old house. Three years later, a Mr Wygod of the Bedfordshire village of Bolnhurst had the misfortune of standing 'under the wall of an old and weak building. By misadventure the building fell on him, breaking the whole of his body.' So flimsy were the walls of common houses that felons and thieves, rather than forcing the doors or windows of a house, broke through them to gain entry. The price of a flimsy wall cost occupants dearly, claiming the life of Henry Ailwit of the Bedfordshire village of Renhold on the night of 9 December 1267. Two years later, in the nearby village of Roxton, thieves emptied one house before going to the house next door where they 'broke its west wall' and struck the occupant 'above her left ear so that her brain issued forth and she immediately died'. The following year in nearby Kempston Hardwick, thieves killed the young daughter of Peter of Hardwick, having 'broken down the west wall' of the house. Only weeks later a similar incident occurred in the village of Henlow, in which the owner, Geoffrey Aylle, was stabbed in his stomach, from where his 'bowels issued forth'. In 1276, thieves used a ploughshare to break the wall of a house in Farndish before fatally assaulting the owner, tying up his wife and removing all their possessions from the house. In 1243, in an incident without fatal consequences, a resident of Portsmouth, Hugh de Stoke, was reimbursed by Henry III 'for damages sustained by the fall through overloading of his house in which the carcasses of bacon sent to the king in Gascony were stowed'. The fragility of domestic structures can also be judged from recommendations in London's first building regulations, drawn up in 1189, which stipulated that town aldermen should be furnished with nothing more than a cord and hook so that they could pull down unauthorised or unsafe houses, particularly in the event of fire.

Lack of maintenance and poor construction were to blame for the generally shoddy quality of domestic buildings, and both factors were related to the perishability of available materials. Before the 13th century, all forms of domestic construction except for the relatively few stone buildings in some towns were compromised by this, whether a wall of cob or plastered wattle in a peasant hut or a massive oak column in an early-medieval hall. All would decay within the owner's lifetime if they came into direct contact with the ground. By raising structural timbers on to stone footings or a continuous sill, this ancient problem was eliminated and domestic construction changed for ever. The increasing permanence of houses impacted significantly on social and economic relations in medieval society. Houses came to be inherited from one

generation to the next, something that the great majority of Britain's population had never had to contend with.

Unlike their immediate and even ancient wooden-structured predecessors, the method of construction and permanence of timber-framed buildings were almost revolutionary. In the first phase of the process leading towards the home's physical permanence, from about the 10th century, wooden elements of the structure were placed on to a non-perishable foundation and secured into a groove or, later, a mortise. In the second phase, starting from the early 13th century, the structure's dependence on gravity was removed. The full timber-framed building was literally a wooden box whose structural integrity derived from its joints rather than gravity, enabling it to remain intact whether placed on its side or, if such a thing were possible, rolled like dice.

The innovation that gave rise to the timber frame was the innocuous mortise-and-tenon joint. This simple advancement in carpentry comprised a narrow peg at the end of one piece of wood, the tenon, being fixed into a hole, the mortise, of exactly the same size at the end of another piece of wood. Helping also in the establishment of timber-framing was the introduction into Britain of the saw in the 12th century, which allowed carpenters to prepare with relative ease the necessary squared timbers. Previously, large timbers were prepared by splitting them with wedges then finished with axes. Medieval carpenters fashioned the timbers for buildings in open areas known as frame fields, often many miles from the site of construction. In these fields, the structural frame would be prepared and assembled to ensure it was sound, then dismantled and transported to the site and reassembled. Westminster Hall was prefabricated in this manner, nearly a hundred miles away in Fareham, Hampshire.

Branchless sections of young to middle-aged oak trees over a century old were ideal for the structural elements of a timber-framed building, known as 'standards'. Standards, commonly about four metres long, were chosen from carefully managed forests by master carpenters, whose trade was by now becoming a professional craft. Felling of the trees and their conversion into usable timbers was done by a sawyer. Standards and other useful materials recovered from the conversion process were then transported to the carpenter's workshop or frame field.

∧ An example of a timber frame sitting on a sill to prevent damp, in this case at the Barley Barn (1205–30) at Cressing Temple, Essex.

> The mortise-and-tenon joint, an innovation in carpentry that was essential to the timber frame.

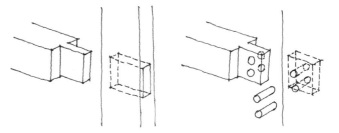

> The aisled interior of the Barley Barn (1205–30) at Cressing Temple, Essex, showing the timber frame which was reconstructed and re-roofed with crown posts, collars and purlins, in the 15th and 16th centuries. The barn has been reconstructed and reduced in size (c 1400 and c 1500) and now measures 36m x 13.6m x 11.3m high.

Each timber was fixed securely into a continuous wooden sill around the base of a structure, which sat on a small stone wall, or stylobate, that protected the timbers from rising damp. The largest timber-framed structures in Britain were at Cressing Temple in Essex, built for the Knights Templar for the storage of barley and wheat, as well as other agricultural produce. The massive Wheat (1259–80) and Barley Barns (1205–30) were the largest timber-framed buildings in the world when built.

A variation of the timber frame was the cruck frame, which formed an A-frame using massive timber members that arched from the ground to the apex of the roof. The principles of cruck-framing, according to the 1st-century BC Roman architect, Vitruvius, in his *Ten Books of Architecture*, could be found in man's first attempt to improve upon the most primitive form of dwellings: 'At first men erected forked spars interwoven with twigs, then covered the walls with mud.' The crucks formed a gable at either end of the building, the space between a pair of crucks forming one bay. The medieval cruck-framed structures built in Britain, particularly in the southwest where this method of construction was most prolific, were physically vastly superior to those that Vitruvius alluded to, but their dependence on massive timbers meant that they were suitable only for the construction of relatively small buildings of one storey with the possible inclusion of a garret, making them a common feature of the homes of the lower ranks of society.

One common application of crucks in domestic construction was in the longhouse of the landed peasant, a narrow permanent dwelling comprising two or three bays and up to 17 metres long that, for the sake of economy, accommodated a nuclear family and their livestock under one roof. The typical layout of a longhouse was characterised by the divided cohabitation of humans and animals either side of a cross passage linking doorways on both sides of the building that formed the entrance.

> An example of a cruck frame in a late-14th-century hall house at the Weald and Downland Open Air Museum, West Sussex. Because these timbers do not extend from the base to the apex, stopping instead at the roof collar, they are known as base crucks.

∨ Diagram showing the different methods of cruck-framed construction.

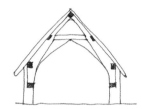

Raised

Upper

Jointed

The frequent passing of humans and animals in and out of the entrance made the floor surface suitable for threshing wheat, giving rise to the term 'threshold'.

On one side of the entrance and occupying the larger area was the domestic space which was often divided in two: a public space containing a central hearth around which food was prepared in pits, beyond which was a private chamber where the occupants slept. Sometimes a mezzanine level supported by the strong cruck frame would also be incorporated and used for sleeping or for storage. On the other side of the entrance and occupying approximately a third of the internal space was the byre. The stone floors usually contained drainage channels to allow the area to be washed out regularly. The proportions of the byre were determined by the size of the oxen, a factor that Vitruvius had determined over a thousand years earlier. To accommodate two pairs of beasts, the length of the stalls inside the byre was fixed to one perch, a medieval unit that was key in building as well as agriculture and was roughly equivalent to 5 metres.

An acre, the basic medieval unit of agricultural land that could be ploughed in a day, was four perches wide – equal to and determined by two pairs of oxen walking abreast (the length of an acre, a furlong (just over 200 metres), being the distance oxen could plough before needing a rest). Nowhere else during the medieval period and perhaps at no other time in history was the spatial arrangement inside the home so precisely defined by and engaged in such an intimate relationship with the functions of society outside the home.

The principal difference, structurally, between the timber frame and the cruck frame was in the way that each supported the roof. The roofs of large timber-framed buildings were supported by a crown post and cross-beam that provided both longitudinal and lateral stability and superseded the triangular roof truss, which the Normans reintroduced to Britain for the first time since the Romans brought it with them over a thousand years earlier. The roof of cruck-framed buildings was supported directly by the crucks, which produced a steeper pitch.

Coverings of roofs varied depending on cost and the region. The homes of peasants were invariably covered in some form of thatch, which was economical and abundant, whereas the nobility, to whom money was much less of a consideration, used every available material. The bird that sang in Chaucer's *The Book of the Duchess* did so 'upon my chamber roofe without, upon the tyles over all about'. Over a century earlier the *Calendar of Liberate Rolls* reveals how the Sheriff of Nottingham was commanded by Henry III to 'lead half the body of the hall of Nottingham Castle', whereas nine years later he was instructed to 'thatch and repair the roof of the king's hall, the bakehouse, and the granary'. For the roof of the hall at his castle in Bristol, Henry III ordered '23,000 shingles to be made in the Forest of Dene', and at his palace in Woodstock ordered all staff quarters and courts to be re-roofed in slate. Years later, at Marlborough Castle, the pecking order of roofing materials is revealed by the king's instruction to replace the wooden shingles on the kitchen roof with lead and the shingles to be reused to replace the straw thatch on the chamber.

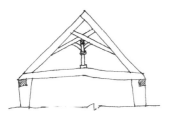

∧ Diagram of a crown post.

∨ The medieval longhouse showing the division of domestic and agricultural space under one roof: the combined home (comprising central living area and private parlour) and byre.

THE HEIGHT OF THE HALL

The ascendance of the hall coincided with and was partly responsible for the decline of the castle. The great age of the fortified castle dominated the turbulent late 11th and 12th centuries, but the costly battlements defended by hired soldiers did not suit the prolonged period of relative calm that followed. Instead, the era of the great hall began. For the next three centuries, this central component of the medieval home grew in size and stature from a rectangular space defining the status of the uppermost nobility to a ubiquitous feature of almost every household above the modest serf.

A distinctive plan for the hall began to emerge in the 13th century, throughout which living and building standards improved appreciably. These developments were owed in part to Henry III, whose reign (1216–72) spanned much of the century and whose desire for progress and an improvement in domestic comfort is evidenced in a number of building projects including the renovation of Westminster Abbey and, more importantly, the introduction of bathing in royal households – a domestic feature absent in Britain since Roman times. Henry was responsible not only for the construction of London's first waterworks in Westminster, laid for the purposes of washing himself, but also for London's first ever water main, which, by 1237, linked the springs of Tyburn, a village formerly located near present-day Marble Arch, and West Cheap in the City of London.

When Henry III came to the throne, the plan of the domestic hall remained much as it had done since before the Norman Conquest, containing a private chamber, or solar, and the main hall, as illustrated in late-12th-century Moyse's Hall, but which can also be seen at the early-13th-century ruin Wilmington Priory, East Sussex and at late-13th-century Old Soar, Kent. Old Soar was a knight's home in the form of a fortified manor. The aisled Great Hall no longer exists, but the private chamber, over a barrel-vaulted undercroft, with attached chapel and garderobe remain. Anglo-Saxon halls commonly had a separate private chamber or bower, often reserved for the ladies of the household. In the halls of the most affluent, these were laid out over two storeys.

The next major development was the addition of extra rooms at the end of the hall opposite to the private chamber. The additional rooms, a buttery and pantry, were service rooms that, combined with the central hall and the private chamber at the opposite end, form a tripartite or H-shaped plan. Among the best early examples of this development in the plan of the home is Penshurst Place in Kent, commissioned in 1338 by the London merchant and four-times-elected Lord Mayor, Sir John de Pulteney, who made his fortune from wine and wool.

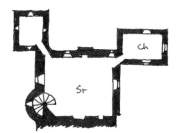

∧ A plan of Old Soar, showing the private chamber with the attached chapel and garderobe. The hall would have been attached to the side wall of the private chamber.

Sr: Solar · Ch: Chapel

> The remains of the 13th-century knight's home, Old Soar (1290), Kent. The existing structure comprises a private chamber raised on a barrel-vaulted undercroft, with attached chapel and garderobe.

The interior of the private chamber at Old Soar (1290), with the chapel leading off at the back left corner.

Wilmington Priory (early 13th century), East Sussex.

The south elevation of the Great Hall at Penshurst Place, Kent, commissioned in 1338 by the London merchant, Sir John de Pulteney, who obtained a licence to crenellate his manor in 1341. The house has been added to extensively throughout later centuries.

Plan of Penshurst showing the original buildings (1338–49).

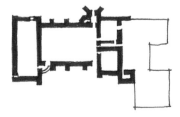

The hall at Penshurst was massive, measuring 19 metres in length and 12 metres in width, with an 18-metre-high roof, making it the centrepiece of one of the grandest homes in the country. At the heart of the hall was an octagonal hearth. The hearth's enduring centrality to the home appears in its Latin translation, *focus*, which refers to the household unit.

The development of the tripartite plan accompanied a shift in emphasis, especially in more peaceable areas of Britain, throughout the 13th and 14th centuries from domesticated fortifications to fortified domestic buildings. This was the age of the fortified manor, whose nominal defences, such as a moat or gatehouse, provided sufficient protection not for repelling a military force but for defence against organised bandits and marauders. The keeps of Norman castles became private chambers or fell into ruin. The open areas within the castle walls were turned over to offices or accommodation for lesser-ranking retainers.

One of the best and most complete examples of a 13th-century hall and fortified manor is Stokesay Castle, Shropshire. Surrounded by a moat and commissioned by the wool magnate, Lawrence of Ludlow, the building was completed in 1291. The estate had been owned by a wealthy Norman family, the

^ The eastern elevation of Stokesay
Castle (1291), Shropshire, viewed
from the courtyard.

>> Stokesay Castle (1291), Shropshire,
seen from the north.

de Says, but fell into decline by the mid-13th century. At the
time, Shropshire had a thriving wool industry that accounted
for half of the country's wool exports and at the heart of this
industry was Lawrence of Ludlow. Having amassed a fortune,
he purchased the de Says' manor in 1281 and, like so many
other wealthy manor owners throughout the medieval period,
requested a licence from the king to crenellate the building.
On gaining the licence, he set about almost completely
rebuilding the manor, except for the north tower, which
he kept and extended by another floor.

Much of what remains today is what Lawrence of Ludlow
commissioned. The central portion comprises a massive hall with
stone walls four bays long and each containing, on the courtyard
side, three gabled partially glazed windows with wooden shutters
and seats set into the sill. A large arched doorway serves as
the main entrance, while a larger doorway on the opposite
wall provided access for coaches and horses. The huge hipped
timber roof was constructed with two braced collar beams
resting on moulded stone corbels, the whole being supported
by massive external buttresses. In the centre of the stone floor
was the hearth. At the northern end of the hall and accessed by
an internal wooden staircase was a first-floor chamber with a
fireplace, glazed windows and walls of timber and plaster that

The Great Hall at Stokesay Castle
(1291), Shropshire.

were cantilevered on timber jetties which extended out over the oldest and original part of the building that was formerly a tower with a cellar beneath and constructed in the first half of the 13th century. At the southern end of the hall were other chambers including another cellar and a private chamber above, access to which was provided by an external staircase. Wooden panelling on the walls and around the fireplace in the main private chamber, along with the construction of the elaborate gatehouse in the 17th century, are among the few modifications made to Stokesay. Beyond the private chamber is the more heavily fortified three-storey tower accessed both via a raised ground floor by an external staircase and along a covered corridor from the private chamber. A narrow staircase set into the thick stone wall provides access between the floors. The irregular polygonal plan of the tower allows the lancet windows to be oriented obliquely to the wall, making it more difficult to fire projectiles into the tower.

Stokesay was among the earliest examples of a standard type of domestic plan that dominated the layout of the medieval home for the next two centuries. With rooms at either end of the hall, there emerged the social delineation of an 'upper end' and a 'lower end'. The upper end of the hall was set aside for the lord and his closest aides, behind which was the private chamber

∧ A room in the south tower at Stokesay Castle, Shropshire.

∨ The first-floor room at the top of the stairs from the Great Hall at Stokesay Castle, Shropshire.

– which later served as a bedchamber, presided over by the chamberlain – with a room beneath used as a cellar or parlour. At the lower end, the recently added service rooms were used to store the medieval staples, bread and beer. The pantry, whose title derived from the French *pain*, reveals its function as a bread store while liquid produce, such as wine and beer, were stored in butts in the buttery, which was presided over by the butler. Dividing these two spaces was often a passage leading out of the building to the sometimes numerous kitchens, which invariably remained separate and often temporary structures throughout the medieval period, though not at Stokesay, which was an exception in having its own internal kitchen. The impermanence and even fragility of some kitchens is evidenced in Henry III's instruction to the Sheriff of Oxford to attend to 'what needs repairing in the kitchen, which lately fell down in part by force of the wind'.

The elevated status of the upper end from the lower end was achieved both physically and symbolically. Physically, the lower end was a busy interchange with up to five doorways used by visitors as well as servants and retainers either to enter and exit the hall or in the course of fulfilling their household duties, particularly in scurrying back and forth from the external kitchen with food. One of the doorways was a main entrance, in the long side of the hall, which was sometimes accompanied

The idiosyncratic gatehouse at Stokesay Castle, Shropshire, built in 1640–41.

The plan of Stokesay Castle (1291), Shropshire.

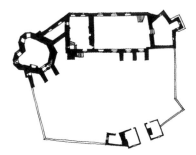

by another doorway on the opposite side of the building. At the end of the hall, perpendicular to the main entrance and facing the upper end, were often three other doorways. These were used by the lord's retinue; the outer two provided access to the two service rooms at the lower end of the hall while the central doorway led to a passage separating the two rooms leading to the kitchens and other ancillary outbuildings. By the early 14th century, a wooden screen inserted across the hall to conceal these doorways from the main hall, and forming a short corridor known as a cross passage, had become a common feature.

Symbolic reverence appeared in the carved decoration on the side of this screen facing the upper end, paying homage to the head of the household. Similar symbolism was repeated in the roof timbers, with the well-dressed 'faces', sometimes elaborately carved, facing the upper end of the hall. The position of the hearth also reflected the social status in the hall. Rather than being positioned in the centre of the room, as it had been for millennia, it moved towards the upper end of the hall, nearer the wooden dais that elevated the lord's seat and table above the rest of the hall. Further raising the status of the upper end was the arrangement of the windows, which often increased in number and size towards the upper end of the hall, letting in more light and, with the advent of glass, allowing for greater comfort

> The private chamber at Stokesay Castle, Shropshire, redecorated in the 17th century.

and ostentatious decoration. Glass was a luxury and while it appeared in churches and the homes of the nobility throughout the medieval period and often in an array of different colours, it was unusual in common domestic buildings until it became increasingly affordable by the 16th century. In the evenings, the hall was illuminated with wax candles or oil torches. The homes of the nobility were therefore bright compared with the gloomy interiors of the almost windowless peasant's home, which relied on glass substitutes, such as wooden shutters, canvas, or linen treated with alum and made translucent and weatherproof with animal fat, before being stretched over a latticed wooden frame called a *fenestral*.

The noble's hall was often sparsely furnished and decorated. Guests' tables were no more than panels covered with a cloth on trestles that could be removed after the meal, along with the benches on which they sat. The only chair in the hall belonged to the head of the household, whose table, or 'board', as it was known, was one of the few permanent fixtures in the hall. In the later medieval period, a canopy and other forms of decoration, such as richly embroidered tapestries and elaborate coats of arms, would be hung above the lord's table and around the walls of the hall, which, along with the other chambers, were painted colourfully. Towards the end of the medieval period a gallery was often erected at the low end of the hall, above the screens passage and facing the dais, from which the sounds of musicians and singers would fill the room. On the uncommon occasions where a private chamber was located at the low end of a hall, the wall behind the dais was often adorned with a large window decorated with elaborate tracery in the gable end. The floor of the hall was made of rammed earth, wood, or stones, covered in reeds or straw and often strewn with strong-smelling herbs, while floors in the private chambers were usually timber boards or tiles.

The vital social function of the medieval hall is colourfully portrayed in the tales of Sir Gawain, nephew of King Arthur, a central character in the Arthurian legends along with Lancelot, Galahad and Perceval. Although these early examples of English literature are based on an Anglo-Saxon subject, they were all written after the Norman Conquest and therefore likely based on contemporary observations. A vivid description of the hall during a large feast appears in *Perceval: The Story of the Grail*:

> Long was the hall and wide, yet 'twas full in every part, and all the tables filled. After them came full twenty chamberlains, young men of noble birth and courteous bearing, who bare napkins and basins, that did the knights mark well; behind them were a great company, bearing candles and candlesticks without number, with that was the hail so light 'twere hard to tell whether 'twere day or night. And there followed thirty minstrels, and others who sang full many a tuneful melody, all with one accord rejoiced and sang praises.

Another appears in the 14th-century story, *Sir Gawain and the Green Knight*, which represents both the acme of the medieval hall and the impending trend for privacy. The author writes of the king and queen hosting Gawain on the dais in the hall, while the knights sit at the lower tables and a roaring hearth burns in the centre of the hall. The first course is served with a 'blast of trumpets and waving of banners, with sound of drums and pipes, of song and lute'. Afterwards, Gawain is led by the lord of the household to his private chamber, which is furnished with noble bedding and 'curtains of pure silk wrought with gold [that run] on ropes with rings of red gold, wondrous coverings of fair cloth all embroidered, and walls hung with carpets of Orient, and the same spread on the floor'. In the privacy of his own chamber, Gawain is served a sumptuous meal of fish on a trestle table laid with white tablecloth, salt cellar, napkins and silver spoons.

The private chamber and service rooms at opposite ends of early halls were initially accommodated under the same roof, effectively forming an extension of the hall, but with the increasing need for more space and a growing desire among the wealthiest and most powerful households to project their status, more ambitious and costly solutions were devised. Contrary to the development of the hall on the Continent, which expanded longitudinally, the medieval hall in Britain grew wings, forming first L- and T-shaped plans, before reaching its apogee in the fully fledged H-shaped plan by the 14th century. The result was a divergence in the relative status of the hall throughout Europe. In France, for example, the eminence of the hall diminished as it was absorbed in an elongated building, becoming anonymous behind a repetitive facade. In Britain, the central position of the hall between two wings not only afforded it special significance

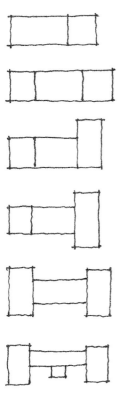

∨ Diagram showing the evolution of the house plan from I-, to L-, to T-, to H- and finally to E-shaped plans.

in its position relative to the plan, but also allowed it to grow to any size in relation to the rest of the building.

The subtle rise of individualism played an important role in the hall's development, manifest in a desire for privacy. Having never played more than a peripheral role in determining the domestic plan, privacy began to dominate it. By the 14th century, the head of the household became less inclined to fraternise with his staff and minor guests on a daily basis. Extricating himself from the large number of guests that ate and slept in the hall, he retreated to the parlour to dine, socialise and sleep in the company only of close family and friends. As William Langland (c 1330–87) wrote in the late-14th-century poem, *Piers Plowman* (X: 96–101):

> Wretched is the hall, each day in the week
> There the lord and lady like not to sit.
> Now have the rich a rule – to eat by themselves
> In a private parlour, for poor men's sake,
> Or in a chamber with a chimney, and leave the main hall
> That was made for meals, for men to eat in.

As the great feasting and communal revelry that once defined life in the medieval hall waned, the space in which these medieval customs had been played out for centuries lived on in the service of status. Although used less and less on a daily basis, the hall remained a vital venue for ceremonial functions, where the lord's obligation to bestow abundant hospitality remained an important means of bolstering the household's name and reputation. At important times of the year, such as religious festivals, food was provided by the household for the hundreds or even thousands of tenants on the manor. If additional space were needed, tents would be erected to provide the temporary accommodation for services such as kitchens or even serve as an extension of the hall itself. One of the expenses in Henry III's accounts for 1230 was 'a new tent for a hall (ad aulum) to be made' measuring 25 metres long.

The centrality of the hall to the projection of a household's power and wealth meant that by the end of the medieval period, much like its Roman predecessor, in the most lavish examples it evolved further still – from the winged hall to the complete courtyard plan and even to the double courtyard. Courtyard plans had been a common feature of ecclesiastical and military establishments for some time, setting a precedent for others, including the embryonic colleges at Oxford, Cambridge and Winchester, and London's Inns of Court. For the wealthy medieval magnates and their copious retinue, the courtyard was a practical response to the problem of accommodation.

A similar problem, albeit with a different cause, confronted the peasant's longhouse. By the 13th century, the cohabitation of

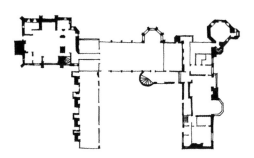

^ Gainsborough Old Hall (1460–80),
Lincolnshire, built by Sir Thomas Burgh.

˅ Plan of Gainsborough (1460–80), Lincolnshire.

humans and animals increasingly shifted to accommodation in separate buildings. Nevertheless, William Harrison commented in the 16th century on the phenomenon of 'stable and all offices under one roof' being 'seene in the fennie [fen] countries (and northerne parts) unto this daie', and it was a practice that persisted in some areas of Britain well into the 19th century. Generally, though, as additional structures were added to the longhouse and its internal functions changed, the small courtyard farmstead emerged as the dominant household type among Britain's rural population. On the much larger scale of the noble's manor, accompanying buildings around the courtyard housed not only the lord, his family and his immense retinue, but also their lodgings, food supplies, horses, offices and equipment. Gainsborough Old Hall (1460–80) in Lincolnshire, built by Sir Thomas Burgh, is one such example and was one of the largest manor houses in Britain at the time.

The social forces that precipitated the rise of the courtyard plan also contributed to the decline of the great halls. The desire for privacy among the nobility increased the number of separate chambers under one roof and the desire for emulation among the increasingly wealthy and mobile groups at the lower end of medieval society undermined the hall and its status.

^ The kitchen at Gainsborough Old Hall
(1460–80), Lincolnshire.

˅ The Great Hall at Gainsborough Old Hall
(1460–80), Lincolnshire.

By the 14th century, the homes of lower-gentry, merchants and yeomen had adopted the hall, where feasting became normal practice and meals were daily set at a high table in front of an open fire. 'Full sooty was her bower and also her hall' was how Chaucer described the 14th-century home of the poor old woman in *The Nun's Priest's Tale*, who lived a simple life with little means in her cote, the diminutive dwelling that gave rise to the modern term *cottage*. The status of the hall was becoming nullified by ubiquity. Few examples reveal this better than the Wealden house.

THE MERCHANT'S AND YEOMAN'S HALL

Named after the once wooded region of southeast England covering Kent and East Sussex, the Wealden house was effectively a miniature matured hall for wealthy yeoman farmers or town merchants. Sharing the same features as the great medieval halls, albeit on a substantially smaller scale and in a compressed form, the characteristics of the Wealden house were its central open hall with screened cross passage flanked by a two-storey private chamber and parlour beyond the upper end, and a buttery and pantry beyond the lower end, all housed under a hipped roof.

∧ A Wealden house (1405–30) originally from Chiddingstone in Kent, but restored at the Weald and Downland Open Air Museum, West Sussex.

〉 Illustration and plan of the typical Wealden house showing the central hall and private chamber beyond the upper end and service rooms beyond the lower end.

P: Parlour · H: Hall · Pa: Pantry
By: Buttery

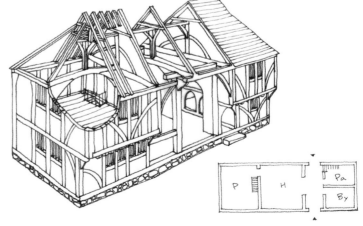

∧ A small late-14th-century medieval hall from Boarhunt, Hampshire, reconstructed at the Weald and Downland Open Air Museum, West Sussex, which comprised three rooms: chamber, hall and service room.

The tripartite plan replicated the internal arrangement of the great halls, but the Wealden house did possess its own distinct characteristics. The most pronounced of these was its jettied first-floor wings.

Jetties were a product of significant improvements in carpentry and methods of construction throughout the medieval period. They provided greater floor areas on the upper storeys and were particularly popular where space was restricted. In Britain's growing towns and cities they extended the upper floors by over half a metre on every side, and by the 15th century they had become very fashionable. Since jetties were dependent on the timber frame being jointed to the floor beams, they first emerged in the 13th century. Many thriving towns would have had jettied buildings, but one of the first recorded examples was a shop on London's Ironmonger Lane in 1246. The fullest expression of the jetty was an extension over the street to form an arcade.

The central portion of a Wealden house contained the hall and comprised two bays, one with windows and one without. As occurred in the halls of the nobility, the windows helped to define the upper end and illuminated the dais. A hearth burned

∧ Left: The hall in the Wealden house (1405–30) from Chiddingstone, Kent (and now in the Weald and Downland Open Air Museum, West Sussex), facing the upper end, showing the central hearth, high table and doorway leading to the parlour and chamber beyond.

Right: A 15th-century open hall from North Cray, Kent, reconstructed at the Weald and Downland Open Air Museum, West Sussex. The plan was very similar to the Wealden type, comprising four bays: the central two containing the hall, with service rooms and chamber in a single bay at the low end and parlour and chamber in a bay behind the upper end.

﹥ The service rooms in the Wealden house: buttery (right) and pantry (left).

in the middle of the space, the smoke from which would have escaped through louvres (from the French *l'ouvert* meaning 'the open one') in the roof, or through the gaps between the roof tiles. Stairs leading to the upper floors in both wings were located internally, one inside the parlour leading to the private chamber where the head of the household would sleep, and the other in the cross passage leading to a chamber above the pantry and buttery. Cooking was done over the central hearth until, by approximately the 16th century, separate kitchens were built within easy reach of the service end of the hall. Kitchens, as in the great halls, were never integral to the main structure, so as to avoid fires engulfing the entire home. Variants of the medieval hall similar to the Wealden house include the most common type throughout much of England and Wales that had a similar plan but in which the first-floor chambers did not project beyond the side wall, and a smaller single-storey type which comprised a central hall with a chamber at the upper end and a service or storage room at the lower end.

∧ The private chamber on the first floor of the Wealden house with stairs leading down to the upper end of the hall and the parlour. The room was well furnished, had shuttered windows and a garderobe is built into the wall overhanging the garden below.

⟩ The parlour on the ground floor of the Wealden house behind the upper end of the hall.

TOWN HOUSES

The placing of homes in medieval towns was defined by a form of property division that emerged in late-Anglo-Saxon Britain known as a 'burgage tenement'. These portions of land were laid out along the street and their size was calculated in perches. Occupation of a burgage tenement depended on the payment of rent to the lord on whose land the town was sited. However, unlike the occupants of rural tenements who generally paid rents to their master through the provision of services or produce throughout the year, the occupants of burgage tenements paid an annual monetary rent that exempted them from all other obligations and afforded them the privilege of doing business in the town and being protected by the fortified perimeter wall, whose gates were shut from dusk until dawn. This single payment was one of the factors that allowed townspeople to enjoy a relatively high level of personal freedom in medieval society, unfettered from the often crippling forms of bondage imposed on the rural population.

Initially, most homes in towns were built from wood with whitewashed walls of plastered wattle or cob and roofs of thatch. As the emerging ranks of merchants attained greater and greater wealth, stone became an increasingly common building material in the construction of homes. This was due in part to the increasing affordability of stone caused by the propagation of castles in the late 11th and 12th centuries, as well as its application in the construction of churches and monasteries. More quarries meant a reduction in the distance stone had to travel to the construction site. Stone offered the advantages of durability and strength, which made it popular among one group of merchants in particular: Jews. Stone buildings suited Jewish businessmen and moneylenders because it provided a secure place to store their assets. The home of a Jewish merchant in Lincoln built in the 12th century still stands and is still referred to as the Jew's House (*c* 1150).

Although small, these early stone houses were comparatively sophisticated and for over half a millennium they surpassed most urban homes in Britain for their durability and convenience. Constructed over two storeys, the ground floor provided a commercial space open to the street with internal and external access via staircases to accommodation on the upper floor. The earliest examples of these stone houses appeared throughout the 12th century in larger towns, such as London, York, Lincoln, Norwich and Southampton. Stone was an excellent deterrent against fire, too. The London Assize of Buildings drafted in 1189 by the Mayor of London, Henry Fitz-Aylewin (*c* 1135–1212), in the reign of King Richard I underlines this characteristic:

In ancient times the greater part of the City was built of wood, and the houses were covered with straw and stubble, and the like. When a single house had caught fire, the greater part of the City was destroyed through such conflagration; when, by reason of a fire that broke out at London Bridge, the Church of Saint Paul was burnt; from which spot the conflagration extended, destroying houses and buildings, as far as the Church of Saint Clement Danes. After this, many of the citizens, to the best of their ability to avoid such a peril, built stone houses upon their foundations, covered with thick tiles, and [so] protected against the fury of the flames; whence it has often been the case that, when a fire has broken out in the City, and has destroyed many buildings, upon reaching such houses, it has been unable to do further mischief, and has been there extinguished; so that, through such a house as this, many houses of the neighbours have been saved from being burnt.

Merchants' stone houses in Britain's towns reached their peak in the late-12th century. Although the Assizes positively encouraged building in stone, a steady decline was under way in the face of more affordable and improved timber construction and the increasing persecution of the Jews, culminating in their expulsion from Britain by Edward I in 1290.

> A 15th-century semi-detached town house from Horsham, West Sussex (and now in the Weald and Downland Open Air Museum), containing two shops on the ground floor with access via a rear staircase to accommodation on the impressively jettied first and second floors.

The reversion to timber structures in expanding towns was to have some detrimental and even devastating consequences over the next half a millennium, as the deterioration of stone structures caused widespread urban dereliction by the late-medieval period. In the 16th century, 'The greatest part of our building in the cities and good townes of England, consisteth onelie of timber', observed William Harrison, 'for as yet few of the houses of the communaltie (except here & there in the West countrie townes) are made of stone.' The proliferation of timber structures was frequently the cause of urban conflagrations that devastated large areas of Britain's towns, none more so than the Great Fire of London in 1666.

As Britain's towns grew and space became scarcer, burgage tenements were subdivided and in new developments burgage plots were laid out as increasingly narrow strips of land aligned perpendicularly to the street. Unlike their Anglo-Saxon predecessors that were generally set back from the street, late-medieval town houses abutted and even overhung it. In older and more densely populated towns such as York and London the process of subdividing burgages began as early as the 10th century, but elsewhere it was a much later phenomenon that became widespread by the 13th century. With a premium on access to the highly prized street frontage, both for the trader and for the landlord who charged rent per property and therefore benefited from high densities, the typically broad facade of the medieval home with its hall flanked by wings shrank in width to maximise the number of properties on each plot.

The characteristics of the home within these growing and increasingly densely populated towns were not fundamentally different to those in the countryside. In just the same way that many of the activities that took place on burgage plots were quasi-agricultural and proto-industrial, including the small-scale rearing of livestock or cultivation of crops and an increasing range of artisan pursuits, the home in the medieval town remained part of a *rus in urbe* tradition. Structurally, dwellings would have been built by the same travelling artisans, and the knowledge, skills and materials required to construct them would not have varied significantly between a rural region and its neighbouring towns.

Variance occurred primarily as a result of constraints on space and the need to exploit the street frontage. The consequence for the home was the reorientation of its plan so that, rather than being parallel to the street, it was aligned perpendicular to it, with its shortest side presenting the principal elevation which commonly, but not exclusively, formed a gable end. In many British towns, houses with their gable ends facing the street were taxed less than those whose sides faced the streets. The tax was called a *gabulagium*, from the Latin *gabella*, meaning rent, and *gabellus*, meaning gable.

> A medieval merchant's town house (c 1290) in Southampton, Hampshire, restored to how it would have appeared in the mid-14th century.

∨ View from within the shop space of a 15th-century town house in Horsham, West Sussex, showing the door and counter. The staircase provides access to accommodation on the first and second floors.

ARCHITECTURE AND AVARICE

THE TUDORS AND EARLY STUARTS
1485–1649

By the late-medieval period, the traditional ties that had bound
society in Britain for centuries were loosening irreversibly,
heralding a more flexible, sophisticated and ultimately more
prosperous order under the reign of the Tudors (1485–1603).
The nation's religious orientation was recalibrated by the
English Reformation (1529–36) and Henry VIII's Dissolution
of the Monasteries (1536–41) – the largest transfer of property
since 1066. And in the front-line of social change helping to
unshackle society from its antiquated ways was the rise of
the merchant classes, whose power and affluence had grown
dramatically throughout the late-medieval period. Land,
presided over for centuries by the monarch's lords and nobles,
was no longer the sole font and repository of wealth. Nor was
it any longer the exclusive ground on which Britain's power
structure was built. Lords, for so long the linchpins in this
structure, were ceding control to a more fluid labour market
that was increasingly able to buy their freedom with wages or
earn it with acquired and specialised skills. This new-found
independence for the common worker gnawed away at the
fabric of traditional institutions and was integral to a rising
material and cultural prosperity that epitomised an age.
Shakespeare wrote the script that defined not only his era but
also his nation's soul, while trade sowed the seeds of Britain's
empire and spawned the East India Company, the world's first
global corporation. Under the Tudors, Britain's art flourished
and its produce was, for the first time in history, distributed
to the world.

A common desire among the many benefactors of Britain's
escalating affluence, whether petty merchants or royal courtiers,
was to convert their riches into a home. Many of Britain's cities
and towns were transformed by a higher standard of home
built by wealthy merchants; evidence of which survives in the
panoply of black and white timber-framing at the heart of many
urban centres, including Chester, Southampton, Stratford-upon-
Avon, York and Ludlow. However, at the very top of society
the home was revolutionised. The spirit of this transformation was
embodied in the Tudor show home – as much a deliberate display
of ostentation as a strategic quest for social promotion. The list
of monumental homes erected for these causes is prodigious.
By exploiting his closeness to Henry VIII, Cardinal Wolsey built
Hampton Court (see pages 122–3). By marrying shrewdly,
the Countess of Shrewsbury built many homes, including the
original manor at Chatsworth and Hardwick Hall (see pages
139–42). By charming a monarch, Christopher Hatton built
his Holdenby (see pages 135–6) and William Cecil (also known
as Lord Burghley) built his Burghley House (see pages 132–3
and pages 136–7) and Theobalds (see page 136–7), Queen
Elizabeth I's favourite home. Entertaining royalty was a passport
to untold wealth and many a British noble spent, and often
lost, their personal fortunes on preparing for the chance.

It was in these epic homes complete with their royal suites and built on fortunes amassed and guaranteed by connections to the crown that the greatest change in domestic planning occurred during the period following Britain's emergence from centuries of medievalism. Here, two developments in particular characterised and dominated the home's evolution over the next two centuries: architecture and avarice. For the well connected few, fortunes could be safely accumulated and might even be bestowed, as the bounties from dissolved monasteries were parcelled out to court favourites. Tudor amendments to England's long-standing Sumptuary Laws restricted most people from displaying wealth above their station, but such legal limitations rarely hampered those that made the law or wooed the lawmakers. The art of architecture and the accumulation and exhibition of personal wealth were not merely novel and momentous phenomena in their own right; they fed one another in a process that saw the construction of unprecedented piles of excess. These stone piles were for architecture what the luxuriant fabrics and costumes were for fashion during the Tudor era – both were arts of affectation expressed exclusively through the attire and abodes of the super-rich and both designed explicitly to elevate social standing. The aristocratic Tudor show home became a venue for extraordinary entertaining – not of staff, travellers or the poor, as their ancestors would have done, but of their own kind and, most crucially, to impress and win the favour of their sovereign.

< Classically inspired columns at Audley
End (1610), Essex, reveal the growing
Continental influence on British design
at the turn of the 17th century.

VIII's reign, and its elaborate and contorted brick patterning decorated with heraldic badges and insignia, were seen as a sign of decadence. William Harrison wrote of 'the multitude of chimnies latelie erected' whereas houses only a few years earlier had no more than two or three. The multiplication of chimneys was invariably a response not to the growing number of rooms, though these were increasing, but to the Tudor predilection for bragging. It was their way of keeping up with the Joneses. These chimneys 'make a shew a far off, and catch Travellers eyes', wrote Thomas Dekker (*c* 1572–1632), 'but coming nere them, neither cast they smoke, nor hath the house the heart to make you drinke'. Greene also commented on this contemporary phenomenon, blaming the nobility for wasting decent bricks and mortar in building glorious palaces with 'some threescore chimnies' yet 'three of them shal not smoke in a twelve moneth'. Hospitality's decline paralleled the chimney's ascent, which was built, quite literally, on the demise of the hearth and the hall. Having endured for centuries, these essential characteristics of the British home could not survive the Tudor's desire for style articulated by architecture.

THE ASCENT OF ARCHITECTURE

As architecture's reputation progressed from the middle of the 16th century, this new profession was not only adopted by the nobility to elevate them literally and figuratively above the rest of society, but it also became a requisite skill of a worthy gentleman. Suggesting architecture was more scholarly than the work of a master mason, the writer James Cleland asserted in 1607 that a gentleman should become acquainted with this new art form, enabling them to decipher the features of building and the classical orders – Tuscan, Doric, Ionic, Corinthian and Composite. Architecture was one of a number of talents in the aristocracy's repertoire that allowed them to feel they were superior. 'He that hath no relish of the grandeur and joy of building,' wrote the lawyer Roger North (1651–1734), 'is a stupid ox.'

On its lofty pedestal, architecture was, in the words of the diplomat and author of *The Elements of Architecture*, Henry Wotton (1568–1639), a mistress who was dressed and trimmed by her 'two principall *Gentlewomen*: Picture & Sculpture'. Architecture meant that the aristocratic British home was no longer satisfied principally by food, benevolence and good cheer, as it had been since time immemorial, but by the superficial veneer of art, the championing of which, particularly during Elizabeth I's reign, was incomparable. The veil of civility shrouding the new ostentatious structures built by Britain's expanding nobility was, like the flagrant fashions and overt opulence of the Elizabethan age, invariably a cloak of conceit reinforcing their distinction and

inviting condemnation. 'Scab'd Cuckows in a cage of gold' is how Joseph Hall in *Virgidemiarum* described patrons of architecture who presided over the moral vacuum left behind by hospitality's retreat. By invoking the classical orders, he employed architecture to mock Britain's nobility:

> Goe se who in so garish walls doth dwell?
> There findest thou some stately *Doricke* frame,
> Or neat *Ionicke* worke;
> Like the vaine bubble of *Iberian* pride,
> That over-croweth all the world beside.
> Which rear'd to raise the crazy Monarche's fame,
> Strives for a Court and for a College name.

Hall's employment of the formal language of architecture reflected a growing awareness of this new art form in Britain throughout the Tudor period. The language was foreign, coming from Italy, France and Flanders, and took time for the native population to master. In the meantime, the practice of building throughout the 16th century remained a largely domestic affair characterised by clumsy attempts at copying classical codes interpreted through the treatises and pattern books of Continental masters, such as Alberti, Serlio and the Dutch architect and painter, Hans Vredeman de Vries (1527–1606). '*Englese Italianato, è un diabolo incarnato*' ['An Englishman Italianate is a devil incarnate'], rang the Italian proverb mockingly in Roger Ascham's *The Scholemaster* (1570). Preceding this period of experimentation was not only John Shute's effort to make the formal language of architecture accessible to an English-speaking audience, but also earlier observations by others unversed in the formality of architecture yet nevertheless interested in building.

Around 1540, Andrew Borde, a keen physician and traveller, published *The boke for to Lerne a man to be wyse in buyldyng of his howse for the helth of his soule, and body, etc.*, an early treatise on building and a unique account of the British home at a critical point in its evolution – when the simple convenience of the medieval type was giving way to a more formal arrangement imposed by the aesthetic order and coded language of architecture. What makes Borde's example so interesting is that it is not inhibited by architecture's obsession with harmony between the plan and the elevation, which came later, but instead concentrates on the site, plan and aspect.

At the core of Borde's hypothetical mansion was the plan of a medieval home. It contained a central hall with a parlour at the top end and buttery and pantry at the low end, and a kitchen beyond. He also described certain developments, such as a pastry house and larder annexed to the kitchen and additional private chambers annexed to the master's chamber, each with a prospect

^ The rear door at Audley End (1610), Essex, showing a mixture of British and Continental motifs.

< Evidence of classical influences in British design of the late 16th century, here at Longleat (1580), Wiltshire.

into the chapel. These extra lodgings were arranged around a quadrangular courtyard in front of the hall with a gatehouse, whose central and adjacent position in relation to the entrance to the hall anticipated Britain's imminent adherence to symmetry in domestic planning. If the house was grand enough to have an outer courtyard, it was laid out in front of the gatehouse and contained offices and stables far away so that odours would not reach the house.

Borde's professional interest in physical and mental wellbeing focused his attentions on the synergy between the building, its layout and its setting – something Henry Wotton later referred to as the 'situation' or 'total posture'. Obsessed by the relationship between the home and its site, Borde appears like a Tudor advocate of feng shui. He claimed the chief prospect of the home should be east/west so as to avoid the 'moste worst' meridian winds. The south wind in particular he thought was corrupting and produced evil vapours, while the east wind, in contrast, was temperate, frisk and fragrant. He also believed a home should always be near water and a wood, with views that are 'pleasant and fayre, and good to the iye'. Outhouses containing malodorous activities such as slaughterhouses and brewhouses should be at least 'a quarter of a myle' away from the mansion and servants should not let 'the fylth of the kytchyn descende in to the mote'. Pre-empting the great 18th-century landscape gardeners, such as Lancelot 'Capability' Brown (1716–83), Borde also suggested the surrounding estate should be replete with herbs 'of a romantyke and redolet savoures' as well as containing a dovecote, fish ponds, rabbits and deer.

Borde's advice echoed the even earlier humanist musings of one of the first British writers on the subject, William Horman (c 1440–1535), former headmaster at Eton. Horman suggested a man's dwelling ought to be sited in 'a plesant place of soyle and holsome ayre. The hylly country rounde about us kepeth awey parellous wyndis and pestylent infections'. Although their approaches were not scientific, their legacy endured, as the 17th-century scientist, Francis Bacon (1561–1626), clearly owed a debt to their ideas when he wrote: 'He that builds a fair house, upon an ill seat, committeth himself to prison.' Borde and Horman's observations show that it was during the early Tudor period that the conscious planning of the home became a subject of popular debate: firstly in its siting, then later in its internal arrangement, which required an architect.

Two decades and five monarchs later, a different kind of guide to building was made available to an English-speaking readership. It was also an early contribution to a process that changed the way the British viewed building for ever. John Shute's illustrated account of the five classical orders, *The First and Chief Groundes of Architecture* (1563), was based on the works of the first and

great Roman architect, Vitruvius, who compiled the first book on the subject: *The Ten Books of Architecture*. Seven years after the publication of Shute's work, the Elizabethan scientist, John Dee (1527–1609), wrote the introduction to Henry Billingsley's translation of Euclid's *The Elements of Geometrie*. Although he felt architecture was too infrequently used in the late 16th century, Dee understood its importance and identified three principal applications. These were fortifications, shipbuilding and housing, the last of which he separated into public 'for Divine Service' and private for 'Mans common usage'.

Dee, like Shute before him, was among a vanguard of British scholars indebted to Continental contact during the 16th century, whether indirectly by reading imported books or directly by travelling to Europe on Grand Tours. Shute travelled to Italy in 1550 under the patronage of John Dudley, the Duke of Northumberland, at the height of the Renaissance, when Palladio was in ascendance before becoming the pre-eminent architect of the age and the defining influence of Inigo Jones (1573–1652), Britain's first Classicist architect. Jones's earliest surviving work, the Queen's House (1616) in Greenwich, is the first and foremost example of an architectural composition in Britain, and was inspired by his recent journey to Italy on which he took a copy of Palladio's revolutionary *Quattro libri dell'architettura* (1570).

Although Shute was no architect, he and Jones were indebted to their experience of Europe, and in particular, Italy. For years, artisans from Europe had come to Britain to help build and furnish royal households, but Shute and Jones were among the first benefactors of early attempts by British patrons to foster a home-grown architectural profession. Travelling was considered a prerequisite of a young nobleman's education and would become a rite of passage in acquiring the proper cultural values that defined 'taste'. Touring Europe not only taught a young gentleman 'wholesome hardship', as Richard Lassels later described in *The Voyage of Italy* (1670), but also afforded him vital experience. In Italy he could 'learn to make a fine house; but not to keep a good house' and in Holland he could 'learn to keep his house and hearth neat [but not] adore his house, and stand in such awe of his hearth, as not to dare to make a fire in it, as they do'. Britain's architectural inspiration came primarily from Italy, the Low Countries, Germany and France. According to Henry Peacham, France 'possessed the best Architects of the world'. Although British practitioners struggled to grapple with this new art form, the result, by the 17th century, was an established and formal architectural language dominated by Palladio's parlance but which nevertheless retained a distinctly British inflection and whose most famous spokesmen were Inigo Jones, John Webb (1611–72), Roger Pratt and Christopher Wren (1632–1723). Through these and many other lesser figures, architecture was firmly established in Britain and would permanently alter the plan of the British home.

ROYAL PALACES AND STATELY MANSIONS

Centuries of instability had left their mark on the built landscape in Britain, from town walls, through substantial stone fortifications, keeps, gatehouses, moats, turrets and crenellation, to arrowslit windows. By the 16th century these defensive devices had become largely redundant and as the century closed even the introverted courtyard mansion seemed anachronistic, surrendering its dominance to the extroverted, architecturally designed, monumental mansion. The plan and external appearance of the British home, as well as its interior accoutrements, were modified by the relative peace and prosperity of the Tudor age as a more affluent population sought to make their homes more private and comfortable.

During the Tudor age, an aristocrat's title was no longer preserved by the physical strength of a fortification as it had been in earlier times, but by its ostentatious emulation. According to Roger Pratt, there were 'three sorts of persons for whom houses are built of any consideration, viz. gentlemen, noblemen, and princes'. One of the first major buildings to demonstrate the British nobility's early predilection for a massive home possessing faux-military features of an increasingly distant age was Herstmonceux Castle in East Sussex. Built entirely in brick, then a novel and exceedingly expensive material, this castle was no fortification.

Unconstrained by cost, the construction of monumental homes employed the best craftsmen and latest materials and technologies. Over time, these were reproduced by others or translated to suit the means of less affluent households, but this process would take decades. Seated at the top of this hierarchy was Henry VIII, who, on becoming King of England in 1509, inherited a country whose coffers had been very effectively replenished by his father. The system of taxation adopted by Henry VII had been in place since 1334 and was based on the fractional system of fifteenths and tenths – where cities, towns and ancient estates paid a tenth and everywhere else paid a fifteenth of gross income.

< A drawing of Inigo Jones's original masterpiece, the Queen's House (1616), Greenwich, the first complete classically composed house in Britain.

>> Herstmonceux Castle (1441) in East Sussex, commissioned by Sir Roger Fiennes, Treasurer to Henry VI. Construction began in 1441 and by the 18th century it had become a ruin. It was restored in the 20th century.

Although it was a simple, reliable but not entirely fair system, it did not generate enough revenue for the Exchequer, so Henry VII introduced an additional tax on individuals based on the value of their moveable goods or the income from their land, whichever was the greater. Relatively high tax thresholds meant the tax only impacted the wealthy, but the dividends were much higher. With few wars or costly pet projects, Henry VII restored the nation's economic footing, but his thrift also allowed his son, Henry VIII, to spend, which he did with abandon. Henry VIII honed the tax system, often lowering the threshold in order to generate even more income for his foreign wars and extravagant palaces. Throughout his 38-year reign he created more sumptuous palaces than any other monarch in British history. By the time of his death he could claim over 60 homes, including Nonsuch Palace, Hampton Court, the Palace at Whitehall, St James's Palace, Knole, Leeds Castle and Ightham Mote. Small wonder then that William Harrison described him posthumously as 'the onelie Phenix of his time for fine and curious masonrie'.

The palace most commonly associated with Henry VIII is Hampton Court, by the River Thames in Surrey, originally the home of Thomas (Cardinal) Wolsey (1473–1530). The Cardinal was one of a select group of courtiers who exploited their close relationship with the king to propel themselves up the social ladder and acquire inordinate wealth in the process. Wolsey excelled in this game and gained riches unmatched outside royalty. He started his career as almoner to Henry VIII immediately after his coronation and rose to become Lord Chancellor as well as Archbishop of York (1514) and Cardinal (1515). These positions were among the most powerful in the land, and to occupy them all made Wolsey untouchable for over a decade. The home he built for himself came to epitomise the Tudor age, when influences from Continental Europe permanently transformed and ornamented building in Britain and recalibrated domestic planning.

Wolsey had originally planned Hampton Court around a single courtyard, to which he added a second, making it one of the earliest examples of rectilinear symmetrical planning. In this regard, it anticipated the imminent, almost slavish adherence to symmetry that would dominate both plan and elevation for centuries. Wolsey's Hampton Court had transformed a medieval manor house into a home of unparalleled opulence and extravagance. The palace was so sumptuous that Henry VIII made it his regular residence, staying in one of three separate royal suites that Wolsey had built for him, his wife, Catherine of Aragon, and their daughter, Princess Mary. When completed in 1525, the complex of buildings invited the ire of many, including Poet Laureate John Skelton, who wrote a satire, *Colyn Clout* (1550), inspired by and aimed at his former friend, the Cardinal:

^ Hampton Court in Surrey, commissioned by Cardinal Wolsey and extended and enlarged by Henry VIII from 1528 to 1540.

∨ General plan of Hampton Court, Surrey (completed in 1525 and extended since).

Buyldyng royally
Theyr mancyons curyously,
With turrettes and with toures,
With halles and with boures,
Stretchynge to the starres,
With glasse wyndowes and barres;
Hangynge aboute the walles
Clothes of golde and palles,
Arras of ryche aray,
Fresshe as flours in May.

Faced with overwhelming enemies in the royal court, Wolsey handed Hampton Court to Henry VIII in 1528, before being stripped of his title the following year. Henry's even grander designs for Hampton Court saw the palace become one of the King's principal residences, commodious enough to accommodate his thousand-strong court and hundreds of state guests. Architecturally, Hampton Court is synonymous with the Tudor Age: its brick body, surrounding gardens, increasingly symmetrical plan, and foreign decoration are all evidence of the social and architectural revolution. When Frederick, Duke of Wirtemberg, visited in 1592, he was awed:

> All the apartments and rooms in this immensely large structure are hung with rich tapestry, of pure gold and fine silk, so exceedingly beautiful and royally ornamented that it would hardly be possible to find more magnificent things of the kind in any other place. In particular, there is one apartment belonging to the Queen, in which she is accustomed to sit in state, costly beyond everything; the tapestries are garnished with gold, pearls, and precious stones ... [it is] the most splendid and most magnificent royal Palace of any that may be found in England – or, indeed, in any other kingdom.

> Nonsuch Palace (1538–47), Surrey, commissioned by Henry VIII.

∨ General plan of Nonsuch Palace (1547), Surrey.

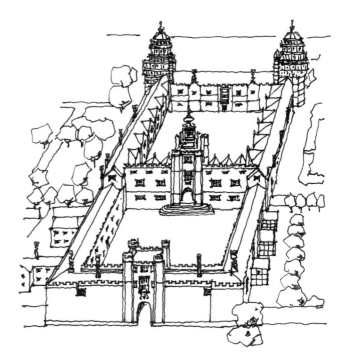

Of all of Henry VIII's many ambitious building projects, none better represented the transition in British building (practically and stylistically) than Nonsuch Palace in Surrey – so named because no such place could compare with it. Nonsuch was built from scratch, so it embodied, more than any other building in Britain at that time, the transition from the convenience of medieval planning to the formal order imposed by architecture. Construction of Nonsuch Palace began in 1538 and was almost complete by the time of Henry's death in 1547. An entire village, including its church, was demolished to make way for the Nonsuch estate. The Palace was immense and its appointments extraordinarily ornate. Throughout the Tudor age, as the Dutchman Emanuel Van Meteren noted, 'the most toilsome, difficult, and skilful works [were] chiefly performed by foreigners', and at Nonsuch it was predominantly foreign artificers that created the unprecedented display of magnificence, wealth and refinement, that Henry hoped would surpass anything belonging to his great French rival, Francis I.

Planned around two courtyards, it closely resembled Borde's hypothetical model of a manor, which was written as Nonsuch was under construction. Access to the palace was gained by an imposing north-facing turreted gateway constructed in brick and stone which led to an outer courtyard, around which were situated private lodgings for the King's entourage. On the adjacent wall, a smaller gateway provided access to the inner courtyard. The buildings surrounding this space were constructed of stone and timber on the ground floor, with the most extensive display of timber-framing ever erected in

Britain above, the spaces between which were embellished with hundreds of ornate stucco panels. The King's residence was situated on the west side of the courtyard and the Queen's on the east. It was customary, as Wolsey had arranged at Hampton Court, for the king and queen to have separate suites within the palace. Although the double-courtyard plan parallels earlier large homes of the gentry, Nonsuch's distinction was a matter of degrees – nothing matched its size, luxuriousness or, most importantly in terms of planning, its symmetry.

Symmetry, later described by Wotton as 'the *conveniencie* that runneth betweene the *Parts* and the *Whole*', had been largely confined to religious and military structures – churches, cathedrals, castles and keeps – but Nonsuch marks the first tentative step in purely domestic planning, albeit on a huge scale, away from medieval utility towards aesthetic order and the formal composition of the facade that would develop over the next two centuries. 'Beautiful it will be if all the great rooms be placed just in the middle,' wrote Roger Pratt over a century later, 'and afterwards that those on each hand of them have alike positions and also dimensions, as we find it in our own bodies ... all the windows on the one side of the house etc. to exactly range with those on the other, and the doors likewise.' Nonsuch was among the first great homes to achieve this.

The symmetry of Nonsuch and the more convoluted development at Hampton Court were evidence of a Continental influence that contrasted with and ultimately usurped British building traditions. The difference between these symmetrical plans and earlier double-courtyard plans, such as at Penshurst in Kent (see page 82–4), is demonstrative of new and the old approaches. Penshurst, like so many British manor houses, had evolved over centuries so that by the 16th century its irregular external form appeared arbitrary but internally it concealed a convenient arrangement of space organised around the central hall and attendant offices and apartments constructed by successive owners. These included Sir John Devereux (d 1393), who built a crenellated stone wall around the manor in 1392; the brother of Henry V, John of Lancaster, the Duke of Bedford (1389–1435), who added north and south ranges (1430–35); and Sir Henry Sidney (1529–86), Lord Deputy of Ireland, who built the west range of apartments that enclosed the double courtyard and a double-storey long gallery in the southwest corner of the site (1573–85). In advance of Henry VIII's earlier visit to Penshurst in 1519, Edward Stafford, the Third Duke of Buckingham (1478–1521), spent the equivalent of over £1.2 million upgrading Penshurst, which was a typically exorbitant sum that nobles were expected to spend hosting their sovereign at home. Unfortunately, Edward's investment was far from rewarding. The king viewed Edward's wealth suspiciously and two years later had him beheaded for treason and appropriated

> The monumental ruins at Cowdray (1530s), West Sussex, showing the integral gatehouse in the front elevation with an obvious urge towards symmetry.

∨ Plan of Penshurst Place, Kent, showing the numerous additions made to the building over two centuries (1392; 1430–35; and 1573–85) that created an irregular double-courtyard plan.

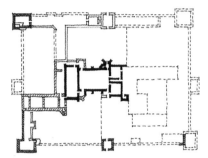

his lavish home. In the 17th century Penshurst was immortalised by Benjamin Jonson's (1572–1637) poem, *To Penshurst* (1616):

> Thou art not, Penshurst, built to envious show
> Of touch, or marble; nor canst boast a row
> Of polish'd pillars, or a roof of gold:
> Thou hast no lantern whereof tales are told;
> Or stair, or courts; but stand'st an ancient pile,
> And these grudg'd at, art reverenced the while.

Separating the rambling forms of these evolving structures and the formal planning of large 16th-century set-piece homes such as Nonsuch was a fleeting generation of stately mansions that were neither disorderly nor disposed. Homes such as Hengrave Hall (1538) in Suffolk and Cowdray in West Sussex, although they served a similar social function as other aristocratic homes, displayed an inclination towards symmetry in certain parts but not yet in the whole.

Cowdray embodies the moment when British conventions, such as those at Penshurst, yielded to modern influences from Continental Europe. Sir David Owen (*c* 1459–1535), Henry VIII's great-uncle, began constructing Cowdray in the 1520s, but it was sold in 1529 to Sir William Fitzwilliam (*c* 1490–1542), who completed it before his death. Fitzwilliam was a friend of Henry VIII from early childhood and maintained his trust throughout his entire life, being appointed Knight of the Garter, Lord Keeper of the Privy Seal, and Lord High Admiral. The home he built at Cowdray was a typical 16th-century noble's household. Much more than a home for his family, it was a miniature realm at the heart of a large estate employing over a hundred members of staff, from a steward who was in charge of the overall management of the estate, to the lowliest scullery man. Most household staff were male, though females were employed as laundry maids and as the personal servants of female members of the household. Although alterations were made to Cowdray after Fitzwilliam's death in 1542, a fire that destroyed the entire main building on 24 September 1793 preserved its original configuration, albeit as a ruin.

Cowdray possessed most of the same features as contemporary royal palaces like Nonsuch. The hall, great chambers, apartments, galleries, lodgings and stores arranged around one or two courtyards were familiar features of medieval and 16th-century homes, but the principal distinction between places like Cowdray and their immediate successors was the degree of symmetry. Echoing contemporary Renaissance ideals, Borde advocated that 'the gate house be opposyte or agaynst the hall dore, and the gate house in the mydle of the fronte entrynge into the place'. His recommendations matched Nonsuch, but Cowdray's imposing three-storey gatehouse was neither opposite the hall door nor in

the middle of the front entrance. Cowdray's almost symmetrical layout is an example of the reluctance among early-Tudor builders to relinquish time-honoured customs and shoehorn modern ideas into medieval planning.

This process of conversion was particularly hampered by the hall and the antique codes that governed its asymmetrical internal layout. When Cowdray was being built, the hall, situated across the courtyard from the gatehouse, was just clinging on to its pre-eminent status inside the home. Aligning the hall centrally with the gatehouse would have required cutting a new doorway in the middle of the hall, which would have destabilised the ancient order of the hall's high and low ends. At Cowdray, Fitzwilliam compromised and retained the entrance at the low end while elevating its prominence by converting it into a Porch of Honour in 1538, in time for the first of Henry VIII's three visits to the house.

To reach the Porch of Honour from the gatehouse, visitors had to cross the courtyard diagonally, passing a towering fountain with figures of dolphins, Medusa heads and a naked male, all believed to be the work of the Florentine sculptor, Benedetto da Rovezzano (1474–1554), which now resides in London's Victoria and Albert Museum. A stone carving of Henry's coat of arms

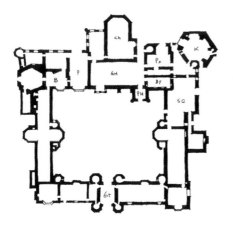

∧ Ground-floor plan of Cowdray (1530s),
West Sussex.

Ch: Chapel · B: Bedroom · P: Parlour
GH: Great Hall · PH: Porch of Honour
Pa: Pantry · By: Buttery · K: Kitchen
SQ: Servants' Quarters · Gt: Gatehouse

hung above the porch's entrance, and inside, a vaulted stone roof carved by Italian craftsmen in a blend of Gothic and Renaissance styles displayed various insignia and motifs. Reverence for heraldic insignia grew particularly strong during the Tudor period. Upon the desecration of Henry IV's household coat and imprese in Shakespeare's *King Richard II*, he claims to have nothing to 'shew the world [he] is a gentleman'. At Cowdray, the Fitzwilliam insignia was accompanied by the Tudor rose and the Prince of Wales feathers to symbolise the recent birth of Henry's son Edward (who later became Edward VI and would visit Cowdray in 1552). As much as these gestures were in honour of the King, they are also evidence of Fitzwilliam's deference to him, for any nobleman who should attempt to surpass royalty in the magnificence and luxury of their home might soon find it confiscated, their position weakened or worse – as Penshurst's Third Duke of Buckingham found out. The Fitzwilliam maxim carved in the oak door between the porch and screens passage, 'LOIAVLAT SA PROVERA' – Loyalty Proves Itself – was no understatement.

Internally, the main hall conformed to the typical medieval arrangement of high and low ends. The low end was marked by a screens passage with three doorways leading to buttery, pantry and the vast kitchen. Separated from the main building, the kitchen was arranged as a tower with thick walls to prevent the possible outbreak of fire and contained three massive ranges that were capable of cooking enough food for up to two hundred people. A chapel was positioned perpendicularly to the hall and located behind it, just as Borde recommended, and could be seen from the private chambers. Above the elaborate screens passage was a musical gallery. At the high end, Fitzwilliam commissioned a huge bay window that extended from the floor to the roofline and was the second largest in Britain at the time. Such expansive bay windows, and their close cousin, the oriel, which projected from the wall and was not carried to the ground, became prominent features of larger Tudor homes. Cowdray's hall would have been richly decorated with tapestries. These costly furnishings would have travelled with the household in medieval times. From the 16th century, as occurred at Cowdray, arrases were replaced by wainscoting in wood, decorated plaster panels or even leather. Above the wainscoting, the walls were adorned with other decorative features. Eleven statues of stags gave the room its name 'Buck Hall'. Finely carved wooden corbels supported a huge hammerbeam roof in the style of Westminster Hall and Hampton Court. By the late 16th century, the hall, as occurred throughout Britain, was no longer used for communal meals. Seeking more privacy, the family retired to the parlour to eat, which was behind the upper end of the hall and beneath the great chamber. On a daily basis, the hall was used by high officials and servants and was only restored to its full medieval-style splendour when used for entertaining.

∧ The exterior of the hall at Cowdray (1530s),
West Sussex, showing the Porch of Honour
in the foreground that led to the low end
of the hall.

A separate development in the building of large homes from
the early 16th century was fuelled by the dissolution of the
monasteries in the late 1530s. Britain's nobility had already
enjoyed several decades of rising prosperity, but Henry
VIII's decision to dissolve the monasteries released abundant
wealth and land into the hands of a few well-placed courtiers.
Confiscated monasteries provided both the site and materials
for many massive Tudor homes, their reconfigured buildings
supplying the skin for new and secular abodes such as those
of Sir Thomas Wriothesley (1505–50) who acquired and rebuilt
Titchfield Abbey, and Lord William Sandys (1470–1540)
who established his family home at Mottisfont Abbey, both
in Hampshire. Wriothesley and Sandys both acquired their
wealth through their association with the king. Wriothesley,
who achieved the rank of Lord Chancellor, was rewarded
handsomely for his loyalty and granted large tracts of formerly
monastic land around Southampton, later becoming the First
Earl of Southampton. Sandys reached the position of Lord
Chamberlain and his home, The Vyne, in Hampshire, hosted
Henry VIII on three occasions. In other cases, such as Fountains
Hall in Yorkshire, the fabric of the buildings was dismantled
and reassembled in completely new guises.

< The stone vault by Italian craftsmen inside the Porch of Honour (1538) at Cowdray, West Sussex, looking out towards the main gatehouse.

> The customary three doorways at the low end of the hall leading to the buttery, kitchen and pantry, depicted here at Cowdray (1530s), West Sussex. The line of holes above the doors would have supported the rafters of a musical gallery.

∨ The massive detached kitchen at Cowdray (1530s), West Sussex.

» Burghley House (1587), Lincolnshire.

By Elizabeth's reign (1558–1603), symmetry began to have a controlling influence on both the plan and the elevation, but at the same time there was also a tendency to axe the large courtyard, which Roger Pratt later described as 'fit only for a large family, and a great purse'. The sprawling courtyard enclosed by lengthy ranges of apartments, chapel, hall and galleries succumbed to the singular structure that was a monumental composition of brick, stone and glass. Throughout the second half of the 16th century many of these monumental show homes were erected, some of which were the most ambitious building projects of this kind in Britain's history. The mansion at Longleat in Wiltshire, commissioned by Lord Burghley's brother-in-law, Sir John Thynne, and completed by 1580, was one of the first of this type. It did not have a courtyard, not in the traditional sense at least, and was built entirely of stone, appearing as one solid mass in contrast to the sprawling medieval homes that comprised a series of loosely connected parts. Unlike her father throughout the first half of the century, Elizabeth I did not partake in this excess, but her attendance was a major factor in stimulating overindulgence among her subjects. Hosting Elizabeth I at home was the greatest aspiration and sometimes the most important duty of an Elizabethan noble. Some, like Elizabeth's darling Sir Christopher Hatton (1540–91), gambled not just their fortunes but also their lives in pursuit of her favour.

Elizabeth's reign was one marked by cultural confidence and economic prosperity. The period's leading figures – Shakespeare, Marlowe, Drake and Raleigh – loom large in British history, as do Elizabeth's successes (not least the defeat of the Spanish Armada) and the homes of the nobility. In the past, wealthy nobles had been content to extend and adapt family homes, but this practice was becoming unfashionable. Pratt warned 'not to patch up an old house, at any great expense, or to make an addition to it', because the old one, after much trouble and expense, will not meet anyone's expectation but will 'look patched and irregular without, and within very little convenience, with low ceilings, and unequal floors'.

∧ Longleat (1580), Wiltshire, designed
by Robert Smythson.

> Ground-floor plan of Longleat
(1580), Wiltshire.

⌄ General plan of Holdenby
(1583), Northamptonshire.

Armed with the latest architectural pattern books from the Continent, Elizabethan aristocrats, 'their heads never idle, their purses never shut', suggested William Harrison, desired nothing more than to build their homes from scratch in the latest style, though the results were regularly a medley. British craftsman were independent from their foreign mentors and their interpretation of Renaissance Italy or Flanders was invariably second-hand. It was not until the early 17th century that the rugged domestic style became refined and tempered by foreign manners.

Nevertheless, the sheer scale of these new brick and stone homes awed many observers, including Harrison who claimed 'the basest house of a baron dooth often match in our daies with some honours of princes in old time'. He even compared the skill of the workmen who built these homes with the Italian masters Vitruvius, Leon Battista Alberti and Sebastiano Serlio, suggesting the dawn of a golden age in the life of the British home. 'If ever curious building did florish in England,' he wrote, 'it is in these our years,' and he was right. Some of the most sumptuous mansions ever raised in Britain were constructed, all of them symmetrical and invariably based on E- and H-shaped plans. Architecturally, these monumental homes were concerned more with vanity than utility, and symmetry was the principle measure of this new-found narcissism. Just as architecture had become a gentlemen's pursuit, so too had symmetry become a means of conveying this acumen – a form of intellectual titillation at the expense of functionality or convenience.

The largest of Britain's 16th-century private homes was Holdenby in Northamptonshire, commissioned by Elizabeth I's darling and Lord Chancellor, Christopher Hatton whose close relationship with the Queen that enabled him to build so prodigiously invited mocking from contemporary satirists. Ben Jonson referred to him in a masque that was performed before the visiting Queen of Denmark in June 1603:

> They come to see and to be seen,
> And though they dance before the Queen,
> There's none of these doth hope to come by
> Wealth to build another Holmby;
> All these dancing days are done,
> Men must now have more than one
> Grace to build their fortunes on.

Completed in 1583, the massive three-storey structure covering over 7,000 square metres was Britain's largest private home. Hatton had his home designed in the most modern manner possible. Its sheer scale allowed it to be built on a double-courtyard plan and it was arranged symmetrically with countless apartments and two state halls, one for him and one for the Queen.

> The inner courtyard at Burghley House (1587), Lincolnshire, more grand and spacious than the diminutive courtyards in similar prodigious homes.

˅ Ground-floor plan of Burghley House (1587), Lincolnshire.

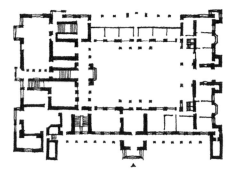

It was decorated with classical architectural features, including a Doric arcade, and boasted 123 huge glass windows at a time when glass was the height of luxury and a conspicuous expression of affluence. The project ruined Hatton, who died in 1591, destitute and childless, though his memory lives on. Francis Drake named the ship in which he circumnavigated the world, *The Golden Hind*, after Hatton's crest because Hatton sponsored his expedition, and London's Hatton Gardens and the nearby primary school retain the name of this once eminent local resident. James I purchased Holdenby in 1607 and after the Civil War it was sold to the Parliamentarian Captain Adam Baynes who razed most of the house, leaving just one wing standing.

Holdenby was rivalled only by Theobalds Palace in Hertfordshire, commissioned by Sir William Cecil (1521–98) – Lord Burghley, Lord High Treasurer to Queen Elizabeth I and another of her most trusted aides. Completed in 1585, Theobalds was built to strengthen Lord Burghley's standing in the royal court, and became one of the Queen's favourite residences, which she visited on eight occasions. In 1592, the Duke of Wirtemberg described Theobalds as 'one of the most beautiful houses in England'. In its 'handsome and delightful hall' stood 40 trees representing the counties of England. Theobalds, like Holdenby, suffered in the Civil War and although it was later restored, it was eventually demolished, though its staircase survives in Herstmonceux Castle.

Theobalds was Cecil's show home, designed for doing business more than enjoying the comforts of domesticity. His true home was Burghley House in Lincolnshire, which he commissioned in 1555 and was completed in 1587. In keeping with the latest fashions, Burghley House was symmetrically designed with vast ranges on an altogether different scale than those earlier in the century built around a small inner courtyard. The south, west and north ranges were all symmetrical, with the exception of

the Great Hall's addition to the eastern end of the south facade, which Cecil added later when his elevated social position was secured and keeping ahead of prevailing tastes in architectural composition was less vital than when he started the project over three decades earlier.

The Jacobean equivalent of Lord Burghley's Theobalds was Audley End in Essex, commissioned by Thomas Howard (1561–1626), who became Earl of Suffolk. A Benedictine monastery had occupied the site of Audley End until Henry VIII granted the land to his Lord Chancellor, Thomas Audley, in 1538. Howard was Audley's grandson and became Lord Chamberlain, Privy Counsellor and Lord High Treasurer to James I. In his commanding position, and like Lord Burghley and Hatton before him, he spent his riches on building a massive home. Audley End (1610) was equal to Holdenby and Theobalds in its audacious scale, boasting 750 rooms and private suites for the King and Queen arranged around two huge courtyards. In 1618 Howard was found to have abused his position and was stripped of his title and power. Audley End, like Holdenby, was simply too large for anyone to maintain. Charles II bought the building in 1668 but it was soon returned to the Suffolks and fell into disrepair, with two thirds of the house being pulled down in the 18th century.

> Audley End (1610), Essex, south elevation showing the extensive glazing that was increasingly common by the early 17th century.

< Audley End (1610), Essex, window detail showing British and Continental influences.

∨ Ground-floor plan of Audley End (1610), Essex.

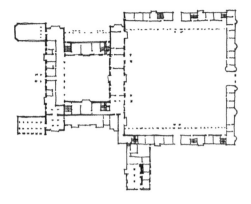

Notable survivors from this prodigious period of monumental home-building are Wollaton Hall in Nottinghamshire, commissioned by Sir Francis Willoughby and completed in 1588, and Hardwick Hall in Derbyshire, commissioned by Elizabeth, Countess of Shrewsbury, better known as Bess of Hardwick (*c* 1521–1607/8). Completed in 1597, Hardwick Hall dispensed with the courtyard layout and, like Burghley, Longleat and Wollaton, was surrounded by expansive parkland that was later landscaped, with the exception of Wollaton, by the renowned 18th-century landscape gardener, Lancelot 'Capability' Brown. All of these show homes were at least three storeys high, with wings, towers and turrets up to five storeys containing chambers that Shakespeare described in *The Two Gentleman of Verona* as being 'aloft, far from the ground'.

Longleat, Wollaton and Hardwick all involved the handiwork of the master mason-cum-architect, Robert Smythson (1534/5–1614), who also had a hand in Doddington Hall (1600) in Lincolnshire and Burton Agnes Hall (1610) in East Yorkshire. Smythson's example demonstrates the economic and social mobility that distinguished 16th-century Britain from the preceding medieval period when movement between social ranks was much less fluid. Starting his career on the bottom rung of the social ladder as a lowly artificer, Smythson used his trade to elevate himself to the rank of gentleman and in the process became one of the most important proto-architects of his time and one of the principal progenitors of the Elizabethan style. Indeed, Smythson's career mirrored the rise of architecture in Britain from the trades to a distinguished overarching profession. Recalling Plato's assertion that the architect was '*Master* over all, that make any worke', the scientist, John Dee, described the architect as 'neither Smith, nor Builder: nor, separately, any Artificer: but the Hed, the Provost, the Director, and Judge of all Artificiall workes, and all Artificers. For, the true *Architect*, is hable to teach, Demonstrate, distribute,

∨ Hardwick Hall (1597), Derbyshire, built by Robert Smythson for Elizabeth, Countess of Shrewsbury, better known as Bess of Hardwick.

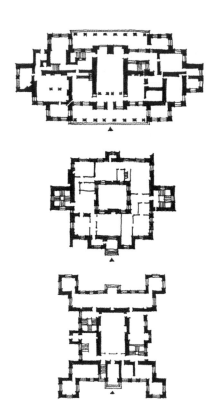

describe, and Judge all workes wrought'. Smythson was the first in Britain to come close to matching this description.

The most refined, compact and ordered of all Smythson's works was Hardwick Hall, whose walls, dominated by great gleaming panels of glass, generated the popular rhyme: 'Hardwick Hall, more glass than wall.' Glass was cheaper in the late 1500s than it had been earlier in the century but it was still a material that boasted a homeowner's wealth. The observation in 1598 by one traveller from Brandenburg that 'glass-houses are in plenty' throughout Britain was telling indeed. However, Hardwick's prodigious application was on an unparalleled scale and was an unashamed attempt to display the owner's vast personal wealth, accumulated through four canny marriages that made her the second-richest lady in Britain and the subject of Horace Walpole's (1717–97) jibing rhyme:

> Four times the nuptial bed she warm'd,
> And every time so well perform'd,
> That when death spoil'd each husband's billing,
> He left the widow every shilling.
> Fond was the dame, but not dejected;
> Five stately mansions she erected.

Hardwick, Longleat, Wollaton, Burghley House, Audley End, and so many other large houses of this era, reveal not only shifting social and economic attitudes in Elizabethan and early-Jacobean Britain, but also architecture's triumph over traditional conventions. Caught in the centre of this battle was the attempt to accommodate the medieval hall into a modern symmetrical plan. Contemporary builders explored various ways of making this marriage a workable one, but it was not possible. The medieval hall, with its weighted scales of high and low ends, was fundamentally asymmetrical and the result was a divorce from tradition.

∧ Top: Ground-floor plan of Hardwick Hall (1597), Derbyshire.

Middle: Ground-floor plan of Chastleton (1612), Oxfordshire.

Bottom: Ground-floor plan of Wollaton Hall (1588), Nottinghamshire.

> The southeast elevation of Wollaton Hall (1588), Nottinghamshire.

∧ The symmetrical facade of Aston Hall
(1635), Warwickshire, showing the
centrally positioned entrance leading
directly into the middle of the hall.

∨ Ground-floor plan of Aston Hall
(1635), Warwickshire.

The hall at Chastleton in Oxfordshire (1612) was arranged inside and parallel to the front of the building. An intermediate vestibule inside the centrally positioned main entrance channelled people into the lower end of the hall. Symmetry with the window in the vestibule was achieved by inserting a bay window at the upper end of the hall. Elsewhere, designers attempted to place the hall perpendicularly to the facade, as at Hardwick, where the main entrance leads directly into the low end of the hall.

By the early 17th century, as occurred at Aston Hall in Warwickshire (1635) and Audley End, the layout of the hall both internally and in relation to other rooms had finally succumbed to the aesthetic demands of symmetry. Aston Hall was designed by John Thorpe and commissioned by Sir Thomas Holte (1571–1654), who was part of a wealthy and powerful Warwickshire family. Holte built Aston Hall some years after being knighted by James I and later purchasing the title of Baronet. The Great Hall in Holte's home was both a grand entrance and a functional space, where business was conducted and servants ate. By this time the hall was no longer a place for the family or important guests to eat. Instead, they dined in the Great Parlour off the main hall or on special occasions they used the sumptuously decorated Great Dining Room on the first floor. Even the servants were eventually removed from the hall and in the 18th

∧ The Great Hall at Aston Hall (1635), Warwickshire, showing the main entrance (right) in the middle of the room opposite the door to the salon (left) which was a later addition in the 1650s.

> The Great Parlour at Aston Hall (1635), Warwickshire, where the head of the household and his family ate following the decline of the earlier tradition of eating in the main hall.

> The Great Dining Room at Aston Hall (1635), Warwickshire, for formal occasions.

˅ Clockwise from top left:
a) Ground-floor plan of Aston Hall (1635), Warwickshire, showing the central position of the entrance and hall, with access from the centre.

b) Ground-floor plan of Chastleton (1612), Oxfordshire, showing the central position of the entrance and hall, with access from the low end.

c) Ground-floor plan of Cowdray (1540s), West Sussex, showing the central position of the hall and asymmetrical position of the entrance providing access from the low end.

d) Ground-floor plan of Wollaton Hall (1588), Nottinghamshire, showing the central position of the hall perpendicular to the entrance, which provides access from the low end.

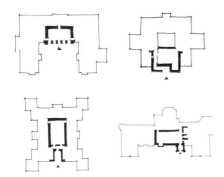

century a separate kitchen and servants' dining room were added to the north wing on the ground floor. In his essay, 'Of Building', Roger North claimed the separate servants' dining room 'ended the antique order of housing'. When Aston Hall was first opened in the 1630s, the main hall was entered from the low end, but the house was soon remodelled and the main entrance was placed centrally to the building and the hall. At Audley End, the huge bay window dominating the central portion of the principal facade illuminated the middle of the large two-storey hall, not the high end. Symmetry also controlled the arrangement of the rear elevation. Both centrally arranged configurations would have been anathema to medieval builders and householders.

At Burghley House the original hall was not even located inside the entrance and instead occupied the eastern range of the rectangular plan before being accommodated in a later extension. In an attempt to offer a solution to the incongruity of ancient and modern ideas, Francis Bacon in *Of Building* (1623) claimed that a perfect palace had to have two sides: 'a side for the banquet and a side for the household; the one for feasts and triumphs, and the other for dwelling ... both these sides to be parts of the front; and to be uniform without, though severally partitioned within; and to be on both sides of a great and stately tower, in the midst of the front, that joineth them together'. Bacon's description closely resembles Wollaton Hall, which overcame the problem of accommodating the hall by placing it in the centre of the building where the inner courtyard would normally have been, and lighting it by a clerestory. A massive tower was built over the hall in the 17th century (see page 146).

Internally, these monumental structures retained the familiar rooms of yesteryear – hall, parlour, great chamber, chapel, buttery, pantry and detached kitchens – although their arrangement was by now more varied and their embellishments eminently more elaborate. The scale of these huge homes reordered the interior of the house socially and functionally,

∧ As hospitality declined, so the servants left the hall and ate in their own dining room, illustrated here at Aston Hall (1635), Warwickshire.

with ground floors dedicated to service, utility and public reception, and upper floors to privacy. To accommodate this new order of things, the once great hall with its lofty roof was increasingly covered over and a great chamber, or master bedroom, built above it with views out over the landscaped gardens at the front of the house.

A momentous consequence of this development was the removal of the ancient and enduring hearth to a wall-mounted fireplace, which in turn became a focus of outlandish ornamentation. Although fireplaces had been a feature of private chambers in larger British homes for centuries, they had never challenged the hearth, whose wholesome smoke, according to William Harrison, 'was supposed to be a sufficient hardning for the timber of the house [and] reputed a far better medicine to kéepe the goodman and his familie from the quacke or pose'. However, its appearance in the hall from the late 15th century was the start of the hearth's slow retirement to the wall-side fireplace, a small journey bearing colossal meaning.

Coinciding with the hall's reduction into a single-storey space was the arrival of the long gallery. The long gallery was an entirely novel and quintessential feature of the Elizabethan home. Elizabethan households and their guests had taken to strolling on the roofs of these vast homes, enjoying the views, exploring their turrets and chimneys, and even dining in specially built pavilions.

∧ An example of a Tudor kitchen, here at Burghley House (1587), Lincolnshire.

> Audley End (1610), Essex, west elevation showing the dominance that symmetry had on the arrangement of the principal facades by the early 17th century.

< The Great Hall at Wollaton (1588), Nottinghamshire.

> The kitchen at Audley End, Essex, built as a later extension and connected to the main house (1610) by a covered corridor.

The long gallery provided an all-weather alternative to this fashionable rooftop or garden promenade, but it was also an opportune space for the householder to show off their swelling collections of art and artefacts.

Long galleries first emerged in the early 16th century and fitted nicely into the space on the first floor adjacent to the great chamber above the single-storey hall or even in the garrets, as occurs at Parham in West Sussex with its 50-metre-long gallery. The galleries at Montacute House in Somerset (55 metres long) and Aston Hall are other fine examples, but the Elizabethan preoccupation with architectural overindulgence invariably produced exceptions, and the gallery at Audley End, measuring 70 metres long and 10 metres wide, was the largest ever built in Britain.

The residents of Elizabethan homes, compared with their forebears, enjoyed a greater degree of comfort everywhere, with often unprecedentedly luxurious furnishings and decorations.

∧ The Long Gallery at Parham, West Sussex, built in 1577 and restored in the mid-20th century.

> The lavishly decorated dining room at Burghley House (1587), Lincolnshire, painted in the 17th century and furnished as it would have been in the 19th century.

The archetypal Elizabethan interior was a riot of coarsely interpreted Continental styles that clashed with indigenous Gothic forms, but regardless of their appearance, their convenience was improving steadily when compared with previous ages. Furniture was more abundant, more refined and more comfortable as upholstery and padded seats made their first appearance.

Walls were painted gaily above oak and leather wainscoting. Windows were glazed, often colourfully. Ceilings were bedecked in intricate plasterwork. Utensils and other innovative devices increased in quantity and popularity, right down to, as Ben Jonson described in *The Devil is an Asse*, 'the laudable use of forks, Brought into custome here, as they are in *Italy*, To th'sparing o'*Napkins*'. Even bookshelves, which Shakespeare described in *The Two Gentlemen of Verona* as being so high 'that one cannot climb it without apparent hazard of his life', evidenced not only the accumulation of furnishings and material possessions, but also a desire for cultural attainment.

Another novel feature of monumental Elizabethan homes was the equally showy staircase. In the 16th century, the staircase was at last elevated above a merely practical mechanism for providing access between floors. Instead, it became the centrepiece and an essential ornamental feature of large houses, and a precursor

The Hell Staircase in Burghley House (1587), Lincolnshire, with late-17th-century paintings by Antonio Verrio.

The old stone staircase (1560) at Burghley House (completed 1587), Lincolnshire, compared with the later main staircase (see opposite).

to the great open stairwell with its cantilevered staircase that emerged in the early 17th century. This entirely new form of staircase should 'be upon a fair open newel, and finely railed in, with images of wood, cast into a brass color; and a very fair landing-place at the top', wrote Francis Bacon in 1623.

The evolving process of architectural braggadocio reached its height at the turn of the 17th century, when builders, architects and their patrons, by now exposed to and bewitched by an increasing variety of examples printed in pattern books from the Continent, clamoured to convey their cultural cognisance. The design of monumental mansions increasingly entered the realm of fantasy. The superstitious Catholic, Sir Thomas Tresham, built the Triangular Lodge (1597) in Northamptonshire, wherein the repeated reference to the number three paid respect to the Holy Trinity. Sir Thomas Gorges' triangular Longford Castle in Wiltshire, completed in 1591, did the same. Construction was supervised by the surveyor-cum-architect, John Thorpe, who is famed for producing a fantastical albeit unrealised design for his own house possessing a plan in his own initials, IT ('I' was then synonymous with the letter 'J'), on the drawing of which he wrote:

> These 2 letters I and T
> Joined together as you see
> Is meant for a dwelling howse for mee
> John Thorpe

These irregular plans characterised the increasingly confused and transitional state of architecture in Britain by the middle of the 17th century and defied Bacon's plea that 'houses [are] built to live in, and not to look on'. His assertion that 'use be preferred before uniformity, except where both may be had' was an attempt to rescue the old manners of convenience from the pretensions of architecture, and echoed Henry Wotton's comments in *The Elements of Architecture* the following year: 'Designes of such nature doe more ayme at Rarity, then Commodity, so, for my part, I had rather admire them, then commend them.'

TOWN AND COUNTRY

While architecture was transforming Britain's wealthiest homes from the sublime to the ridiculous, the homes of the vast majority of the population, from the point of view of the plan, changed little throughout the 16th and 17th centuries. The features that had characterised the British home for centuries prevailed – a hall, chambers, a parlour, bedchambers, a buttery, a pantry and a kitchen, albeit in different configurations to suit the parcel, the purse and new building practices. As the bonded labour of medieval times was replaced by waged labour, freedom could be purchased and skills could be sold. Britain's labouring ranks became more independent, socially, financially, professionally and geographically. This modern worker could build a larger home possessing a greater degree of comfort and quantity of possessions than his forebears. 'The furniture of our houses,' wrote William Harrison in 1577, 'also exceedeth, and is growne in manner even to passing delicacie, and herein I doo not speake of the nobilitie and gentrie onelie, but likewise of the lowest sort in most places of our south countrie.'

Strangers' Hall in Norwich exemplifies the sophisticated urban home of members of the new wealthy merchant class throughout the 16th and 17th centuries. It is concentrated around a Great Hall built in the 15th century by a successful cloth merchant, William Barley, and was improved in the 16th century by the Sotherton family, who added the large stone-mullioned bay window. Further chambers were added over time, including the parlour, built by Thomas Cawse next to the hall and accessed near its low end. In 1627, Francis Cook, a grocer who became the Mayor of Norwich, built the stone staircase from the high end of the hall to the Great Chamber, which was decorated by Sir Joseph Paine, a rich hosier who was knighted for presenting Charles II with a thousand pounds in gold from the inhabitants of Norwich after the Restoration (1660). Cook and Paine were typical examples of successful 16th- and 17th-century merchants who were able to convert their wealth into political power. The home, with its lavish interiors, such as carved oak panelling, curtains, furniture, tableware and artwork, was emblematic of the growing wealth of the middling classes and their capacity to display this wealth.

∧ The Great Hall in Strangers' Hall, Norwich, the home of a number of wealthy merchants and persons of public standing. The hall was built in the 15th century and appears here as it would have done in the 16th century when the Sotherton family had made improvements, including the large stone bay window (left). The entrance to the parlour can be seen to the right.

> A parlour added to Strangers' Hall, Norwich, probably by Thomas Cawse in the late 15th century, and decorated here as it would have been in the 17th century.

∧ The lavish interior of the Great Chamber in Strangers' Hall, Norwich, seen here as it would have appeared in the 17th century when occupied by Sir Joseph Paine, a rich hosier.

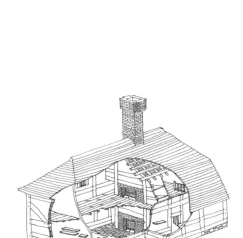

∨ A 17th-century farmer's cottage showing the central fireplace and chimney stack that replaced the hearth and allowed the construction of an upper floor and continuous range of bedrooms.

In lower-ranking homes, such as those owned by skilled labourers, the removal of the hearth to a fireplace allowed the hall to be covered over and the void in the roof converted into a private chamber linking the existing first-floor chambers at each end of the building. The completion of a continuous range of first-floor chambers generated a corridor providing separate access to each room, but this convenience came much later. Up until the 18th century access was invariably provided through each of the rooms from a staircase at the low end of the hall. In some cases, a separate staircase provided exclusive access to the great chamber. In *The Touchstone of Complexions* (1576) the Dutch writer, Levine Lemnie, offers an account of a typical mid-sized dwelling in late-16th-century Britain:

> The neate cleanlines, the exquisite finenesse, the pleasaunte and delightfull furniture in every point for household, wonderfully rejoysed mee, their Chambers and Parlours strawed over with sweete herbes, refreshed mee, their Nosegayes finelye entermingled wyth sondry sortes of fragraunte floures in their bedchambers and privie roomes, with comfortable smell cheered mee up and entierlye delighted all my Sences.

Houses continued to be built from local materials, as transportation was slow, unreliable and expensive. Stone was abundant in the southwest and northeast of Britain and brick was common in the east where the majority of foundries were. Monuments such as the grandiose gatehouse of Layer Marney (1520) in Essex or the late-15th-century Oxburgh Hall in Norfolk still stand in honour of this new manufactured material and the industry it cultivated. The even older Herstmonceux Castle was another pioneer in the use of brick in Britain, though its unique circumstances, which required the importation of bricklayers from Flanders for its construction, set it apart from any subsequent brick trade. Wood remained the most common building material: 'Never so much [oak] hath beene spent in a hundred years before, as is in ten yeare of our time,' wrote William Harrison in 1577, claiming that:

> in times past men were contented to dwell in houses, builded of sallow, willow, plumtree, hardbeame, and elme, so that the use of oke was in maner dedicated wholie unto churches, religious houses, princes palaces, noblemens lodgings, & navigation: but now all these are rejected, Desire of much wealth and ease abateth manhood, & overthroweth a manlie courage.

The voracious consumption of oak and other types of wood during the building boom in the second half of the 16th century became a major problem that threatened the nation's security. The navy, being a principal means for the defence of the realm at a time when it had to confront the Spanish Armada, was in desperate need of oak but the depletion of stocks was

Left: Pendean Farmhouse, a small yeoman's cottage from Midhurst, West Sussex, built c 1609 and reconstructed in the Weald and Downland Open Air Museum in 1976. The hearth has been converted into a central fireplace allowing the roof space to become a range of bedrooms. The main entrance is on the right of the picture.

Right: The main bedroom on the first floor of Pendean Farmhouse, showing the fireplace (left).

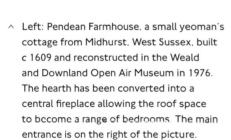

» The outer buildings at Layer Marney (1520), Essex, showing the end of the Long Gallery (right) and the Tower all constructed in brick, which was then a new and very expensive material.

exacerbated by house building, which in turn was precipitated by rising wealth, the redistribution of monastic lands following the dissolution of the monasteries, and, following the slow decline of the wool industry, Queen Elizabeth's promotion of arable farming over sheep farming, increasing the number of rural farmsteads. The late 16th century was a time therefore when not only the rich were building, but 'everie man almost [was] a builder' and, continued Harrison, even the commoner, once he 'hath bought any small parcell of ground, be it never so little, will not be quiet till he have pulled downe the old house (if anie were there standing) and set up a new after his owne devise'.

The exhaustion of supplies of oak was so severe by the early 17th century that builders turned to inferior timber, such as beech, which greatly concerned King James I, who believed it would bring about 'the notorious peril and decay' of the capital of the realm. London's houses were invariably three or four storeys high and built of wood with a thatched or tiled roof, but James I wanted to wean Londoners off timber and to use brick instead, which he proclaimed in 1615 was far more durable, safe from fire, beautiful and magnificent. In 1604, he issued a proclamation forbidding anyone to build a new building, house or facade within one mile of the suburbs of London, and beyond that boundary any such construction must be only carried out in brick or stone. Failure to obey this decree would result in a fine or imprisonment.

Persuading Londoners to surrender timber for brick proved difficult. Brick was more expensive and was only used by wealthier merchants. Between 1604 and 1630, Kings James and Charles issued eight proclamations outlawing the use of timber for construction. It was James's wish in 1615 that, just as the first Emperor of Rome was said to have 'found the city of Rome of bricke and left it of marble', he, being 'the first King of Great Britaine', would be remembered for having 'found Our Citie and Suburbs of London of stickes, and left them of Bricke'.

CONCLUSION

The fundamental changes that transformed the home in Britain between the medieval period and the late 17th century were concerned primarily with the upper echelons of society, whose indulgence of change was matched only by an equally spirited shirking of social responsibilities. Architecture had arrived through varied Continental sources which British practitioners and builders plundered for inspiration and produced the eclectic styles that characterised Elizabethan and Jacobean homes. Order had been achieved in building, just as it had made its mark on contemporary poetry, painting, gardening, music and fashion, as Rules now dominated art.

For the home, this triumph was achieved at the expense of both age-old customs that had implanted themselves in the plan over centuries as well as more recent decorative features. Aesthetically, the gables, turrets, chimneys and crenellation that created the romantic Tudor rooflines were levelled out. The gatehouses retreated into the porch. The stone mullions and tracery that characterised Tudor fenestration were replaced by orderly lines of rectangular openings all formally calculated within a proportioned facade that paid homage to classical precedents. Inside, luxury, whether relative or absolute, became commonplace. For the internal plan, the triumph meant a slow evolution of established spaces within the home to suit modern uses – the hall became a vestibule inside a porch, the parlour a dining room, the private chamber a drawing room, the great chamber a master bedroom, the lady's chamber a boudoir, the buttery and pantry were amalgamated into a larder, and the kitchen was accommodated under the same roof. Connecting all these elements were lengthy tracts of corridor and increasingly grand staircases.

In the overall plan, the sprawling squares created by the single or double courtyard steadily reduced in size and prominence throughout the 16th century, and were eventually subsumed at the core of new monumental mansions, before disappearing altogether with the emergence of the double-pile plan in the 17th century. Compactness became an unstoppable trend that was to reach its climax in the next century, causing larger homes to have a greater number of smaller rooms, and allowed the less affluent to build smaller mansions and the emerging middle classes to dwell in urban terraces.

Architecture's ascent throughout the 16th and 17th centuries, despite its perceived advantages and disadvantages, could not escape its association with the problems of modern life and its asphyxiating avarice. By the late 17th century, as a unified Britain under a restored monarchy looked back on the past, a wistful fantasy was formed. It was an illusion of a golden age when, as Gervase Markham put it, 'Golde was so smally regarded', when a quiet rural life predominated and everyone knew their place and cared not for power or architectural aspiration, as the poet Katherine Philips (1631–64) described:

> This was the first and happiest life,
> When man enjoy'd himself;
> Till pride exchangëd peace for strife,
> And happiness for pelf ...
> Secure in these unenvy'd walls,
> I think not on the state,
> And pity no man's case that falls
> From his ambitious height.

> Detail of one of the two front entrances at Audley End (1610), Essex, showing the fusion of British and Continental styles.

THE COMPACT COMMODITY

CIVIL WAR AND FOUR GEORGES
1649–c 1830

Since time immemorial, rooms in Britain's homes had been arranged in rows, whether just two rooms in the smallest single-storey dwellings or hundreds of rooms arranged around multistorey courtyards. The single pile endured for so long because of the inherent problems associated with the double pile. Chief among these were the provision of access to inner rooms and the construction of a necessarily much wider roof. With rooms arranged in single rows, access was provided either between rooms, via an external corridor, or directly from a courtyard as Roman and Tudor builders did. The single pile had many drawbacks. Roger Pratt, amateur architect and Commissioner for rebuilding London after the Great Fire, mentioned not only the inconvenience of rooms being 'subjected one to another' or their exposure to 'all winds, and weather, and having through lights [that] look too glaring', but also that the single-pile house occupied too 'much ground and consequently requires a great deal of walling'. Despite their massive outward appearances, Longleat, Wollaton, Hardwick, Burghley House, Audley End, Aston Hall and all other Elizabethan and Jacobean homes were single-pile in plan.

The double-pile home was compact, occupying a small area that allowed many rooms to be arranged with independent access via an internal corridor. It also reduced the amount of walling and roofing, though the wider plan demanded a new type of roofing or else the conventional gable roof would have been impractically high. The first solution was a complex system of intersecting gables, which gave way later in the 17th century to the hipped roof. Compactness was seen by many as offering a great improvement to domestic planning and eliminating the inefficient sprawling ranges of medieval and early-Tudor homes. Not everyone was happy with the change though. Some criticised the double pile for being too boxy, likening it to a wasp's nest in which noises and smells travelled everywhere.

Despite their shortcomings and quite unlike their introverted predecessors that retained in their insular courtyards the defensive spirit of medieval times, double-pile houses were fundamentally outward-looking and would not only dominate domestic planning hereafter, but would also provide the backdrop for entirely new architectural expressions. The first double-pile plans were realised in early-17th-century mansions before becoming fully accomplished in the second half of the century. Swakeleys (1629–38) in Middlesex, built by Edmund Wright, a City of London Alderman, Sheriff and, later, Mayor; the Surrey mansion of a Dutch merchant, Samuel Fortrey, which later became Kew Palace (1631) in Kew Gardens; Broome Park (1635–8) in Kent, built by Sir Basil Dixwell, a Warwickshire man who inherited a number of Kentish estates; and Barnham Court in Sussex, built by a wealthy tenant on the Barnham manor in the mid-17th century, are all examples of the first tentative steps

An enfilade at Burghley House (1587), Lincolnshire, where the arrangement of through access between rooms along the entire first-floor front of the house has been deliberately designed for formal effect. The space was originally an Elizabethan long gallery before being converted into a series of rooms in the 18th century.

in this direction. They are also examples of a period in which Dutch and Flemish architectural influences, with their carved brickwork, ornate gabling and chimney rows, surpassed those of the Italian Renaissance, which, together with French influences, lasted throughout much of the century.

The immaturity of this transitional phase is evident in the way rooms were accessed. Corridors and passageways leading to staircases or main entrances were limited, and so the lingering memory of the single plan was maintained in those rooms which could only be accessed by passing through other rooms. Not until the 18th century did independent access into each room in a home become the norm, whether from a lobby, staircase or corridor. It has remained this way ever since, with the exception of the enfilade, which reached its apogee during the late-Baroque period. Introduced from France, the enfilade took the idea of a series of interconnected rooms and dramatised it to great effect, turning it into a processional space along which important guests would pass to reach their private suite at the end. Many older mansions, such as Chatsworth and Burghley House, were converted in the 18th century to accommodate the fashionable enfilade.

Corridors, lobbies and grand staircases in double-pile homes created new forms of communal space that came to have on architecture since Shute's *The First and Chief Groundes of Architecture* one and a half centuries earlier. Campbell's work was one of the most important architectural books of the 18th century as well as a piece of nationalistic braggadocio at the dawn of the Georgian era. Britain's recent buildings, Campbell claimed, 'far surpassed our contemporaries of every other country [and] furnished us with an opportunity of convincing the world and posterity, that architecture was brought to as great a point of perfection in this kingdom in the eighteenth century, as ever it was known to be among the Greeks and Romans'. As a catalogue of drawings, it was also a flattering and canny piece of publicity for his own work and that of his friends and favourite architects, such as Christopher Wren and 'the immortal' Inigo Jones.

Among his own published works was Burlington House (1716–18) on London's Piccadilly. Now housing the Royal Academy of Arts, Burlington House was originally the home of the wealthy and landed Yorkshireman Richard Boyle (1694–1753), Third Earl of Burlington, who was one of the 18th century's foremost patrons of architecture and the first among the British aristocracy to have practised architecture. As a staunch Whig he was very active in the prevailing attempts to create a national style of architecture. He not only designed and commissioned important building projects but also sponsored publications. He paid for the publication of *The Designs of Inigo Jones* (1727) by the architect William Kent, and *The Four Books of Andrea Palladio's Architecture* (1738) by Isaac Ware was reproduced from original drawings in his extensive collection that he had gathered during his Grand Tours of the Continent from 1714 to 1719 and purchased from the antiquarian and architectural hobbyist, John Talman (1677–1726). 'Your giving me access to your study wherein many of the original drawings of Palladio are preserved,' wheedled Ware, 'are such instances of your love to arts, and your friendship to me, that I cannot too publickly return Your Lordship thanks for favours that surpass all acknowledgement.' A decade earlier, Burlington had designed his own house at Chiswick (1729) in west London, resembling Palladio's Villa Capra (1567–80) in Vicenza (generally known as 'La Rotonda'); but Ware's seminal book, which was distributed sparingly to members of Burlington's inner circle, offered readers access to authentic and accurate reproductions of this master's work and consequently were instrumental in stimulating the enthusiasm for neo-Palladianism in Britain throughout the 18th century.

The subsequent Palladian appearance of stately homes and public buildings across Britain throughout the Georgian period can be credited almost exclusively to the efforts of Burlington and his close ring of protégés, such as Campbell, Kent and Ware. However, their efforts were far from universally applauded. Burlington's haughty ambition to revive the spirit of ancient Rome in Georgian Britain and his doctrinaire imposition of Rules

Chiswick House (1729), London, by Lord Burlington and based on Palladio's Villa Capra (1567–80) or 'Rotonda' in Vicenza.

Burlington House (1716–18), London, designed by Colen Campbell for Lord Burlington.

of Art not just in building but also in music, painting, gardening and sculpture attracted the ire of critics and satirists alike. Hidden behind its wall on Piccadilly, one observer remarked in 1771 of Burlington House 'how many are there, who have lived half a century in London, without knowing that so princely a fabrick exists. It has generally been taken for a jail'. When Burlington was at the height of his powers, the satirist Alexander Pope (1688–1744) dedicated his scathing epistle *Of False Taste* (1731) to him:

> You show us, *Rome* was glorious, not profuse,
> And pompous Buildings once were things of use
> Just as they are, yet shall your noble Rules
> Fill half the Land with *Imitating Fools* ...
> Shall call the Winds thro' long Arcades to roar,
> Proud to catch cold at a Venetian door;
> Conscious they act a true Palladian part,
> And if they starve, they starve by Rules of Art.

Being the youngest of the circle of acquaintances in Burlington's orbit, Isaac Ware's influence extended furthest into the Georgian period with his designs, such as Wrotham Park (1754) in Hertfordshire and Clifton Hill House (1750) in Bristol, and his seminal, scholarly and ambitiously comprehensive treatise, *A Complete Body of Architecture* (1756). More than merely an attempt to collect all the previous works on architecture into 'a library on this subject to the gentlemen and the builder', Ware's book sought to highlight the necessary and useful in architecture – 'to instruct rather than amuse'.

Ware's focus on instruction rather than amusement mirrored a more applied approach to the art of building that had been growing since the late 17th century and produced countless publications on the subject over the next two centuries. These books included William Halfpenny's *The Art of Sound Building* (1725) and *The Builder's Pocket-Companion* (1731) and Francis Price's *The British Carpenter: or a Treatise on Carpentry* (1735), or more substantial bodies of work such as those of garden and building designer, Batty Langley (1696–1751), in the first half of the 18th century or the architect-carpenter, William Pain, in the second half. Rather than catering for Britain's culturally and financially rich, these textbooks sought to disseminate among the building trades the method of reproducing classical designs in smaller houses belonging to persons of modest means. From Langley's *Practical Geometry Applied to the Useful Arts of Building* (1726) to his *The Workman's Golden Rule for Drawing and Working the Five Orders in Architecture, etc* (1750) and from Pain's *The Builder's Pocket Treasure* (1763) to *The Practical House Carpenter* (1790), the works of these two dominated the popular market for building publications throughout the 18th century and helped

Clifton Hill House (1746–50), Bristol, commissioned by the linen merchant, Paul Fisher, and designed by Isaac Ware.

> The music room at Clifton Hill House, Bristol, built as an extension to the original dining room four years after the writer Dr John Addington Symonds purchased the house in 1853.

∨ Ground-floor plan of Clifton Hill House (1746–50), Bristol, by Isaac Ware, showing the 19th-century extension.

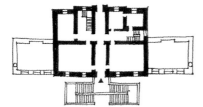

to transform the way in which amateur architects, builders and craftsmen approached domestic design. Uneducated in method and tastes, these artisan instructors attracted a wide readership as well as many detractors. Langley's *Gothic Architecture Improved by Rules and Proportions* (1747), which attempted to create five new Orders in the Gothic style, was said by the art historian Horace Walpole to do nothing but 'massacre that venerable species'.

Orbiting high above these unpretentious practitioners throughout the decades between the Great Fire and the Victorian era were some of Britain's greatest architects – Inigo Jones (1573–1652), Christopher Wren (1632–1723), John Vanbrugh (1664–1726), Nicholas Hawksmoor (c 1662–1736), Robert (1728–92) and James (1732–94) Adam, John Nash (1752–1835) and John Soane (1753–1837) – whose work dominated the period and can still be seen in rural and urban landscapes across the country. However, irrespective of such formidable talents, whose combined portfolios include St Paul's Cathedral, Blenheim Palace, the towers at Westminster Abbey, Syon House, the Bank of England and London's Regent Street, these masters could only be afforded by very few and consequently had little immediate impact on ordinary homes inhabited by the vast majority of Britain's population.

Only through imitation and emulation did these epic structures touch the average British home in the 18th century, as Palladian Classicism found its way on to the facades of modest villas and workers' cottages. The meticulously proportioned facade that concealed all evidence of internal function, the grand stairway leading to a pedimented porch held aloft by a pretentious colonnade, or any one of the various types of ornamentation that these architects espoused revealed little or nothing of the evolution of the domestic plan. Form, not function, was the chief concern for Britain's aspiring Classicists, as outward appearance eclipsed internal convenience.

The great houses of the new and prosperous era that replaced the restraint of the late 17th century all competed to outdo one another for size, style and splendour. Following the tradition established by Elizabethan aristocrats, these vast homes sat among expansive estates with landscaped gardens and were seats of nobles of one kind or another – the Duke of Devonshire's Chatsworth House (1686–1707), Derbyshire; the Duke of Marlborough's Blenheim Palace (1705–24), Oxfordshire; the Earl of Carlisle's Castle Howard (1699–1712), Yorkshire; Lord Burlington's Burlington House (1716–18), London; Admiral George Delaval's Seaton Delaval Hall (1718–28), Northumberland; Robert Walpole's Houghton Hall (1722–30s), Norfolk; the First Marquess of Rockingham's Wentworth Woodhouse (1725), Yorkshire; and the Earl of Leicester's Holkham Hall (1734–64), Norfolk.

As much as these homes sought to emulate the latest interpretation of the Renaissance styles, they were also a barometer of the nation's political leadership in the 18th century. Chatsworth was originally built in the mid-16th century by the formidable Bess of Hardwick, who passed it on to her son, William Cavendish, soon to become the First Earl of Devonshire. The Cavendish family's wealth descended from their close connections to the Crown and their titled position. The Fourth Earl was a prominent Whig and was promoted to the First Duke of Devonshire in 1694, after which he substantially remodelled Chatsworth House. Blenheim Palace was Queen Anne's reward to the First Duke of Marlborough for his role in defeating the French at the Battle of Blindheim (Blenheim) (1704) during the War of the Spanish Succession. Castle Howard was built by the Third Earl of Carlisle, a member of the affluent and influential Howard family, who own the title of Duke of Norfolk extending back to 1483. Houghton Hall was home to the First Earl of Oxford and Britain's first Prime Minister, Robert Walpole, and Wentworth Woodhouse was the home of peer and Whig politician Thomas Watson-Wentworth.

To create these celebrated homes, the owners employed equally celebrated architects, such as William Talman (1650–1719), John Vanbrugh, William Kent (c 1685–1748) and Colen Campbell. Architecture was employed not as a practice of convenience but as an art of affectation – a means of boasting the resources and cultured taste of wealthy patrons. The highest class 'have all the apartments of the middling class, but frequently on a larger scale and more richly decorated', wrote John Claudius Loudon (1783–1843). Further separating them from other classes was their ability to add other apartments to their homes, such as galleries, oratories and wardrobes, all of which were 'not now necessarily confined to the prince or the peer'. It was suggested that the epithet of one of the architects of these sprawling mansions, the dramatist and amateur architect John Vanbrugh, who was responsible for the monumental Blenheim Palace, should be: 'Lie heavy on him earth, for he Laid many a heavy load on thee.'

Aware of such allegations, leading architects sought to provide a defence. In a thinly veiled apologia for elitism, William Chambers (1723–96), in *A Treatise on Civil Architecture* (1759), claimed that architecture was no mere instrument of luxury but had many purposes, including 'the preservation, the amusement, and the grandeur of the human species'. For him, architecture was the basis of civilisation, greasing the wheels of industry and cosseting its captains for the common good. By creating commodious rural dwellings for the political elite of the 17th century, Chambers argued that architecture was the font of commerce, wealth and luxury because it provided a place in which the nation's statesmen could breathe temperate air, sleep securely and work undisturbed so that they be 'active, inventive, and enterprising, with bodies fit for labour, and minds turned to contemplation'. On a similar note, Ware cautioned that we must not be too 'captivated by [architectural] pomp, leaving the more serviceable part neglected', and in respect of the plan he was right – these great 18th-century piles were too varied and complex, and their numbers comparatively few. Many large mansions were extensions of former houses such as Chatsworth, redeveloped or extensively redecorated to keep abreast of the kaleidoscopic trends throughout the period, particularly in their interior ornamentation.

ˇ The exuberant Baroque interior of the Great Hall, Moor Park, Hertfordshire, commissioned by Benjamin Styles after he purchased the house in 1720 and had it remodelled. The plasterwork and paintings were created by Italian artists, including Giacomo Amiconi.

The exuberance of late-17th-century British Baroque was brought into line by Palladianism, against whose monotonous surfaces the floridity of Rococo briefly reacted, and in turn was surmounted by Gothic romanticism, foreign exoticism and then a return to Classicism, by then rebranded as Neoclassicism of the late 18th century.

Despite the different styles that coloured the surfaces of homes throughout the Georgian period, the underlying structure remained broadly classical. In the second half of the century, as scientific discoveries and technological developments caused the first stirrings of the Industrial Revolution, Classicism resurfaced as the dominant style of the age. This was the era of the sublime and the beautiful – magnificence and simplicity. For a building to be sublime it must have uniformity and 'greatness of dimension', though not too great as vast designs 'are always the sign of a common and low imagination', wrote the philosopher Edmund Burke (1729/30–97). For a building to be magnificent, claimed Burke, it had to possess a 'great profusion of any things which are splendid or valuable'.

The period was dominated by the Scottish architects and brothers, Robert and James Adam, and their pursuit of a total uniformity in design that brought about, in their own words, 'a kind of revolution in the whole system of this useful and elegant art'. The brothers' father, William Adam, was a renowned architect and stonemason who ran the family business in Edinburgh and attempted to publish *Vitruvius Scoticus* (1780), the Scottish riposte to Campbell's *Vitruvius Britannicus*, though it was never published in his lifetime. Robert took over the business when his father died. With his brothers, James and John, the Adams became the most celebrated family of architects in Scotland's history. Convinced that the classical style of ornament exceeded all others for interior decorations, the Adam brothers, became the most inventive re-interpreters of Palladian Classicism. They excelled in creating a comprehensive design process, from the layout and appearance of the building to the smallest stucco detail. Working closely with other leading designers and artists, including the furniture designer, Thomas Chippendale (1718–79), their bright and florid style was far removed from the tenebrous wooden wainscoting of former times and, despite making few contributions to the development of the plan, their playful use of elliptical or round-ended rooms produced an element of surprise and variety in the internal arrangements of the houses they designed.

By the late 18th century, the inventiveness of the Adam brothers was giving way to imitation. The imitative tendencies of revivalism towards the end of the 18th century assumed many guises. James Wyatt (1746–1813), or 'Wyatt the Destroyer', as the 19th-century architect Augustus Welby Northmore Pugin (1812–52) labelled him, designed and redesigned in his signature

^ An 18th-century dining room in a wealthy household, here at Strangers' Hall, Norwich, decorated with the latest furniture in the most fashionable styles, including chairs based on Thomas Chippendale's designs.

>> Brighton Pavilion (1787–1823), designed by John Nash for the Prince Regent (later George IV).

Gothic style. Interest in Gothic architecture, which Palladians such as Ware regarded as 'a wild and irregular manner of building', was ignited by Langley's writings and further boosted by Horace Walpole's Strawberry Hill (1749–76) in Twickenham before becoming *de rigueur* in the 19th century. Exoticism was another facet of imitation that had been stimulated by Britain's increasing engagements in Africa, the Americas and the Near and Far East. Chinoiserie, the decorative art movement of which the works of William Chambers and William Halfpenny were a vital architectural component, survives in garishly lacquered furniture and willow-patterned crockery in homes all over Britain and, architecturally, in the Pagoda at Kew (1759) by Chambers, along with other types of exotic expression in the similarly fantastic Pavilion at Brighton (1787–1823) by John Nash for the profligate Prince Regent, or in Sezincote House (1805), Gloucestershire, by Samuel Pepys Cockerell.

The panoply of styles throughout the 18th century conceals more substantial changes taking place inside larger houses that distinguished them from their Elizabethan or Jacobean predecessors. Palladian precedents imposed a slavish adherence to symmetry in both the plan and the elevations.

In the plan a common pattern occurred, wherein four principal rooms of reasonable and consistent height occupied each floor, the overall proportions of which were invariably between square and sesquialteral – the ratio of one and a half to one. The result was a compactness that was absent in the mansions of former times and which gave rise to the familiar four-up four-down.

While the internal functions of Britain's 18th-century mansions are infinitely varied, general trends in their layout did materialise. Formal rooms, such as the parlour, sitting room, dining room or antechambers, where people might wait to be received, were located at the front of the building, and private rooms, such as the library, study, withdrawing room, or an additional sitting room, were at the rear. In Britain, unlike the rest of Europe, the dining room played a pre-eminent role in the home, whereas in France, as the Adam brothers observed, they 'meet there only at meals, when they trust to the display of the table for show and magnificence, not to the decoration of the apartment'. The British dining room was the principal apartment of conversation, where a significant portion of time was spent. It was therefore 'desirable to have them fitted up with elegance and splendour', wrote the Adam brothers, and 'finished with stucco, and adorned with statues and paintings'.

A new addition to some grand homes of the late 18th century, at least in name, was the salon, a large and stately room extending two storeys in height and richly decorated with paintings and tall windows. A descendant from the French influence in planning, the salon in the British home replaced the function of the great chamber or dining room. It was usually located in the centre of the house, behind the now diminished hall, or at the end of a gallery. Although the salon appeared in a variety of sizes and shapes, from square to oblong, it

^ A plan of the compact double-fronted villa (showing the position of dining room, parlour, kitchen and library with a hall and lobby between), which set the standard for this type of house for over a century.

K: Kitchen · L: Library · P: Parlour
Lb: Lobby · H: Hall · D: Dining Room

> An example of a dry laundry – shown here as a later extension to Audley End (1610), Essex – which was one of the ancillary offices accommodated in outbuildings beside large houses of the 18th and 19th centuries.

dictated the symmetry of the building. Rooms leading off the salon increased in privacy, from the semi-private withdrawing room, through the more private bedroom culminating in the sacrosanct closet or annexed chapel. Socially, the salon was place of formal and sumptuous entertainment where Georgian high fashion was displayed in interior decor, furniture, food and clothing. Ware was cynical about such foreign influences, claiming the salon satisfied the present custom of 'seeing all one's friends at once and entertaining none of them', while architecturally it loaded and 'generally discredited the rest of the edifice'.

On the first floor were bedrooms and dressing rooms, the best at the front of the house and the lesser-ranking ones at the rear. Servants' rooms were sometimes attached to the guest bedrooms, but increasingly they were removed to self-contained apartments in the attic or sharing the basement with the kitchen and other offices. The arrangement of these ancillary offices was often determined by the site, especially food stores, which were always located on the north side of the building, while others, such as dairies and laundries, might occupy flanking wings or outbuildings if space permitted. By the 18th century, most houses of note were positioned with the principal elevations facing south or southeast, unless, in the case of towns and cities, the site rendered it impossible.

Whether north- or south-facing, Ware claimed that Palladio laid 'down one excellent and universal rule; which is that in all buildings, the most beautiful and noble parts should be placed most in view; and those of a meaner kind as much concealed from sight as possible'. In the context of rural or suburban detached villas, this rule determined that the most important elevation was always the front, which was dominated by the main entrance approached by a flight of steps and set beneath a pediment. If the purse permitted, a portico stood proud of a parapet encircling the top of the building and concealing the shallow hipped roof, which had supplanted the lofty pyramid roofs of the late 17th century. Examples of this stately gesture include Moor Park in Hertfordshire, built in 1678–9 for James, Duke of Monmouth and illegitimate son of Charles II, and purchased by the city trader, Benjamin Styles, who had it remodelled by Giacomo Leoni in *c* 1720 in a Palladian style with Portland stone facings and Corinthian portico; Berrington Hall (1778–81) in Herefordshire, designed for Thomas Harley by Henry Holland, who was the son-in-law of Capability Brown, who produced his last ever design at Berrington; and Basildon Park (1776–83) in Berkshire, where the grand stairway to the main entrance is incorporated internally. If the rear served as a secondary entrance, then it too would be well treated architecturally and the services retained in side wings. Irrespective of rank, all sides of the building were symmetrically arranged.

Inside the principal entrance, a small hallway provided access to adjacent offices and a lobby beyond, attached to which were two more offices on either side of the building. The centrepiece of the lobby and at the heart of the house's plan was usually an ornate staircase which, unlike the cantilevered staircases of the 17th century that created a stairwell, was increasingly a monumental flight often divided by a landing and giving plenty of open space to the upper floor. A second staircase to the rear of the house was used by the domestic workers. The alignment of the lobby and staircase on a central axis forced the chimneys and fireplaces to the sides of the building, the recess on either side of which was often filled with display cabinets to flaunt ornaments.

The Palladian obsession with symmetry and order meant that windows were contrived where the plan did not require them or, worse still, were omitted where the plan did require them. Symmetry, argued Loudon, was 'the chief source of most of those deformed clumps of masonry which shock the feelings of the tasteful traveler in all parts of the country'. The fixation with proportion, rule and exterior effect resulted in many inconveniences. Awkward corners and voids between rooms in larger mansions were populated by spaces with sometimes invented functions – studies, music rooms, storerooms, dressing rooms and billiard rooms – which helped to uphold prevailing classical rules on the exterior, while closets and other small spaces fitted in unwanted recesses in or between rooms helped to honour these rules on the interior. One new and ultimately revolutionary room type that began to appear in larger houses from the mid-18th century, and which Ware understatedly describes as 'a useful addition', was the water closet, the forerunner to the modern lavatory, the widespread espousal of which took a further two centuries. All the functions of a modern lavatory were carried out by servants, who hauled bathing water and waste water up and down the stairs in a tireless routine that continued in some country homes until the early 20th century.

∧ The dining room at Moor Park (c 1720), Hertfordshire.

› Right: Moor Park, Hertfordshire, built in 1678–9 for James, Duke of Monmouth and remodelled by Giacomo Leoni in 1720.

› Opposite: An example of the cantilevered staircase, here at Moor Park in Hertfordshire, which was succeeded throughout the 18th century by the monumental double-flight staircase with landing.

> A private chamber in Burghley House (1587), Lincolnshire, as it would have appeared in the 18th century with the later addition of a water closet (far right).

Beneath the top flight of monumental mansions owned by the Georgian aristocracy appeared a second class of house best described as smaller mansions, or villas, owned by emerging professionals – bankers, lawyers and wealthy merchants – or the rural retreats of the very rich. These two groups were 'the middling and higher classes of mankind' who, according to Loudon, required 'a considerable number of apartments; because, having more time and wealth, they consequently can enjoy more frequently, and in a greater degree, the luxury of assembling their friends'. These new aspirational homes were a product of their time. Funded by the newly rich whose wealth was tapped from Britain's growing stature internationally and its globally connected economy, these Georgian villas were rarely designed by architects. Instead, they were the work of learned builders who had access to the surfeit of pattern books on classical rules and taste and were by now well-versed in classical methods, albeit through their own interpretation. Different classes of villa served different clients, and potential owners were able to select their home according to their place in society. The architect, Charles Middleton (1756–*c* 1818), identified three types of villa. The first was the occasional and temporary rural retreat for the city-dwelling aristocrat, such as Lord Burlington's Chiswick House. The second was the country home of the wealthy citizen or official, such as Benjamin Styles's Moor Park. And the third was the smaller kind of provincial edifice, sufficient for a hunting residence or the home of an affluent country gentlemen.

These compact villas were far removed from the sprawling facades of aristocratic mansions, but nevertheless sought association with them through the arrangement of classical features laid out on a smaller canvas by trained builders. Their aspirational motives caught the attention of the satirist and Sussex vicar, James Bramston (*c* 1694–1744), who mocked them in *The Man of Taste*:

From out my honest workmen, I'll select
A *Bricklay'r*, and proclaim him architect;
First bid him build me a stupendous dome,
Which *having finish'd*, we set out for *Rome*;
Take a weeks view of *Venice* and the Brent,
Stare round, see nothing, and come home content.
I'll have my *Villa* too, a sweet abode,
Its situation shall be *London* Road.

Elegance, compactness and convenience were the desired characteristics of these villas. Most were raised on a rusticated ground floor that provided a base on which the principal storey, the *piano nobile*, stood aloft to afford decent views of the surrounding country. This Palladian-inspired development was distinct from its Baroque predecessor, whose principal floor was on the ground and indistinguishable from the first floor. By raising the principal apartments on to the first floor, the servants' quarters and other utilitarian rooms could be kept on the ground floor. In the Georgian mansion, everyone knew their place.

These neatly proportioned homes were often located in the countryside near transport routes that put them in easy reach of a nearby town or city or on the urban periphery – the suburbs. Similarly arranged on a square plan over two floors sandwiched between a basement and attic, these villas provided the expanding professional classes with a home that was spacious but not capacious. Sufficiently showy, yet not economically encumbering, these pretentious and decorated boxes allowed Britain's moderately wealthy to enjoy a level of comfort that their forebears could only have dreamed of, though their layout was not yet constrained by bathrooms or modern plumbing. They took their cue from the homes of aristocrats and socialites of the day, such as Henrietta Howard's Marble Hill (1724–9) in Twickenham, Middlesex; Kenwood House (1764–79) in Hampstead, north London, redesigned by the Adam brothers for Lord Mansfield; Robert Adam's Apsley House (1771–8) at Number 1 Hyde Park for Baron Apsley; and Danson House (1766) in Kent designed by Robert Taylor for Sir John Boyd.

Because the design of these villas was often straight out of a book, they took little account of site or aspect, and although the user was free to designate the function of each room, the overall plan remained remarkably consistent across the country and throughout the period. The general composition whereby the ground floor was occupied by public rooms at the front and utility rooms at the rear with private bedrooms above foretold the common arrangement of the British home ever since.

A similar evolution occurred in the homes of rural workers, whose 18th-century farmhouses differed from wealthier homes

primarily on account of their scale, materials and fittings. *The Twelve Beautiful Designs for Farm-Houses* that William Halfpenny produced in 1750 'for Gentlemen, Builders, etc.' were all neatly proportioned and symmetrically arranged and some even included the very modern convenience of a lavatory, but few would be clad in classical ornament or possess the modern sash windows that replaced the hinged casement from the late 17th century. The basic farmhouse was often a core consisting of 'the same number of rooms, and in general the same number of offices' so that the house could increase in size in line with the household wealth. After one or two generations, explained Ware, it would 'no longer be considered as a farm house, but as a house of a person of some fortune, who intends to live as those independent of business do, but withal to have some farming in his eye'.

Just as there could be no precise rule governing the use of rooms in villas and mansions, so too were farmhouse interiors equally enigmatic from the outside. There might be less cause for the rural farmer to enjoy the niceties of inviting crowds of friends and acquaintances to his home or indulging in the comfort of withdrawing rooms, salons and libraries, but every farmhouse needed a parlour and kitchen, which, along with a pantry, scullery, and storerooms if space allowed, would occupy the ground floor

∧ Apsley House (1771–8), London, designed in brick by Robert Adam for Baron Apsley. Subsequent alterations included the facing in stone and the addition of the Corinthian portico (1824) by the Duke of Wellington's family, who took over the house in 1807.

< South elevation of Kenwood House (1764–79) in Hampstead, London, redesigned by the Adam brothers for Lord Mansfield.

– or outhouses if space was lacking. It was from small farmhouses that the custom of eating in the kitchen became popular. As this custom became increasingly entrenched, the kitchen grew in size and standard and the dining room or parlour declined. Just as occurred in larger houses, the first floor was predominantly private, containing the bedrooms; the best ones at the front and secondary rooms at the rear. Servants' quarters were, as ever, in the garret.

Other offices, such as dairy, laundry, brewhouse and bakehouse, were accommodated in single-storey wings attached to the main building and laid out around a courtyard that also housed barns, stores and animal sheds. The rural courtyard of the small farmer had not been seen in Britain since Roman times. Ware even recommended the country gentleman looking to build a noble farmhouse would find the 'best instruction from the villas of the ancient Romans'. After the 18th century, although English farmyards were often irregular, Loudon observed a greater uniformity in areas of East Lothian and Berwickshire, where the main farmhouse was flanked by extending wings of offices, stables and servants' accommodation around a courtyard that was enclosed on the fourth side by a low wall.

Despite the quiet rural setting seemingly adrift from urban or foreign influences, classical proportions made their way into the arrangement of windows and scale of rooms, as well as in the increasing symmetry of the facade and lofty ceilings of British farmhouses. The height of each floor varied but, unlike the largest mansions with their exceptional range of differently sized rooms, would be consistent on each floor, with the ground floor around 3.7 metres and the first floor 3 metres, which were slightly lower than those in a villa.

The artist and social critic, William Hogarth (1697–1764), claimed that 'the greatest part of the effects of beauty results from the symmetry of parts in the object', and it had taken over two and a half centuries for symmetry in the plan and elevation of British homes to descend from the great palaces to the humble farmer's dwelling. But just as the farmhouse was catching up, trends were once again shifting and as Hogarth prophesied: 'I am very well persuaded, this prevailing notion will soon appear to have little or no foundation.' He was right. The inevitable reaction to centuries of symmetry was the proliferation of asymmetry throughout the 19th century.

Such aesthetic concerns were superfluous in the homes of rural workers on large estates, though that is not to say their quality was wanting. Throughout the 18th century, workers' cottages were improved by rural landowners, who replaced the old timber fabric with stone and brick. Where timber prevailed in certain areas of the country, weatherboarding was used to conceal the outdated appearance and was popular towards the late 18th century, boosted by a tax on bricks from 1784 to 1850. Weatherboarding played a much greater role in the life of the American home, which, having been exported by 18th-century emigrants, became synonymous with the British 'Colonial' style. Built in pairs or small rows of single-fronted dwellings, where the house was two rooms deep and one room wide, with the main entrance leading to a stair, these novel conjoined housing types for labourers found their true calling in the cities and their sprawling suburbs over the next two centuries.

At the lowest end of the housing scale, rural cottages were inhabited by poorer rural workers, who continued living as they had done for centuries. Their homes were neither considered worthy of attention nor were they built to last, leaving little evidence of their existence despite accommodating a significant proportion of the population. 'The part acted by the cottager in the great drama of life,' wrote Loudon, 'though important when viewed collectively, is nevertheless, as to the operation of the individual, scarcely discernible.' So their homes receive no acknowledgement in the piles of architectural histories written since, giving the impression that the vast majority of the population simply muddled through in unexciting abodes. Although scant evidence remains of the lowly rural worker's home, it can be said with certainty that it was untroubled by the taste or rules of foreign architects or by the domestic precedents of former ages. These humble structures were built by their owners according to their immediate needs in any assortment of brick, stone or timber, finished in rough plaster and topped with thatch or shingle. They were, as workers' cottages had always been, 'the work of necessity', explained Middleton, 'for which no rules can be given'.

SUBSTANCE WITHOUT STYLE

The greatest contribution that Georgian architects, builders and craftsmen made towards novelty in domestic planning was found not among the calculated proportions and classical orders that characterised the pretentious Palladianism pedalled by the nobility, nor in the emulating square plan of the four-up four-down that characterised the medium-sized mansions of the emerging middle classes, but in Britain's towns and cities, where the growing wealth and settled state of all social ranks caused orderly rows of houses to propagate. London was the seedbed of this new housing type, where it was at first crudely fashioned, then nurtured to a state of unassuming eminence before colonising other towns across the country, from Brighton and Weymouth, through Bristol and Bath, to Newcastle upon Tyne and Edinburgh.

The compact row house, or terrace, was an exemplar of its time. Having emerged as a pragmatic solution to the realities of urbanisation, the earliest examples were hastily erected and visually incoherent. Over time, the basic concept was honed and refined until it formed a dignified composition whose aggregate created entire streetscapes. These collective ensembles epitomised the Georgian character of urban Britain, from whole districts in large cities to singular squares or stately streets designed to bypass the dense and labyrinthine medieval cores in smaller towns.

Since the 16th century, the proliferation of early pattern books had caused a cross-pollination of architectural ideas that germinated an interest among the British nobility in the art of building. By the 17th century, a similar phenomenon occurred that affected less prodigious houses and was fostered by the publication of handbooks aimed at builders, tradesmen and developers wishing to erect convenient, comfortable and cheap homes. It was in these dwellings, 'not in the showy evolutions of buildings', argued Samuel Johnson, that 'the multiplicity of human habitations are crouded together [where] the wonderful immensity of London consists'.

One of the first of the publications that contributed to creating this intense urban setting was *The Art of Fair Building* by Roger

L'Estrange. Initially aimed at a Parisian audience, it was translated into English in 1670. As a form of proto-catalogue describing different types of building suited to different urban plots and status of occupant, this early edition summarised the essential requirements of an urban home: 'In the framing of every Building we must have regard to the durableness thereof, to the pleasantness and conveniency, to the comly proportion, and to the healthfulness of each room.'

The Great Fire of London – which, over the course of four days in September 1666, devoured a quarter of the City, destroying over 13,000 houses, tens of thousands of homes, and rendering 100,000 homeless – generated a hunger for pattern books for lower-ranking houses in the late 17th century by opening up swathes of prime urban land to development. Only months earlier, most of London's minor streets, lanes and alleys which accommodated a wide range of different qualities of house types had been redesignated 'high streets' or 'lanes of note', with the intention of reducing existing distinctions and raising overall standards. After the fire, six commissioners, including Christopher Wren and Roger Pratt, were appointed to make recommendations for the rebuilding of London, which led to the London Building Act of 1667. This Act regulated street sizes and building materials (only brick and stone), and stipulated four types of permissible house within the City of London: (1) a cellar plus two floors with an attic, situated on the smallest type of street; (2) Type 1 plus one extra floor, situated on larger streets; (3) Type 1 plus two extra floors, situated on main roads; and (4) detached mansions of no more than four floors, plus cellar and attic.

Advancing many elements of previous proclamations by Elizabeth I, James I and Charles I, the London Building Act began the process of standardising urban housing and provided a basic model for building regulations that would later be adopted not only throughout the whole of London, but in all cities and towns throughout the country. The Act also ended the monopoly that the City guilds held on the building trades, allowing for the first time artisans from outside the city to work within its walls, increasing competition and reducing prices. Further Acts in 1707 and 1709 extended these regulations to areas of London outside the old City walls, proscribing features such as wooden cornices and exposed sash window boxes, and requiring windows to be relieved by at least four and a half inches (11.5 centimetres) from the surface of the building.

The origin of the terrace lies in the 16th century, though they comprised only a few houses, not entire streets. Little remains of the few examples of row houses predating the Great Fire. The only survivor in London stands far beyond what was then the northern periphery of the City and comprises four houses built in 1658 facing Newington Green. The gable ends of this proto-terrace reveal the independent roof above each of the four units. This inconvenient configuration and its seemingly outdated appearance were discarded in most terraced houses built after the Great Fire, whose combined roof was concealed behind a parapet, giving the entire block a greater sense of unity.

After 1666, London desperately needed to house its homeless and despite the first Building Act, earlier royal proclamations to limit building and reduce urban densities were relaxed. The result was the erection of street upon street of cheaply built standardised multiple-occupancy units erected by property speculators from all ranks of society. One of the first and most renowned speculative builders was Nicholas If-Jesus-Christ-Had-Not-Died-For-Thee-Thou-Hadst-Been-Damned Barbon (c 1640– c 1698). Known also as Barebones, Barbon was the son of the Puritan Parliamentarian, Praise-God Barebones, who gave him the hortatory middle name. Barbon was a classic example of the mixed backgrounds from which late-17th-century speculative builders came. He was a trained physician, economist and Member of Parliament, who combined his interests in finance and building by establishing fire insurance. As a ruthless developer, Barbon was responsible for many of the 'ill-formed masses of brick and mortar' deemed by the likes of Johann Wilhelm von Archenholz (1741/3–1812), a Prussian officer, historian and publicist, as 'dark, and without taste' that linked the City with what was then the rapidly expanding West End.

Much of Bloomsbury, including Bedford Row and Red Lion Square, was built by Barbon. 'Things [that] are of no use, are of no value,' wrote Barbon towards the end of his career; 'there are two general uses by which all things have a value: they are either useful to supply the wants of the body, or the wants of the mind ... satisfying desire [and] contributing to the ease, pleasure, or pomp of life.'

> Terraced houses on Newington Green (1658), the oldest surviving terrace in London.

> Bedford Row, London, built by Nicholas Barbon in the late 17th and early 18th centuries.

∨ Illustration showing the limited ways in which variety could be achieved in planning two homes in the space occupied by two terraced houses.

As more and more people sought to profit from London's development, a 'pinching spirit', as Roger North described it, materialised whereby there was 'allwais some scantyness that spoyles all', whether 'pinching for room to increase the sale of houses' or decking 'a dining room, withdrawing room, and perhaps a closet with some new fingle fangle, to tempt her gay ladyship'. Developers would stop at nothing to secure a profit. Barbon so frequently transgressed the law that it was only parliamentary privilege, on account of his becoming an MP later in his career, which allowed him to escape prosecution.

Property speculators such as Barbon would have been armed with the first published handbooks for the building trades, the earliest of which, Stephen Primatt's *The City and Country Purchaser and Builder* (1667), was published immediately after the Great Fire for the purposes of rebuilding London. Primatt's book contained plans and detailed costs of different types of economical terraced house for households of varying size and financial means. Unlike the gargantuan architectural publications that were produced to flatter more than inform, these handbooks were literally books for the hands-on builder. William Pain's *The Builder's Pocket Treasure* (1763), published a century later but

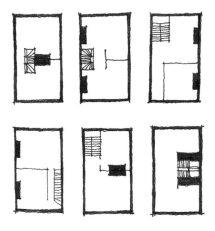

^ Diagram showing the different configuration of a two-room terraced house depending on the location of stair and chimney.

∨ An illustration showing an 18th-century terrace with a typical interior configuration for a single room on each floor and a side staircase.

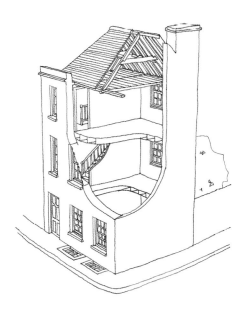

in the same idiom, was intended to fit in a builder's pocket and could not have been further removed physically and figuratively from such prodigious publications as Campbell's *Vitruvius Britannicus* (1717–25). Primatt's assorted plans are conspicuous for their uniformity. The highly standardised and flexible spaces arranged vertically appealed to commoners and nobility alike, guaranteeing their survival for centuries and their reverence today, though such qualities did not invite acclaim at the time.

The most influential factors to determine the character of the terrace were the ground rent and lease. With 31-year leases and annual ground rents payable to landowners, developers' profit margins were tight, but the equation was simple: the higher the density, the higher the income. Even after the standard leases had been increased, some extending to 99 years by the late 18th century, this short-sighted custom was blamed for what Archenholz described as 'the want of solidity in the houses, and the few master-pieces of architecture which we meet with in London'. With the smallest possible plot size, speculative developers sent terraces both upwards and downwards. This in turn set the character of the street frontage and gave rise to the basic model of the standard terraced house as a narrow multistorey structure with one or two rooms on each floor. With the width (5 to 6 metres) and depth (10 to 12 metres) of each house remaining relatively constant, eminence was achieved in the number and height of storeys. Almost all houses ranged from two to four storeys, excluding a cellar for storage and utilities, and a garret for servants' quarters or accommodation for poor tenants.

Any attempt to seek variety in the layout of these rigidly rectangular single-fronted units proved a challenge. Inserting a nook in the party wall gave the front of one house a wider span than the other and vice versa at the rear. The space occupied by two houses could be divided unevenly so that the larger unit had access to the front and rear, while the smaller unit only had access to the front. Internal variations were even more obscure. So standardised were the early terrace configurations that the only role left for architecture was, as Primatt suggested, 'in the placing of Chimneys and Stair-cases'.

Chimneys and stairs could be placed adjacently in the middle of the plan and used to divide the two rooms, preventing the need to build a partition wall, but this also undermined the flexibility of the space and so was less popular. The central staircase with the fireplace on the party wall was among the most common early configurations. It began in the higher end of the housing market and remained popular at the lower end up to the end of the 18th century because it usefully divided a shop at the front and accommodation at the rear and also because it was effective in accommodating the separate spaces created by a subdivided terrace occupied by multiple tenants.

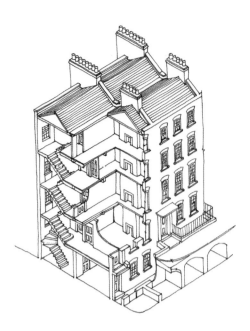

The most common layout, particularly among the larger terraces, was to have the stair against the party walls or at the rear of the house, which rendered the front room spacious, light and unobstructed, although it encroached on the space in the back room and made the entrance way and connecting corridor dark. A folding double door inserted between the front and back room improved lighting and allowed the two separate spaces to be opened up as one. To overcome the problem of a gloomy corridor behind the main entrance, windows were inserted above the door. Arranged in arced or semicircular shapes with slender tracery projecting in rays from the hub, they were named fanlights. Fireplaces were commonly omitted from the ground floor if it was occupied by a shop, which was common. London was a city of shops, and one in 10 of its workers owned one.

The greatest divergence from the standard single-fronted model of terrace was the double-fronted plan, which, rather than having two rooms on each floor in a rectangular plan with an entrance to one side, had four rooms in a square plan with the entrance in the middle, much like the middling villa type that occupied the suburbs. The double-fronted terrace was comparatively rare and on account of its larger frontage and overall plan it was built only by the very wealthy.

The simplicity of the terrace plan was its greatest asset and is the chief cause of its pervasive influence across the country ever since. Such simplicity arose out of specific circumstances, particularly economy and the absence of a client, which gave the terrace its greatest claim to novelty. Designed cheaply for no one, it had to cater for everyone. Consequently, the terrace was an unadorned empty space built with the principal intention of renting to tenants, often one family to a room with beds everywhere, but it was equally suited to a single family occupying the whole terrace. In this case, the dining room, the principal public room, was located at the front of the building on the ground floor with the drawing room above. Sitting rooms and studies were at the rear of the house, with the kitchen in the basement. Bedrooms occupied the upper floors at the front and rear, and up to four or five servants slept in the attic.

The exterior appearance of the single-fronted terrace altered little throughout the late 17th and early 18th centuries. A standard terraced house of two to four storeys sandwiched between a cellar and garret was composed in a similar manner to the classical orders: a base, middle and top. This tripartite composition was often accentuated with plaster detailing on bare brick, particularly from the late 18th century, when the entablature and ground-floor walls were entirely plastered and painted white to appear like stonework. Decorative detailing, such as pilasters and cornices, increasingly found their way on to the once austerely bare brick facades. By the early 19th century,

A typical speculative development, here in Great James Street, London, which was an early-18th-century extension of Bedford Row to the south.

Diagram of a typical 18th-century London terraced house with two rooms on each floor, rear staircase, attic, basement and undercroft at the front.

rough Georgian brickwork, like the people's pocked complexions hidden beneath a layer of white make-up, was concealed behind a skin of brightly painted plaster.

The bases of Georgian terraces extended to a cellar or lower-ground floor, as it is now called, whose buried position Ware described as 'damp, unwholesome, and uncomfortable'. It was not a space for living (except for servants if space elsewhere was lacking) but for cooking and storage, with adjacent stores and water cisterns vaulted beneath the pavement. The insertion of a cellar defines the way the terraced house engaged with the street and gave rise to the distinctive Georgian streetscape made up of road, pavement, railings and uniform facades. To allow natural light into this subterranean annexe, the terrace was set back from the street, cordoned off behind neat rows of iron railings. Access to the ground-floor entrance was provided by a series of steps or paving bridging the void between the pavement and the house. At the rear, the cellar opened out directly into a yard or garden. 'Almost every Body, whose Business requires them to be constantly in Town,' wrote the renowned gardener, Thomas Fairchild, in 1722, 'will have something of a Garden,' since 'every one in London, or other Cities, may delight themselves in Gardening.'

Inside the main entrance, the passage led to an internal staircase set either at the front of the house inside the doorway, or in the middle, between the two rooms on each floor, or at the rear. If the stair was placed at the front or middle, the larger-sized room at the rear became most suited to a parlour, allowing the front room to become a form of hall or reception room, though this was not always applied in practice. A small room, or closet, was often attached to the rear of the house to provide additional storage space without impacting on the internal arrangements of the house.

The first floor of medium-sized or larger terraces was treated as the *piano nobile*, visually expressed in the external appearance of the building through the taller windows extending almost the full height of the floor and divided into larger lights by slender bars. Ornate iron balconies were also affixed to the walls in front of these tall windows. With its elevated position and large windows affording the best views over the street, the function of this principal room was invariably the main dining room – the great seat of public entertainment in the modern 18th-century British home. The rear room would be a withdrawing room overlooking the garden or, in smaller houses, could be a principal bedroom with an adjoining closet over the same on the ground floor. Bedrooms in all terrace types were located on the upper floors, with men and women sometimes on separate floors and servants in the garret. A family of four would likely have at least as many servants, if not one or two more.

Windows throughout were of the sash type, except in the garret, where dormer windows penetrated the steep roof concealed behind a brick parapet. The windows of the earliest terraces were set almost flush with the surface of the building and had flat heads, but the Building Act of 1709 forbade this, stipulating that they should be set back at least four and a half inches (11.4 centimetres) from the surface of the wall and have arched heads. A consequent practice was to plaster the recesses and paint them white, which is continued to this day. Most terraces had two windows on each floor, while larger houses had three or even four, though their size in proportion to the overall facade was a point of considerable contention. Too much brick and the house 'resembled a prison, where the windows were only holes to let light into separate dungeons', wrote Ware, and too much window and the brickwork served 'only as ribs to hold the glazing together', giving the building the appearance of a 'lanthorn'. It was a fine balance between 'a house of glass [and] a heap of brick'.

The general plan of the London terraced house had become virtually standard by the end of the 18th century, though the same could not be said of its inhabitants. It was the terrace's simple form and unique internal flexibility that made it suitable for occupants of all financial means. The shape that Ware called the 'long square', formed by two rooms and a stair, was suited not only to east London workers, but in more commodious configurations it also served as a home for the country's nobility. The consequent indistinction was often scorned. In *Critical Observations on the Buildings and Improvements of London* (1771), James Stuart wrote:

> How many a nobleman, whose proud seat in the country is adorned with all the riches of architecture is content with a simple dwelling, convenient within, and unornamented without ... When we hear of a Grafton house, a Gower house, an Egremont house, we expect beyond roominess and convenience; the meer requisites of a packer, or a sugar baker. Would any foreigner, beholding an insipid length of wall broken into regular rows of windows ... ever figure from thence the residence of the first duke of England?

Whether accommodating the poor or wealthy, domestic conditions in the 18th century showed a general upward trend. Quiet improvements in the domestic economy raised the standard of living and transformed the interiors of common British homes, as more and more people could afford extravagances such as soft furnishings, hygienic apparatus and labour-saving devices that improved comfort and convenience.

> Eighteenth-century workers' houses in Woodseer Street (formerly Pelham Street), east London.

As the wealth of the nation was growing, so too was the demand for private possessions, from the rudimentary, such as cutlery and crockery, to the rarefied, such as eyewear and timepieces.

'The English are unfortunately led away, beyond all other countries in Europe,' wrote Archenholz, 'by the luxury of dress ... even those of the middling class, wear very excellent linen, and change it daily.'

From aspirational attire to newfangled domestic devices, new commodities were manufactured in terraces that doubled as factories and workshops for tradespeople, artisans and craftsmen. Up to a half of London's population was engaged in manufacturing in cottage industries turning out all sorts of products, from leatherwear to lace, from gin to jewellery, and from deluxe furniture to dried fish. London's homes had not only become a commodity, but, long before anywhere else in Europe, they produced commodities. Cottage industry remained a feature of London's domestic landscape well into the 19th century, but throughout the 18th century it was usurped by larger and more specialised manufacturing facilities that consumed vacant land beyond the City's perimeter or near its main artery, the Thames, whose fetid waters licked the walls of warehouses, factories and docks, poisoning the lifeblood of the city.

In the midst of this increasingly dystopian drama that characterised modern urban life, the gentry began their westward migration, away from the hubbub by the river and the densely populated areas encircling it, where the streets and manners were deemed debauched and dangerous. Places such as Alsatia on the western edge of the City, so called because until the end of the 17th century it enjoyed legal sanctuary and consequently had attracted all forms of vice, reinforced negative perceptions and spawned a flood of artistic and literary commentary on the condition of the modern metropolis, from Hogarth's print of *Gin Lane* (1751) to the anonymously written poem *Hell-on-Earth*:

> This great, wicked, unwieldy, over-grown Town, one continued hurry of Vice and Pleasure; where nothing dwells but Absurdities, Abuses, Accidents, Accusations, Admirations, Adventures, Adversities, Advertisements, Adulteries, Affidavits, Affectations, Affirmations, Afflictions, Affronts, Aggravations, Agitations, Agonies, Airs, Alarms, Ailments, Allurements, Alterations, Ambitions, Amours, Amphitheatres, Anathemas, Animosities, Anxieties, Appointments, Apprehensions, Arrests, Arrogances, Assassinations, Assemblies, Assessments, Assurances, Assignations, Attainders, Audacities, Aversions, etc.

Convinced of the squalor and carnality in and around the City and along the South Bank, the westward migrants moved to the open land around Westminster, where Archenholz observed 'the most fertile fields and most agreeable gardens [were] daily metamorphosed into houses and streets', creating nascent suburbs and new urban districts. Capitalising on London's unprecedented urban expansion and migration were the owners of the Great Estates – the Russell family who developed the Bedford Estate from the mid-17th century encompassing much of Bloomsbury; the Grosvenors who bought up Mayfair in 1677; the Cadogans who purchased large tracts of Knightsbridge and Chelsea in the early 18th century; and the later estates such as Viscount Belgrave's Belgravia. These vast estates were the modern-day equivalent of the medieval manor, with their aristocratic landowner reaping the financial rewards of leasing the land at a huge profit. Buildings, not crops, were the staple earner on London's estates.

As west London developed, so too did the taste of those speculating in its homes. In contrast to the bare brown brick of Bloomsbury rose the shimmering stuccowork of Belgravia, Pimlico and Knightsbridge, whose whitewashed walls aspired to better things. East and west London differed not only in their

∧ Eighteenth-century silk weavers' terraced houses in Shoreditch, east London.

< Eighteenth-century terraced houses over shops in Shoreditch, east London.

'government; regulations; privileges; manner of living; every thing', wrote the French traveller, Louis Simond, but also in their 'taste and arrangement of houses ... Every minute of longitude east was equal to as many degrees of gentility minus, or towards west, plus.' Residents of the east looked upon 'the people who lived at the west end of town with luxury, idleness, effeminacy, and an attachment to French fashions; while the others speak of a citizen as a dull, fat animal, who place all his merits in his strong box'. London's rapid transformation and the distinction between its east and west ends was dramatised by the playwright, David Garrick (1717–79), in *The Trip to Scarborough*, performed at the Theatre Royal in Drury Lane in 1781:

> What various transformations we remark,
> From East Whitechapel to the West Hyde-park!
> Men, women, children, houses, signs, and fashions,
> State, stage, trade, taste, the humours and the passions;
> Th' Exchange, 'Change-alley, wheresoe'er you're ranging,
> Court, city, country, all are chang'd or changing;
> The streets, some time ago, were pav'd with stones,
> Which, aided by a hackney coach, half broke your bones.

It might have been correct to assume, as did the man of letters and founder of *The Spectator* magazine, Joseph Addison (1672–1719), that 'the Inhabitants of *St James's* are a distinct People from those of *Cheapside*, who are likewise removed from those of the *Temple* on the one side, and those of *Smithfield* on the other, by several Climates and Degrees in their ways of Thinking and Conversing together', but behind the facades of their respective homes, and irrespective of fixtures, fittings and furnishings, there remained a striking uniformity in their plan. Inevitable exceptions aside, the most common types were single-fronted with an entrance on one side that led to a rear staircase mounted on the party wall with a formal room at the front of the house and withdrawing room behind. Living rooms or studies were on the first floor, bedrooms on the second and third, with servants' quarters in the garret and basement. Kitchens and other utilities were also in the basement or in outhouses at the rear, where mews began to line the streets behind.

As far as the plan was concerned, the principal difference between the single-fronted stuccoed terraced houses sprouting up beyond the newly laid Hyde Park and those in east London was one of scale. The new homes being erected in west London in the late 18th century could be as much as twice the width of those in the east. Four east London terraced houses could fit into the front room and entrance hall of some of their west London counterparts. Some west London terraces even extended to six floors from basement to garret. The depths also increased towards the end of the 18th century, as cheaper land was made available beyond the fringes of existing developments.

> Houses (1820–40) on the Lloyd Baker
> Estate, Finsbury, London.

Regardless of location, attempts were made to arrange terraces in a more orderly and cohesive manner, often in the style of country mansions around a park area, forming squares of different shapes and sizes, from the grandiose in more salubrious areas of west London to the diminutive around the periphery of the City, as in the case of the Lloyd Baker Estate in Finsbury. However, the scale of these often ambitious projects and the price of land undermined their development and London's planning was piecemeal, forever retarded by economic precedents. Places such as Bloomsbury Square (1660 and initially called Southampton Square) or St James's Square (1670s), among the first residential squares to be laid out in London, were quickly occupied by insipid lengths of wall perforated by regular rows of windows rather than the sumptuous detached mansions that their owners had intended. In a bid to avoid the monotony that these lines of houses created, attempts were made to treat the whole facade as one palatial frontage, crowning the central section with a pediment and adorning the outer terraces with pilasters or other details that hinted at the wings of former rural mansions. This unified treatment of a facade appears throughout the country, from the grandest scale, as on the north side of Bedford Square (1775–83) in Bloomsbury, London, down to the smallest, as in the row of two-up two-down houses in Albert Terrace (1820), Norwich. The financially driven nature of London's residential development put paid to any attempt to realise the full grandiose extent of these set-piece urban ensembles, causing them to end up being, according to James Stuart, 'gardens, parks, sheep-walks; in short, every thing but what they should be'.

London was not suited to urban planning. This great trading city was and always had been a town fuelled by finance. Speculation, not planning, had caused the formerly independent

cities of London and Westminster and their surrounding villages to become one. Following the mad process of 'roofing all the county of Middlesex with tiles', Archenholz described London as 'a monstrous aggregate, to which there are neither limits or regulations'. Joseph Addison similarly referred to it as 'an aggregate of various nations distinguished from each other by their respective Customs, Manners and Interests'. With the construction of over 43,000 new houses in London between 1762 and 1779, Archenholz asserted that 'it cannot now be doubted that the English have the misfortune to possess a capital infinitely more extensive than the French'.

London was, in the context not only of Britain but also of Europe, another world. Its homes and residential districts were the result of accumulated individual speculations, not of any conscious plan. The property speculators that waded into this city in the late 17th century not only built on the city's tradition of trading, but in erecting the lines of brick terraces literally helped to build the city's future traditions. Under such conditions no individual or organisation, whether the wealthiest landowner, the government or the church, had the means to impose or undertake anything more than a civic square or part of a street. But 18th-century Britain did experience architecture on the novel scale of town planning, and to witness this one must look westwards to the former Roman settlement at Bath where, according to the French traveller Louis Simond, 'there is more good architecture in private buildings than in any town in the world'.

The most ambitious and wide-ranging residential designs of the Georgian era were carried out by the Bathonian architect John Wood (1704–54) and his son, also called John, though their influence cannot be entirely detached from London. As a young adult, Wood went to London and worked as a carpenter and joiner for Lord Bingley who, like many wealthy landowners

< The north side of Bedford Square (1775–83) in Bloomsbury, London, showing the central pediment and eastern portion providing a unified design to a series of single-fronted four-storey terraced houses, including garrets behind the pediment.

> Albert Terrace (1820), Norwich, individual houses designed as a complete ensemble unified by a central pediment and cornice.

in London at the time, was developing swathes of land either side of Oxford Street. The piecemeal development of London's Great Estates made a big impression on Wood. In 1727, having purchased a plan of Bath, he began working 'towards the Improvement of the City by Building' and produced two plans, which he presented to the landowners. Describing these plans in his 'Essay Towards the Description of Bath', he 'proposed to make a grand Place of Assembly, to be called the *Royal Forum of Bath*; another Place, no less magnificent, for the Exhibition of Sports, to be called the *Grand Circus*; and a third Place, of equal state with either of the former, for the Practice of medicinal Exercises, to be called the *Imperial Gymnasium* of the City'. For Wood, Bath presented an opportunity to physically and symbolically surpass the classically inspired Palladianism that the likes of Burlington were using to try to forge a national architecture, and, instead, fuse Roman and Grecian architecture with the mystical patterns of the ancient Druids, whose influence was not only strong in the region but who Wood believed had even inspired their Mediterranean successors.

When Wood returned to Bath, the city, like many in Britain at the time, was enjoying a period of prosperity and expansion. International commerce was driving Britain's economy forward at breakneck speed. 'What is a commercial nation, but a collection of commercial towns?' wrote George Chalmers in his *Estimate of the Comparative Strength of Great Britain* (1794), citing 'London and Bristol, Birmingham and Sheffield, Manchester and Leeds, Whitehaven and Newcastle, Glasgow and Paisley, Greenock and Leith' as leading commercial centres. Throughout the 18th century, these and many other towns and cities were shaking off the tight-knit and timber appearance that had characterised their centres since medieval times and were being refurnished in brick and stone. This description of early-18th-century Birmingham by the historian William Hutton (1723–1815) was typical of many British towns:

… less than one hundred straggling huts, without order, which we will dignify with the name of houses; built of timber, the interstices wattled with thatch, boards of sods: none of them higher than the ground story. The meaner sort only one room, which served three uses, shop, kitchen, and lodging room; the door for two, it admitted the people and the light. The better sort two rooms, and some three, for work, for the kitchen, and for rest; all three in a line, and sometimes fronting the street.

By the mid-18th century, such primitive scenes composed 'of wretched dwellings, replete with dirt and poverty' were swept away, as new elegant buildings were erected and the foundations were laid for Britain's modern cities: 'grand, populous, extensive, active, commercial – and humane'. Wider streets and stately squares rose up around the peripheries of medieval cores. Internally, homes were acquiring an air of respectability and comfort unseen beneath the rank of the nobility, as the swelling ranks and purses of merchants and traders helped to form a new middle class, or what Daniel Defoe described as 'the upper station of low life … not exposed to the miseries and hardships, the labour and sufferings of the mechanic part of mankind, and not embarrassed with the pride, luxury, ambition, and envy of the upper part of mankind … but in easy circumstances sliding

Royal York Crescent (c 1791–1820),
one of the largest unified speculative
developments in Bristol.

Charlotte Street, Bristol, laid out by
Thomas Paty (c 1713–89) and his son
William (1758–1800). The iron balconies
are early-19th-century additions.

Detail of the terraced houses in the
Royal Crescent (1767–75), Bath, designed
by John Wood the Younger.

gently through the world'. The hardness of stone and wood
floors was softened by carpets and rugs. Flimsy fixtures and
fittings gave way to polished brass and solid decent timber.
Furniture grew in comfort and quantity and novel devices and
tame trinkets began to litter the home. Even the painted walls
and serious wainscoting were invigorated by the novelty of
gaily patterned wallpaper. Pipes too began delivering water into
homes, though it would be some time before these would be
used for heating the home or disposing of waste. In most
of Britain's cities, it was a time of progress and indulgence.

Bath was a little different however: it was a place devoted to
leisure, not commerce – a town where, according to Simond,
'half the inhabitants do nothing, the other half supplies them
with nothings'. While the invigorating waters of the springs
served visitors all year round, at the heart of Bath's calendar was
the social season, when the cream of Georgian society would
flock to the city to rub shoulders with one another and be seen
to be seen. Evening entertainment centred round the Assembly
Rooms, designed by John Wood the Younger in 1769, where
visitors played cards, listened to lectures, or danced the night
away in endless balls, as enterprising mothers busied themselves
with the task of marrying off their daughters to the nearest
eligible bachelor. Property in Bath was therefore propped up
by the temporary resident.

∧ King's Circus (1754–67), Bath, initiated by
John Wood (the Elder) and completed by
his son, John Wood the Younger. Note
the basement floor, access to which
creates the characteristic Georgian
terrace set back from the street.

> Plans (ground and first floors only) of
different flats in King's Circus (1754–67),
Bath, showing the versatile arrangement
of the staircase with two rooms on
each floor.

The Royal Crescent (1767–75), Bath, designed by John Wood the Younger.

The elder Wood's first major work in Bath was Queen Square (1728–36), whose unity in design surpassed anything since Inigo Jones's Covent Garden a century earlier, including its massive namesake in Bristol (1699–1727) or London's early speculative squares, such as Bloomsbury and St James's, whose individual plots betrayed any consistency in design. However, where Wood's Queen Square set a high standard in aggregated unity, it was his later work which was continued by his son that would take this coherence to a new level, which would set it apart not only from the Georgian developments springing up in and around its mercantile neighbour, Bristol, but also from the rest of the country, including London. The monumentality and majesty of King's Circus (1754–67), Britain's first circus, and the Royal Crescent (1767–75) derived from the simple repetition of elements and their aggregated whole, which Simond described as leaving the town looking 'as if it had been cast in a mould all at once; so new, so fresh, and regular'.

Construction of King's Circus (now known simply as 'The Circus') began the year before Wood died, leaving the completion of the plan to his son. John Wood the Younger designed the extension of Gay Street (1755–60), connecting his father's Queen Square to King's Circus, and then Brock Street (1760s), connecting the Circus to the Royal Crescent. Although Wood the Elder had conceived these designs earlier in his career, many years separated the projects and they took two lifetimes to complete. Between them, the Woods had elevated the urban terrace to an entirely new plane that, although still a speculative development in its own right, went far beyond the cumulative developments built in London up to that date.

Only John Carr's Crescent (1779–90) in Buxton, Derbyshire was comparable for its time, and not until Nash produced his plans for Regent Street and Regent's Park in the early 19th century would London see anything quite like what Woods had created in Bath. Even then however, Nash's painted stuccowork on brick and unusual interpretation of Classicism could not compare with the Woods' originality in design and the unrivalled finish of the fine local stone from which their buildings were fashioned. Stone, as every aristocrat knew, possessed a finesse far superior to brick. 'Brick, Mr. Pitt, brick,' said George III disparagingly to George Pitt when he witnessed the construction of his Dorset home, Kingston House (1717–20).

While the creativity of Bath's majestic plans set them apart from anywhere else in Britain, their internal arrangements were less original. The basic plan of most Bath terraces was akin to those found in London from the late 17th century, with a standard width of 6 to 7.5 metres and a depth of 11 to 15 metres accommodating two rooms per floor separated by a stair. There were notable exceptions. In Queen Square, Wood mixed single-fronted and double-fronted houses in the north terrace, placing a double-fronted unit in the middle so that it formed a centrepiece beneath a pediment to present a palatial appearance

∧ Plan of a terraced house in the Royal Crescent (1767–75), Bath, designed by John Wood the Younger.

∨ The Royal Crescent (1767–75), Bath, viewed from the western end.

∧ The north side of Queen Square (1728–36), the first major work in Bath by John Wood (the Elder), where he designed the entire terrace as one symmetrical palatial elevation with pedimented central portion flanked by wings.

∨ Plan of houses in Queen Square (1728–36), Bath, designed by John Wood, showing ground and first floors of double-fronted and single-fronted houses in a terrace.

to the entire range. In the later King's Circus, all 33 houses were three storeys and 13 metres high with basement and attic, but internal arrangements differed subtly to suit the site – sometimes the principal room was at the front of the house and elsewhere it was placed at the rear. In both King's Circus and the Royal Crescent, the Woods managed to maintain a rectilinear configuration of rooms despite the curved plot on which they stood, the angle of the curve being accommodated in the thickness of the walls rather than the room.

The function of each space inside these terraces conformed to the prevailing pattern. Basements were occupied by kitchens and servants' quarters, and the ground floor contained the dining room and parlour, with a side hallway leading from the entrance to a stair at the centre or rear of the house. The first floor, just as in London's later Georgian terraces, was the principal floor containing the withdrawing room which, in the case of King's Circus, had almost full-length windows. One distinguishing feature of first-floor rooms in the Royal Crescent was that they occupied the entire floor rather than being separated. Bedrooms and dressing rooms were on the upper floors, with servants' accommodation in the garrets above.

∧ Park Square (1823–4), London, designed by John Nash, linking Park Crescent with Regent's Park.

Bath's terraces were the first and foremost examples of housing design on the scale of town planning in Britain and preceded numerous other, though often less monumental, examples across the country. As the developments in Bath were drawing to a close, similarly ambitious plans were being launched in Edinburgh. In 1766, the young Scottish architect, James Craig (1739–95), won a competition for the masterplan of the New Town to the north of the Old Town. His design comprised a series of streets and squares laid out on a gridiron pattern dominated by Princes Street, George Street and Queen Street, with St Andrew's Square at one end and St George's Square at the other. The latter, renamed Charlotte Square before construction, was the last part of the scheme to be built, and is its crowning glory, with palace-fronted terraces designed by Robert Adam in 1791.

In London, the only way such extravagant schemes could be realised was through the irresponsible profligacy of a wayward royal. In 1810, just such a person appeared from the shadow of the incapacitated King George III following a second bout of mental illness. In early 1811, the Prince of Wales became Prince Regent and following the death of George III in 1820 became King George IV (1762–1830). Many unworthy and unpopular monarchs had ruled parts of this island over the centuries, but few were as disliked by their subjects for their outrageous extravagance as George IV. His ostentatious taste and fondness for luxury were unsurpassed. No architect benefited from the Regent's predilection for costly construction more than John Nash, who began work for the Regent almost immediately.

Nash's first contribution was a grandiose urban plan linking the Prince's residence in Carlton House at the southern end to the open ground that is now Regent's Park at the northern end. The grand route that carved its way through London's 17th-century street pattern either side of Oxford Street, via Piccadilly Circus, Oxford Circus and the Adam brothers' Portland Place provided the first opportunity in London for a large-scale urban plan. Regent Street (1813–20) was the first component of this plan to be finished, followed by Park Crescent (1806–21) at the north end of Portland Place, linking it to the third part of his scheme comprising the terraces and villas on the fringe of Regent's Park (1818–27). The final constituent of the masterplan was the construction of Carlton House Terrace (1827–32) on the site of the Prince Regent's former residence. Assisting Nash on several of these schemes was the young architect Decimus Burton (1800–81).

Burton and Nash worked together on Carlton House Terrace, whose two monumental blocks each contained nine mansions, the sale of the leases of which helped to bankroll the Prince's conversion of Buckingham House further down The Mall into

∧ The south elevation of the easternmost
of the two blocks comprising Carlton House
Terrace (1827–32), London, designed by
John Nash on the site of Carlton House
on the north side of The Mall.

> Ground-floor plan of Carlton House Terrace
(1827–32), London, showing a two-up two-
down arrangement with two staircases
(one main and one for servants).

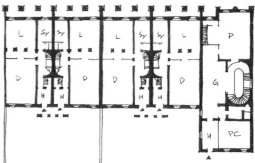

L: Library · Sy: Study · D: Dining Room
H: Hall · P: Parlour · G: Gallery
PC: Parlour (Common Room)

Buckingham Palace. The houses in Carlton House Terrace, despite their immense appearance, continued the terrace tradition of stacking rooms in a vertical manner with public rooms near the ground floor and private rooms on the upper floors that had begun in London over a century earlier. The difference here, just as in west London throughout the 18th century, was one of scale. Each residence was arranged over three storeys with a basement and attic and a broad single frontage allowing the rooms to be wider and taller, with two flights of stairs (one for show and one for service) against the party wall. One break from the norm was the double basement at the rear, which was permitted by the steep fall in the topography of the site from the front to the back. To accommodate this idiosyncrasy, Nash designed a heavy Grecian colonnade along The Mall that removed the mews, which was then an essential appendage to any respectable town house, and presented a formal frontage to The Mall with views over St James's Park.

The most conspicuous facet of Nash's works for the Regent was the gleaming painted stucco over brick. Inferior to the masonry that both Woods used in Bath, stucco was adored and abhorred in equal measure and caused Nash to be the subject of ridicule by an increasingly critical public. W Hillary jibed in 1825:

> Augustus, at Rome, was for building renown'd,
> And of marble he left what of brick he had found:
> But is our Nash too, a very great master?
> He finds us all brick, and leaves us all plaster!

After the death of George IV, Nash's career came to an abrupt end, but his influence lived on, most completely in the seaside resort of Brighton where he had built the fantastical Pavilion for the Prince Regent. Brighton's expansion in the early 19th century mirrored that of Bath a century earlier as a place of leisure and

∧ Brunswick Terrace (1828), Brighton,
designed by Charles Busby.

‹ Regency Square (1817–30), Brighton,
which introduced bay windows to
the flat facade of the Georgian terrace.

pleasure for the aristocracy and increasingly affluent middle class.
Several squares were laid out towards the end of the 18th century,
but it was not until the construction of the Royal Crescent (1799–
1802) some distance to the east of the town centre that a planned
development was built facing the seafront. The Prince Regent did
much to raise Brighton's popularity, with the town's population
trebling in the first two decades of the 19th century from 7,000 to
21,000, a faster rate than any other town in Britain. Throughout
the first half of the 19th century, Brighton's development spilled
into neighbouring Hove to the west and climbed the cliffs beyond
Kemp Town to the east, as terrace upon terrace was laid out along
the seafront: Regency Square (1817–30) with its bay windows on
all but the top floor providing views of the sea; the massive Lewes
Crescent flanked by Chichester and Arundel Terraces by Amon
Wilds (1762–1833) and Charles Busby (1788–1834); Montpelier
Crescent (1843–7); Brunswick Square and Terrace (1825–) by
Busby; Amon Wilds the Younger's string of conjoined two-storey
Palladian villas in Hanover (c 1814–23) and Park Crescents
(1849–54) and the massive Adelaide Crescent (1830–60s), which
was originally designed by Nash's assistant, Decimus Burton.
Financial difficulties halted Burton's project in 1834 after just 10
houses had been built and it was not resumed again until 1849,
by which time Burton's rather tired neoclassical plan had been
substantially revised.

In contrast to the fresh appearance of sun-drenched stucco, Brighton's Regency houses were a dying breed and represented the end of an era of domestic planning spanning three centuries. The flexibility of the multistorey terraced house, the hard currency of property speculation when Britain's cities were booming, was not able to withstand the new and mounting pressures that came to define domestic developments in the 19th century. Industrialisation and the concomitant romanticism that it evoked would, more than anything else, shape the course of domestic planning for the next hundred years. For a new generation of architects who would flourish under a new monarch and a new era of industrialisation and empire, the dubious taste of each villa and terrace in Brighton was surpassed only by the royal palace itself. It would be extremely difficult, if not impossible, argued AWN Pugin in the 1830s, to find one example 'amongst the immense mass which could be handed down to succeeding ages as an honourable specimen of the architectural talent of the time'.

Brighton's Regency houses were symptomatic of the extravagance of an ailing and addled architecture in desperate need of reorientation. Architecture, like society itself, had become decadent, distasteful and dishonest. Architecture, 'that grandest of sciences', as Pugin called it, had become a mere trade, conducted not by artists but by businessmen. Assorted styles collected from around a world in which Britain was becoming increasingly dominant had been placed incongruously into Britain's cities, towns and countryside and presented an architectural menagerie that betrayed the nation's history. 'The peculiars of every nation form a mongrel species in England,' wrote James Malton (1761–1803) despairingly, 'the new fashioned windows of Italy, opening to the floor, with lengthened balcony, originally intended to survey the lawns, the vistas, and the groves of Claude, in their summer attire, or the canals of Venice ... are now to be seen in every confined street of London.' Pugin concurred, railing at the motley internationalism he saw around him in the form of 'Swiss cottages in a flat country; Italian villas in the coldest situations; a Turkish kremlin for a Royal residence; Greek temples in crowded lanes; Egyptian auction rooms; and all kinds of absurdities and incongruities'. The miscellaneous collection of imitations was for Britain's new generation of architects a national disgrace, and, argued Pugin, 'so it will remain till the plaster and cement, of which it is composed, decay'.

Such sentiments were an attack on the present condition of architecture as much as a response to industrialisation's omnipresence. William Blake's 'dark Satanic Mills' cast a long shadow over Victorian Britain. Faced with wholesale change, an enduring facet of the human condition to look back rather than forward materialised in architecture, as it did in all the arts. A search for roots and the picturesque was under way,

> Adelaide Crescent (1830–60s), Brighton,
designed by Decimus Burton.

and the Gothic revival that Halfpenny and Walpole had begun several decades before became the dominant theme of domestic architecture for the rest of the century as Britain's population sought security in the snug cosiness of the home. Motivated by the moralistic pursuit of building a new Jerusalem in England's green and pleasant land, the next chapter of domestic planning was characterised by a dichotomy between the romantic pursuit of a domestic idyll and the unsettling reality of industrialisation with its consequent urbanisation and the explosion of the suburbs.

John Nash's scheme for London, parading its way pompously from The Mall to the fringes of Regent's Park, was as much a closing statement reverberating from a passing age that promoted the urban terrace at its most grandiose, as it was a declaration of intent in a new era defined by confronting the problems associated with the gathering urban poor. By sweeping aside some of London's most impoverished neighbourhoods, Nash's gleaming stuccoed plan for London's affluent was, among other things, an ambitious act of urban cleansing and a portent of the chief challenge that Britain and, in particular, its cities faced during the next stage in the life of the British home. The Georgian terrace, ideally suited to all manner of occupants for nearly two centuries and perfectly placed to provide the steady densification that characterised Georgian towns and cities, could not survive the forthcoming transformations. The new age of iron, fuelled by revolutionary industries and methods of communication, propelled Britain's towns and cities to the brink of unprecedented expansion. The life of the British home was about to be shaken to its core by the Industrial Revolution.

HOME SWEET HOME?

THE INDUSTRIAL AGE
c 1830–1910

Following the death of George IV in 1830 and that of his successor William IV seven years later, a new monarch was waiting in the wings. Her name would define the next and, some would say, most glorious age in Britain's history as much as the names of the previous four kings had defined the urban terrace from the previous age. Under Queen Victoria's reign, Britain's social and physical landscape was totally transformed, though the seeds of change were sown long before.

Throughout the 18th century, Britain's wealth and population had been growing steadily. From around 6 million in 1700, the country's population nearly doubled to 10 million by 1800. During the same period, trade, industry and warfare transformed Britain into a global superpower where, for nearly a century, it enjoyed a hegemonic position. The Georgians had laid the foundation of Britain's industrial and commercial supremacy by digging the first canals, laying the first railways and constructing the first iron bridges, but the Victorians would take industrialisation to new heights.

Eminent industrialists like John 'Iron-Mad' Wilkinson (1728–1808) had steered Britain towards a new iron age in which the components of the Industrial Revolution were forged. Bridges, boats, machines and cannons all turned to iron, which in turn enabled new technologies like steam and rotary engines, revolutionising factories, mills, furnaces and forges. '[T]hings are changing ev'ry day, / And ev'ry thing's improving,' chimed the poem *The Iron Age* (1827); 'Then for the shining age of gold, / The poets can but sigh on, / For this, as iron's all the rage, / Must be the age of iron.' In the 19th century not only did Britain become the world's first industrialised and urbanised society, but its population nearly quadrupled, reaching 35 million by the end of Victoria's reign in 1901. The provision of housing for these extra tens of millions dominated the next chapter in the life of the British home and produced its foremost examples of novelty in domestic planning. The site of these new houses was overwhelmingly urban – the population of Britain's towns and cities having increased from 3 million to 25 million during the 19th century.

Urban migration was not a 19th-century phenomenon, but its consequences in that century could no longer be ignored. Britain's rising wealth and population throughout the 18th century was satisfied by the property speculator, whose consistent contributions to domestic planning were characterised more by the densification of existing urban centres that remained within easy reach of the countryside than by their expansion and detachment from it. Population increases towards the end of the 18th century and throughout the 19th century were on a different scale entirely, and demanded a more purposeful approach than that which speculators could provide on their own.

Help was needed in accommodating Britain's rapidly growing population, and philanthropic associations were the first to step in, followed in the next century by the state in the form of council housing. London, whose population exceeded one million by 1801, remained Britain's largest city by some distance and consequently faced some of the most acute problems associated with overcrowding, but other cities experienced higher rates of growth and sometimes greater suffering as a result of poverty and a lack of planning: Birmingham, Bristol, Cardiff, Edinburgh, Glasgow, Leeds, Newcastle upon Tyne and Nottingham, whose populations were less than 60,000 in 1801, all had populations of between 250,000 and 500,000 a century later.

Compared with these unique challenges, the concerns of the rural homes of the affluent, whose overriding obsession throughout much of the 19th century was their style of dress, appear palpably trivial. Between the two extremes, hierarchically and geographically, were the homes of the now firmly established middle classes, whose aspirations aped those above them and whose incentive was to leave behind those below them. The result was the suburb and the stimulus was the railway. In the 19th century, connected to the urban centres by expanding iron filaments of the world's first urban railway network were endless rows of cloned cottages, some conjoined, some detached, and others terraced. These new suburbs produced an altogether different scene from the pockets of middling villas that were built beyond the perimeters of prosperous towns and cities in the previous century.

In an age of unprecedented change, the home assumed an almost mystical reverence – a harbour that protected its inhabitants from the gathering storm. 'Home, sweet home' and 'There's no place like home', words from *Clari* (1823) by the American playwright John Howard Payne, struck a chord. The 19th-century British home was a moral temple, a spiritual sanctuary and a place of refuge – a place to bury one's head in the sands of time.

In its material manifestation, it also defined one's place in society – tendering clues in architectural details, in the number, arrangement and function of its rooms, and in the size and location of its site. An analysis of these different facets and functions of the British home in the 19th century could fill libraries, forcing this exploration to concentrate on the ongoing evolution of planning trends that brought about that increasingly elusive quality of originality. It is no minor fact that by the end of the 19th century a significant proportion of British homes were made in old housing stock accumulated over several centuries. The very existence of these older models of housing influenced the century's architects, builders and clients, exciting various degrees of imitation and disavowal that were most forcefully expressed in the 'Battle of the Styles', in which the appearance and values associated with Gothicism and Classicism were pitched against one another in a lengthy skirmish during which Charles Barry's (1795–1860) Gothic-styled Houses of Parliament (1835–68), whose details bore the distinctive mark of Pugin, and Robert Smirke's (1780–1867) neoclassical British Museum (1823–52) were major victories for both sides.

The search for originality and appropriateness continued just as eagerly as it always had done and can be found lingering in all types of housing, though nowhere more pervasively and prominently than in the homes of the less well-off, whose dwellings not only transformed Britain's towns and cities, but also created much of the urban fabric that we take for granted today.

THE WORKER'S HOME

From the 18th century trade, industry and empire became bedfellows in a cosy, profitable and triangular relationship that lasted nearly two centuries. Paralleling this extraordinary rise, zenith and fall was the stampede of Britain's new labouring classes from the countryside to the city. Though most acute in the nation's capital, this almost biblical migration consumed all Britain's towns and cities. In the hundred years from the late 18th century, Liverpool's population grew from 70,000 to 700,000, outpaced by neighbouring Greater Manchester which grew from 25,000 to nearly 1.5 million. In 1845, a member of Liverpool's newly established Health of Towns Association observed that 'Within the last thirty years the wealth and resources of this country have increased in an unprecedented degree, but by a strange anomaly, the physical condition of the people has deteriorated.' Liverpool, like many cities in Britain, had experienced a sharp decline in living standards and a corresponding increase in mortality rates. Life expectancy was just 17 years, compared with 20 in Manchester, 21 in Leeds and 26 in London. From a healthy town

< Queen's Gate Terrace (1850s),
  Kensington, London.

> The towering five-storey terraces (plus
  basement) three bays wide known as
  'Albert Houses' (1855–60s) along Queen's
  Gate, Kensington, London, designed by
  CJ Richardson.

in the 18th century, Liverpool was described in 1845 as 'the most unhealthy town not only in Lancashire, but in the kingdom' and the Health of Towns Association laid the blame squarely at the 'mal-arrangements in our towns and dwellings, especially [those] inhabited by the poorer classes'.

By the mid-19th century, urban authorities could no longer ignore the problems associated with urbanisation. In the *Adventures of Benjamin Bobbin the Bagman* (1855), Glasgow was described as a place in which 'Abomination, poverty, and uncleanliness seemed to reign supreme.' Paradoxically, such scenes of utter destitution were a consequence of the nation's growing prosperity and their remedy was a societal responsibility, though society was slow to offer any assistance. The earliest attempts to provide a solution were opportunistic and often morally moot, merely moving the problem elsewhere. Workers' dwellings erected on the fringes of the city or anywhere that space allowed were torn down and their inhabitants forcibly evicted.

Here began a process of expulsion and resettlement that lasted for much of the remainder of the century. Following Britain's victory over France in the Napoleonic Wars in 1815, the government focused its attentions on improving London, and Regent Street was planned. 'One great reason for its formation in the line it took,' wrote William Gilbert in 'The Dwellings of the London Poor' (1872), was that 'it would destroy an immense number of poor dwellings.' The wretched inhabitants were ejected in their droves without compensation or provision, only to migrate to other parts of town, such as the Strand, Westminster and across the river into Lambeth. When it came to improving the Strand and Trafalgar Square, the same excuses prevailed. And so it continued – each round of eviction moving the problem elsewhere and causing it to grow in size and intensity. St Giles, wrote Gilbert, became so crowded that 'the whole parish was threatened with an overwhelming mass of pauperism'. New Oxford Street and Endell Street were laid down on countless miserable homes belonging to London's poor. With the improvement of Westminster, the poor were driven into Chelsea from Pimlico and Belgravia, where miniature palaces and stucco terraces descended over former fields like a plague in the creation of new districts such as Kensington.

At the same time, railways started to infiltrate inner-city areas, providing the ideal pretext for continued slum clearances. The route of the Charing Cross Railway 'was to a considerable extent adopted by the promoters in consequence of the cheapness of the property it would destroy,' claimed Gilbert, 'but not one single dwelling was erected for their accommodation, nor a question raised as to where they might go'. The scale of these clearances caused eminent figures to intervene. Lord Shaftesbury (1801–85) was one such champion for the cause of improving urban housing for the poor who helped to bring about changes in the legislation and regulation concerning working-class housing. The fountain in Piccadilly Circus, *The Angel of Christian Charity*, modelled on Anteros, the Greek god of requited love, and often mistaken for his brother Eros, was erected in 1893 to memorialise his efforts.

While many of Britain's romantic poets and painters were busy painting a whimsical myth of a rural idyll, Victorian writers, such as Charles Dickens, fed on the inequities and hardships of life fabricated in part by the country's property speculators, immortalising the urban dystopia through characters such as Oliver Twist, Amy Dorrit and Sissy Jupe. The popularity of the ubiquitous terraced house, the speculator's staple salary, ultimately brought about its downfall, as more and more people were packed into smaller and smaller spaces. Terraces were subdivided and many degenerated from respectability into slums. In London's Soho 'the very houses which were the town mansions of the nobility a century ago are today inhabited from basement to attic, by the Heavy-rented', wrote George Haw in

> Stafford Terrace (1860s),
Kensington, London.

1900. 'Go to some of the manufacturing towns,' exclaimed Rufus Usher indignantly, 'go into Edinburgh, Glasgow, and Liverpool, and take the average in the abodes of the Irish poor, where in some instances bedding for fourteen persons is spread over a space not exceeding twelve feet square. Go and take the average in London, where one-third of the human race expire in infancy.'

Overcrowding was not confined to London. Gateshead, Newcastle upon Tyne, Sunderland, Plymouth, Halifax and Bradford were among the country's most densely populated cities by the end of the 19th century. Larger cities such as Liverpool had been grappling with the problem of overcrowding for decades. Some districts of Liverpool had densities of over a quarter of a million people per square kilometre. 'One cannot help wishing that such streets had never been built,' wrote the Christian minister, Hugh Stowell Brown (1823–86), 'and that the act of building such houses were made a criminal offence, for they are most destructive of public health and public morality.'

Morality was an emotive argument in favour of improving the living standards of the poor. Victorians staunchly believed that the home was able to regulate the health and morals of the people, but the problem was identifying which came first. Christian moralisers often viewed alcohol as the root of the problem and the promotion of abstinence became a key policy of Christian outreach organisations such as the Salvation Army, which was established in London in 1865. 'A good house requires a good tenant,' wrote Brown, 'as long as there are pigs there will be pig-styes.'

For others, the problem lay with the dwellings, for which the capitalists who built these houses and profited from the poor's pitiable condition could be blamed. 'No class of people are so ill-lodged as the working-people,' wrote the author of 'Domestic Arrangements of the Working Classes' (1836): 'Their dwellings are rarely built purposely for them ... Even in houses built on purpose for them, their conveniences are little attended to.

And wealthy are they sure to be who supply the wants of the poor on a large-scale. Where the builder makes five or seven per cent by the dwellings of the rich, he makes twenty-five by the dwellings of the poor.' As long as housing the poor in poor conditions remained a lucrative business, conditions were not going to improve. 'As long as the construction of homes for the poor was governed by the sordid hand of avarice, when nothing is looked forward to but a weekly pittance wrung from the scanty earnings of the most haggard, wretched, and sickly of mortal beings,' decried Rufus Usher in his essay 'Cottages of the Urban Poor' (1877), then such homes would be fit only for 'disease, for vice, and for ignorance to dwell in.'

The economy of scale between renting to the rich and to the poor was a telling facet of Victorian property speculation. It exacerbated overcrowding and was largely responsible for the appalling conditions of the labouring classes because the rent paid by a pauper for a shared room in a teeming tenement was, as a lead article in *The Times* in 1861 noted, proportionally as much as a nobleman paid for his mansion in Belgrave Square. Throughout the 19th century, as this questionable practice began to affect the lives and health of all city-dwellers, it attracted increasing reprobation.

The condition and character of urban working-class homes were infinitely varied. At the bottom of the pile and among the largest and most despicable obstacles preventing the advance of modern civilisation were the shared tenements, or rookeries, where thousands of destitute inhabitants lived together in abject poverty. These miserable places, to which the title 'home' is inappropriately munificent, would, as Reverend Mearns (1837–1925), the author of *The Bitter Cry of Outcast London* (1883), suggested, fare unfavourably in terms of health and comfort with 'the lair of a wild beast'. Tenements came to define the problems associated with 19th-century overcrowding, and, although they were common, they were far from ubiquitous for the urban poor. As un-homely as any place could be, they were little more than a wretched last resort. Malodorous gases greeted the visitor before they even breached the entrance. Raw sewage and other waste flowed liberally throughout the tenement, whose walls and ceilings sweated with vile liquids that saturated the building's fabric. The unfortunate souls that lived in these awful spaces shared them not only with the dead and dying but also with vermin, and domestic and wild animals. Mearns describes one sanitary inspector who came across a 'father, mother, three children and four pigs' in the cellar of one block.

The surest means by which one could liberate oneself and one's family from such misery and afford a better place to live, somewhere that could be called home, was through business. The simplest type of businessman was the costermonger, or humble street hawker, whose modest home comprised a single room of varying quality. The home of the poorest type of costermonger was akin to a single room of no more than 3 metres square comprising a shack or lean-to. Furniture consisted of a mattress on the floor and a carpet sewn together from old matting. Ornamentation, if such personal niceties existed, stood on the mantelpiece: 'an old earthenware sugar-basin well silvered over', observed Henry Mayhew (1812–87), the cofounder of *Punch* and author of *London Labour and the London Poor* (1851), with a couple of cracked teacups and saucers either side of the fireplace to give the appearance of tidiness.

The middle-ranking costermonger, though still struggling, had a slightly better standard of dwelling. Sharing a bed, the impoverished but proud occupants made the usual attempt to make the fireside comfortable. He might paint the stone sides and furnish the mantelpiece with a few choice knick-knacks. One resident proudly revealed to Mayhew her cat and kitten by the fire, which not only kept the vermin away, but also gave 'a look of home'. Modest furnishings aspired to homeliness. Curtains, tables and mahogany chairs suppressed the reality of living in a cellar and demonstrated that every effort had been made 'to give the home a look of comfort'.

More comfortable still was the home of the prudent and business-minded costermonger, which, though small, was hygienic, airy and cosy. Here, the floor was cleanly planed, the walls were papered and covered in pictures, and the mantelpiece was bedecked with a better quality of trinket – 'a row of bright tumblers and wine glasses filled with odds and ends' between which 'stood glazed crockeryware images of Prince Albert', wrote Mayhew. Furniture was more abundant and substantial, with possessions such as chests of drawers, dressers, and a bedstead with a decent quilt aspiring to the lifestyle of a reasonably paid worker.

The homes of 19th-century skilled or semi-skilled workers, like those of the impoverished costermonger, possessed few characteristics that, beyond convenience and cheapness, were either novel or distinctive. Whether in the city or in the country, although a worker's home comprised just one or two rooms with no services or utilities and required no entertaining rooms or servants' quarters, internal arrangements were nevertheless varied.

In the countryside, the ubiquitous home of the poor and labouring class was the cottage – that 'primitive invention of our peasants', described Richard Elsam in *An Essay on Rural Architecture* (1803). The most rudimentary cottage comprised a single room. Conditions were hardly better than those in the city, except the air quality was perhaps better and there was less chance of catching various diseases from contaminated water.

Most rural cottages were detached and comprised one room on the ground floor which served as a kitchen and living room, with a bedroom above, where the whole family, often in excess of 10 people, would sleep. With such basic means inside, it would be unlikely for such small cottages to have a garden or outhouses.

A garden was highly prized for what it brought to the dinner table. Fruit, vegetables, chickens and even pigs were commonly found in the garden of the British home, and so a small piece of land was consequently the preserve of a slightly better type of cottage that had two rooms on each floor, separating the function of kitchen and living room on the ground floor and providing separate sleeping arrangements for parents and children upstairs. Unskilled, casual or temporary workers could not have afforded such a large home, whose tenants would have been skilled employees of an estate. It was incumbent on the landlord to provide housing for his workers and sometimes even the homes and public buildings of an entire village including schools, shops and other amenities. Improving economic conditions throughout the 19th century, especially among the landed classes, encouraged the improvement of these types of rural workers' cottages, whose designs were often straight out of pattern books produced and distributed by builders and architects.

A typical worker's home on a country estate was cheap and functional, and usually two-up two-down. They were sparsely but adequately finished, with plaster walls and flagstone or wooden floorboards. The ground floor comprised a sitting room and a bedroom for boys, with two bedrooms above for parents and girls. Ground-floor bedrooms, recommended John Birch in his 1871 pattern book for labourers' cottages, are a 'very desirable arrangement in cases of sickness, infirmity, or where the tenants may have a lodger, friend or aged relatives'. As the 19th century progressed, life expectancies in all but the most impoverished inner-city areas were generally rising, with the effect that it became increasingly common to find more than two generations living in one house, or even one room. Each room had a fireplace with cupboards occupying the recess either side. A scullery containing copper sinks and baking oven, and a pantry were built at the rear of the house, with outhouses, such as pigsties, a privy, woodsheds, cesspit and ashpit, further down the garden.

The worker's home in the city was quite different from its rural counterpart. Conditions were invariably more cramped and less clean, these inconveniences being offset by the hope of better pay and a better future. Workers' homes in the city often accommodated both man and machine, with families working and living in the same room, carving out a living from a single dwelling space. It was the separation of these two functions that contemporary theorists such as Max Weber (1864–1920) believed enabled capitalism to take shape – the

> A weaver's house in Shoreditch, London, built in 1778 and altered in the 19th century. The wide second-floor window allows more light into the workshop, which contained the loom.

distinction of business and home 'which completely dominates modern economic life' and later assumed legal significance in the separation of private and commercial property. In London's Spitalfields, the homes of the silk-weaving descendants of the Huguenots, the religiously persecuted migrants who fled from France after the Edict of Fontainebleau in 1685, exemplified the proto-industrialisation of 19th-century urban dwellings. The architect-journalist and champion of housing reform, George Godwin (1813–88), rebuked these homes in *London Shadows*:

> His home – alas! Scarce worth the name –
> A room some few feet square,
> With bed and loom crammed in one room,
> And children huddled there.
> With such a sense before one's eyes,
> To be condemned to toil,
> Half clothed, half fed, – much better dead
> Beneath the peaceful soil.

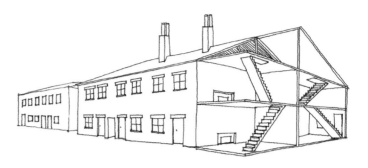

Wretched though these factory homes were, they were superior to their neighbours' in London's impoverished East End and, collectively, formed a better streetscape than many areas of the city. The same relative respectability could be observed throughout Britain, with artisans often occupying decent homes and living in relative comfort compared with the unskilled workers in the cities. The failed weaver and radical reformer, Samuel Bamford (1788–1872), describes rows of flannel weavers' houses in his native Lancashire in 1844 as being 'uniformly neat and clean' with small gardens. Each house contained a front room with fireplace, oven and boiler. The kitchen was put at the rear, and two large bedrooms on the first floor. As in the Spitalfields homes, these would have contained looms. Improvement was concerned chiefly with the size of rooms and the provision of a garden or external 'area' where residents could grow food or build outhouses, sheds or privies.

The comparatively high standard of living, provision of space and comfort within and outside the home meant that, for a county that had endured appalling poverty and only 25 years earlier had experienced the Peterloo Massacre caused by demands for voting reform, there was, according to Bamford, 'no outward sign of distress ... nor any great demonstration of discontent'.

Bamford's description of a Lancashire dwelling is typical of a decent mid-19th-century worker's cottage. The compact two-up two-down plan accommodates two bedrooms above a living room and a scullery. Throughout the early 19th century, the various functions of a scullery and outhouses, such as washing of clothes, storage of utensils, and preparing, cooking and eating of food, were increasingly consolidated in one room – the kitchen. The aggregation of these functions within the kitchen increased its size and significance within the home. Building dwellings in rows and setting the first floor beneath a pitched roof economised on building materials and made them cheaper to maintain and heat. Fireplaces, despite the comfort they provided, were a constant drain on resources and were employed sparingly in most workers' homes, except those in mining towns, where coal was often freely available.

∧ Illustration of a row of typical back-to-back houses showing the compact arrangement of one room on each floor.

∨ Site plan of a typical configuration of back-to-back houses around a courtyard containing shared amenities.

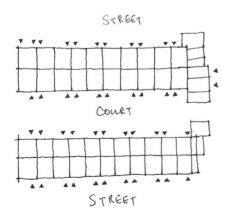

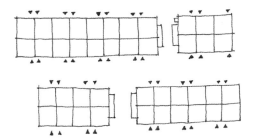

> Site plan of a typical configuration of
back-to-back houses without a courtyard
and with alleys, known as tunnels,
separating the blocks of houses.

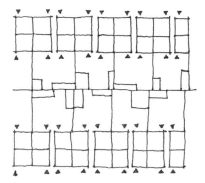

∧ Site plan of a typical configuration of
back-to-back houses without a courtyard
and with alleys separating each pair of
houses, each of which has a small yard at
the rear.

∨ Top: Site plan of typical back-to-back
houses with alleys separating each pair of
houses and leading to a court.

Bottom: Site plan of typical back-to-back
houses with a yard set within the row
containing shared amenities.

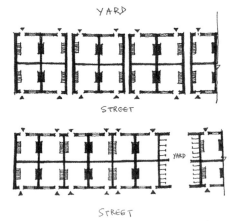

In the north of England and the Midlands, the rapid expansion
of manufacturing industries precipitated the equally hurried
development of poorer-quality workers' housing, epitomised by
the omnipresent rows of 'jerry built' brick houses without gardens
or independent utilities. The most common and contentious was
the back-to-back, which was built in a variety of configurations,
but all possessing the essential characteristic of having two rows of
houses placed back-to-back under one roof. Where the common
terraced house took advantage of the savings made by arranging
houses lengthways in rows, the back-to-back took even greater
advantage of this method of economising by arranging houses in
both length and depth, often with just one room on each floor. The
back-to-back plan provided a very high density of accommodation
that was basic but an improvement on the squalid rented tenement
or cramped sublet room inside an old subdivided terrace. One
common problem was the lack of light, since each room had only
one window, the three other walls being shared with neighbours
to each side and the rear. The most uncomfortable aspect of the
back-to-back was the communal utilities in the courtyard. Rows
of privies were shared by all the residents, as was the brewhouse,
where water was boiled for the all too infrequent practice of
washing clothes and bathing. Even cooking was done in a
communal kitchen in some of the earlier back-to-backs.

Conditions in the back-to-backs were often so bad that some
municipal corporations banned their construction, but gradual
improvements in building standards, local and national regulations
and the incomes of workers caused their survival until the 20th
century. The better type of back-to-back was up to three storeys
high with a cellar, and had two rooms on each floor arranged side
by side. Sculleries became kitchens and were brought inside the
house, unlike the privy, which, although each house later tended
to possess its own, was never accommodated under the same roof
and stood at the end of the backyard. Improved ventilation and
decreasing densities saw some designs of back-to-back acquire
alleyways that separated units and provided access to the rear
courtyard like the entrances to a termite mound. Improving
standards also prevented the entire enclosure of the once closed
and claustrophobic courtyard, which became open at both ends
of the street and could also be separated by an alleyway, giving
rise to the 'through terrace'.

These types of improvements were brought about in part by the plummeting life expectancy of the lowest classes and the frequency of epidemics, which Victorians believed were caused by noxious gases and poor air quality. Miasma, the theory that diseases such as cholera were airborne, cast a chilling shadow over Victorian Britain and caused the obsession with 'through-ventilation' in house design. The theory terrified people from all classes, but the reality principally affected the poor, who, in London alone, died in their tens of thousands in cholera epidemics during the mid-19th century. As Godwin wrote:

> They call it a fever,
> Putrid or low;
> But I and the weaver
> Both of us know
> That the fetid well-water, and steaming styes,
> And the choked drains' gases, that unseen rise,
> Subtle and still,
> Sure and slow,
> Certain to kill
> With an unheard blow
> Are the fiends who poisoned that maiden's breath,
> And cling to her still as she sleeps in death!

The solution was found not so much by the discovery that the miasma theory was flawed and water was the source of the problem, but, in part, by a product that brought about one of the most significant amendments to the plan of the home in centuries: the flush lavatory. As more and more people used flush lavatories (especially the middle classes), London's antiquated sewerage system failed to cope with the confluence. Cesspits overflowed into streets and rivers of waste poured directly into the Thames rather than being transported to willing farmers' fields as fertiliser, as was formerly the custom. Investigations into the improvement of London's sewerage system were already under way when the problem came to a head in the unusually hot summer of 1858, causing London's 'Great Stink'. With the prevailing theory of miasma still widely accepted, the foul odour was a trifling inconvenience in comparison with the apocalyptic potential of airborne cholera. The putrid blend of substances flowing literally under the noses of the powerbrokers in Westminster accelerated the calls for a revolution in sanitation, and within a matter of years the remarkable system of sewers built by Victorian engineers that London has relied on ever since was constructed. Motivated by the fear of the odour, the Victorians invested heavily in a solution to cholera and, inadvertently, found it.

Technological innovation was a hallmark of Victorian Britain and no event crystallised this trait more than the Great Exhibition of 1851, held in London's Hyde Park. Among the exhibits in

> Prince Consort Lodge: model dwellings for workers designed by Henry Roberts and displayed at the Great Exhibition of 1851. It was later rebuilt in Kennington Park, south London.

∨ Plan of Prince Consort Lodge, designed by Henry Roberts for the Great Exhibition of 1851, showing a pair of small three-bedroom flats around a living room with central staircase.

B: Bedroom · PB: Parents' Bedroom
Lv: Living Room · Sc: Scullery
WC: Water Closet

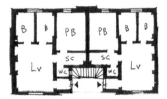

and around Joseph Paxton's revolutionary Crystal Palace were two diminutive houses that appeared innocuous in comparison to the swathes of innovative products and manufacturing devices peddled by Victorian designers that promised a better and brighter future. Throughout the first half of the 19th century, housing the poor had received scant attention from the architectural profession, which was more concerned with bickering over the rightful claimant to authenticity between Classicism and Gothicism.

There were others though who believed in a much nobler cause. Usher was one such person, asking: 'How much needless suffering, and needless expense too, might be saved by making architecture subservient to its noblest purposes, namely, the health and happiness of the people.' The two houses designed by the architect Henry Roberts (1803–76) at the Great Exhibition were among the first attempts to provide an answer to this rising problem. These structures were model dwellings for workers and offered a new approach to designing good-quality high-density workers' housing. Arranged on a two-storey double-square plan with a central communal staircase, each block contained four units. Each dwelling had a lobby, living room, three bedrooms, scullery and lavatory. The central space was the living room, which was accessed from the main entrance via a small lobby. Three other doorways led from the living room, two to small bedrooms and one to the scullery, from which entrance was provided to the main bedroom and lavatory. Although the space was extremely compact, it was convenient and healthy – far superior to anything that the intended occupants would have been previously used to. An innovative hollow brick devised by Roberts was used for the walls, which improved ventilation, and the floors were concrete to minimise any risk of fire.

Roberts was a pioneer in the design of workers' cottages and was a founding member of both the Institute of British Architects and the Society for Improving the Condition of the Labouring Classes (SICLC), whose first President was Prince Albert and Vice-President was Lord Shaftesbury. Among the SICLC's contributions, besides pioneering new housing designs, was to lobby for the abolition of the long-standing taxes on windows (1696–1851) and bricks (1784–1850), which had hindered the construction of cheap, functional and well-ventilated housing, and contributed to the appalling conditions endured by the labouring classes. The tax had little impact on the houses of the wealthy. Speculative developers devised various avoidance schemes by building in other materials, such as mathematical tiles, but such taxes had a grave impact on more modest dwellings. Giving evidence to a House of Commons Select Committee in 1840, a Dr Southwood Smith said: 'At present no more regard is paid in the construction of houses to the health of the inhabitants than is paid to the health of pigs in making sties for them.' From 1850, the repeal of the tax greatly increased the use of brick and brought down the cost of building. With such influential backing, Roberts was able to design many houses and housing estates, including the Prince Consort Cottages (1855) in Windsor for the Royal Windsor Society under the patronage of Prince Albert. Here Roberts designed an entire estate around a central green. Each unit was two storeys high, comprising a living room and scullery on the ground floor, and bedrooms on the first floor contained in the roof space and lit with dormer and gable windows.

Roberts's designs pioneered a new concerted and coordinated approach to housing workers and heralded a new age of large-scale housing. Considered by many as the source of infinite nuisances, from rampant epidemics to moral decline, workers' housing was one of the most emotive issues of the 19th century, attracting a wide range of professional consideration, from architects to evangelists. 'To talk of education and temperance and morality' when housing standards were so poor, lamented Henry Clarke, the author of *Dwellings for the Poor* (1884), was 'like one constructing a house on rotten piles sunk in a quagmire'. Throughout the second half of the century, the provision of workers' housing became firmly established as a social obligation, though it remained the responsibility of privately funded philanthropy. Motivated by profit as well as moral improvement, various organisations including the Peabody Trust, the Artizans', Labourers' and General Dwellings Company, the Four Per Cent Industrial Dwellings Company, and the Society for Improving the Condition of the Labouring Classes in London or, elsewhere in Britain, the Newcastle upon Tyne Improved Industrial Dwellings Company, the Chester Cottage Improvement Company, and, in Edinburgh, Pilrig Model Dwellings Company and the Edinburgh Co-Operative Building Company, began building model housing for the labouring classes.

∧ Prince Consort Cottages (1855). Windsor,
designed by Henry Roberts.

These were noble bodies fighting noble causes, but because the standard of accommodation they provided was good and they had to recoup their investment through rent, it was still beyond the reach of the poorest, such as the costermonger. These were initiatives that, in spite of their philanthropic or moralistic motives, were designed to make a profit by purchasing land cheaply from local authorities and deriving a rental income from the housing constructed on that land, though the rent was proportionally less than that which could be gained from building tenements. 'What are the respective advantages first of all to the owner between tenement houses that are sublet; of flat houses, that is to say blocks let in flats?' asked a commissioner when questioning the builder, Mr Dudley, during the Royal Commission on the Housing of the Working Classes; to which Dudley replied: 'I should say that the [tenement] houses would be of greater value to the owner.' 'For the occupier which do you consider more advantageous?' was the commissioner's response, to which Dudley replied: 'The blocks [of flats]; there is no doubt of that.' Developers like Dudley had to admit that flats afforded better accommodation and were better ventilated and easier for the landlord to keep clean and regulate. Their problem was that they made less profit.

Through the process of flat-building, builders and philanthropic bodies became landlords, just as speculative builders had done

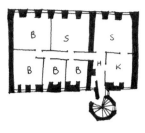

∧ Plan of Riddles Court, Edinburgh, an apartment block designed in 1726 showing sitting rooms, bedrooms and kitchen all on one floor accessed by an external spiral staircase.

B: Bedroom · S: Sitting Room
H: Hall · K: Kitchen

∨ Plan of flats in Victoria Street (1853), London, the first flats erected in the city. Each block was 36 metres long, 14 metres deep and 25 metres high and constructed in iron, cement, brick and stone, making it fully fireproof. Six shops occupied the ground floor in each block, with eight apartments above.

B: Bedroom · DR: Drawing Room
D: Dining Room · St: Store · Sc: Scullery
K: Kitchen

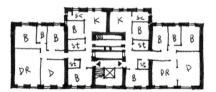

the ground floor, and even several floors above that, given over to shops or offices, while private apartments occupied the upper storeys. The problems associated with this arrangement of 'lands', as they were called, were the communal staircase and the lack of cellar for those living above the ground floor. Fire was a constant hazard. Following the Act of Union of 1707, Edinburgh ceased building 'lands' on the scale it had done in the 16th and 17th centuries. Peace allowed construction to spill out beyond the city's walls and although flats continued to be built, none matched the prodigious height of former centuries and most were no more than four storeys high including the attic.

In the 19th century, the apartment lifestyle spread throughout Europe and to America, where it was taken to new heights and defined urban living in the modern world throughout the next century. Modern construction techniques and materials and technological innovations made the high-rise apartment both possible and highly desirable. The use of iron and steel in construction reduced the weight of buildings while retaining their strength, allowing them to rise higher and higher. The invention in 1852 of the safety brake for lifts by American inventor Elisha Otis (1811–61) enabled the rapid espousal of the passenger lift and paved the way for vertical living.

The story of the development of the apartment in Britain in the late 19th century was one marked predominantly by socially driven resistance and indifference. The use of modern materials, such as iron, steel and reinforced concrete, in the construction of buildings occurred throughout the 19th century, but the sight of entirely novel structures such as Decimus Burton and Richard Turner's iron and glass Palm House (1844–8) at London's Kew Gardens and Joseph Paxton's Crystal Palace for the Great Exhibition of 1851 helped to revolutionise architecture and represented the boundless possibilities of these new materials. Some even suggested that iron was the ideal material for building housing for the poor as it was cheap, a natural disinfectant, easy to paint, hard wearing, and needed no foundations. In just a few years, the world's first iron and glass office building, Oriel Chambers (1864), was built in Liverpool, designed by Peter Ellis. However, the almost universal denigration the building received not only caused Ellis's premature retirement from architecture but was also a portent for British attitudes to modern building and house design in the decades ahead.

The apartment was not entirely alien to Britain and could be said to have certain indigenous precedents throughout history. For centuries, castles and royal palaces possessed self-contained and shared accommodation for large numbers of staff of various ranks that had to be kept separate from royalty. London's Inns of Court had provided temporary accommodation and office space in the city for their members since the late-medieval period. Throughout the 16th and 17th centuries, rent-paying tenants had occupied multistorey terraces in the centres of Britain's major towns and cities. By the 18th century speculative builders had so successfully refined the notion of flexible living in a terrace that these rows of houses just as often housed one family on each floor as they did one family to an entire unit with servants in apartments in the attic. The conversion of York House (later called The Albany) on London's Piccadilly, designed by William Chambers, into bachelor apartments in 1804, which included the construction of two rows of maisonettes on the long garden, was one of the earliest examples of flats being provided for owner-occupants in London. By the 19th century, the design of several dwellings under one roof, like Henry Roberts's early examples of two-up and two-down for the Great Exhibition, heralded a new era in high-density urban living. Once homes could be stacked in pairs around a communal stair, the process only needed to be multiplied and the fully fledged apartment block emerged, although in Britain a stigma remained from its origins in the philanthropic movement. Certain members of the middle classes abhorred the idea of living in buildings resembling those of the class beneath them. Until the 1860s, the only flats in all of London built for and occupied by middle-class tenants was a block on Victoria Street constructed in 1853. Built by Mr Mackenzie according to his own designs, this block of flats was described in an article in *The Builder* in 1853 as supplying 'what has long been a desideratum in London, namely, complete residences on flats, as in Edinburgh and Paris'. By the late 1860s, the idea of building high-rise apartments all over London in order to meet the needs of the rapidly growing populace was gaining widespread approbation among developers, architects and investors, but the public remained reticent.

The apartment's initial lukewarm reception from potential tenants made speculative builders cautious about investing in them, but by the 1870s social customs and attitudes were starting to change and the most affluent city dwellers began to appreciate the convenience of having a self-contained home in or near the city centre. 'The "flat" system, borrowed from France,' wrote the Victorian writer, Thomas Escott (1844–1924) in 1879, 'has now existed in a considerable scale in London some fifteen years, and at the present time is in great and growing favour.' Flats, like terraced houses, were speculative investments, unlike some larger houses, which might be built by their owners. Blocks were managed by a company and all charges aggregated in a single fee that was far simpler to settle than the infinite number of charges facing the owner of a suburban or town house. Built from modern materials, such as reinforced concrete, flats required less maintenance, and their compactness meant fewer servants. They could also be vacated at a moment's notice and left in the hands of a porter, leaving the tenant secure in the knowledge that his home was safe from any means of danger or unwanted visitors.

Over the course of the late 19th century, apartment blocks sprang up all over London and in the centres of other major cities, catering for a more and more diverse range of tenants, from the large and wealthy family with numerous servants who would have occupied 12 Hyde Park (1903), St George's Terrace (*c* 1905–7), or Gloucester House (1904) down to the lone young professional living in Audley House (1907) or Marlborough Chambers (1902–3). It was only a matter of time before this dwelling type filtered down the social scale where the middle classes eagerly sought the comforts and conveniences of the centrally located apartment, such as The Mansions in Sloane Gardens. One fact that 'no architect should forget when designing a block of flats for the middle classes', wrote Frank Verity in the early 20th century, is that 'members of the middle classes are called upon to keep up a position more or less beyond their means, because they can afford still less the danger either of living in a way that might stamp them as failures, or of

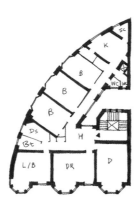

∧ Plan of The Mansions, Sloane Gardens, London, showing one flat on a floor.

L/B: Living Room/Bedroom
DR: Drawing Room · D: Dining Room
Bt: Bathroom · Ds: Dressing Room · H: Hall
B: Bedroom · K: Kitchen · Sc: Scullery
WC: Water Closet

> The Mansions, Sloane Gardens, London, designed by Edwin T Hall in the early 20th century.

> St George's Terrace (c 1905–7), London, designed by Paul Hoffmann.

∨ Plan of a portion of St George's Terrace (c 1905–7), London, showing large apartments arranged around small courtyards

K: Kitchen · B: Bedroom · DR: Drawing Room
H: Hall · Bt: Bathroom · Sc: Scullery · SB: Servant's
Bedroom · D: Dining Room · WC: Water Closet

dressing in a style that their clients or employers might regard as too negligent or too poor'. By the end of the century, flats had become a dwelling type accessible to all social classes.

> Gloucester House (1904), Piccadilly, London, designed by Thomas Collcutt and Stanley Hamp.

∨ Plan of a luxurious flat occupying a whole floor of Gloucester House (1904) on London's Piccadilly.

B: Bedroom · Ds: Dressing Room · DR:
Drawing Room · Bt: Bathroom · H: Hall
Bo: Boudoir · D: Dining Room · V: Vestibule
Sm: Smoking Room · BP: Butler's Pantry
SH: Servants' Hall · La: Larder
KS: Kitchen/Scullery

> Sandringham Court (c 1901–8), Maida Vale,
London, designed by Boehmer & Gibbs.

∨ Plan of Sandringham Court (c 1901–8), Maida
Vale, London, showing four flats on each
floor for families of moderate income.

B: Bedroom · R: Reception Room
Bt: Bathroom · H: Hall · K: Kitchen
WC: Water Closet

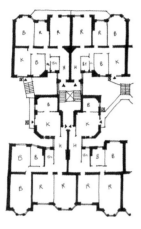

> Marlborough Chambers (1902–3), Jermyn
Street, London, designed by Reginald
Morphew, containing luxury bachelor
flats and shops on the ground floor.

∨ Plan of Marlborough Chambers (1902–3),
Jermyn Street, London, containing luxury
bachelor flats and shops on the ground floor.

S: Sitting Room · Bt: Bathroom
B: Bedroom · H: Hall · Sm: Smoking Room

∧ Albert Hall Mansions (1880–7),
Kensington, London, designed by Richard
Norman Shaw and Driver & Rew.

∨ Plan of one of the blocks in Albert Hall
Mansions (1880–7), Kensington, London,
by Richard Norman Shaw.

B: Bedroom · K: Kitchen · Bt: Bathroom
D: Dining Room · DR: Drawing Room
WC: Water Closet · H: Hall

If the site was on a main commercial street, the ground floor was occupied by shops which delivered a high rental income; otherwise it would be partially occupied by a public area or lobby containing a lift and staircase. In contrast to their Continental counterparts that housed service and main staircases together and their owners and servants on separate floors, the Victorian snobbery that underpinned the new class system in Britain (class was very different from status which had once defined one's position in society) ensured that in most British apartment blocks, such as 12 Hyde Park, Gloucester House, Sandringham Court (*c* 1901–8) or Albert Hall Mansions (1880–7), master and servant would not cross paths. Servants were accommodated in separate rear portions of the apartment, and the main access to each apartment was gained via a public lobby on each floor. Although the plans of individual apartments were diverse, each block tended to contain a number of differently sized units, so appealing to a broader clientele. The plan of each apartment tended to be the same on each floor, except for the ground floor, which invariably had a dual function of private and public or commercial space.

Since a flat was considered a substitute for a house, the private rooms, public rooms, entertaining areas, utilities and servants'

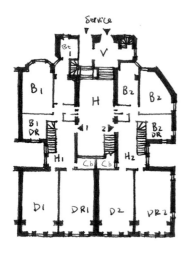
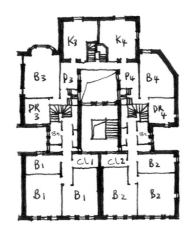
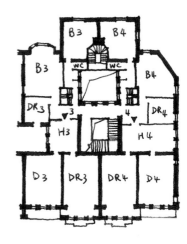

∧ Ground- (left), mezzanine- (middle) and first-floor (right) plans of Albert Hall Mansions (1880–7), Kensington, London, designed by Richard Norman Shaw.

B: Bedroom · DR: Drawing Room · H: Hall
D: Dining Room · WC: Water Closet
Cl: Closet · P: Parlour · K: Kitchen
V: Vestibule · Cb: Cupboard · Bt: Bathroom

∨ Section through Albert Hall Mansions (1880–7), Kensington, London, by Richard Norman Shaw, showing a form of scissor plan that allowed a double-height dining room at the rear and maisonette at the front of the flat.

B: Bedroom · S: Sitting Room · K: Kitchen
P: Parlour · D: Dining Room
DR: Drawing Room

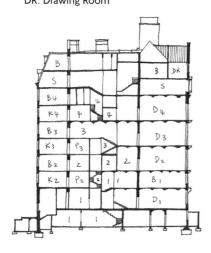

quarters had to be accommodated and arranged conveniently on one floor. Inside the main entrance, a lobby or hallway formed a type of threshold before entering the public rooms, such as the living room, drawing room, morning room and dining room. Private rooms, such as the study, library and bedrooms, were beyond. The passage from public to private space was rooted in the Continental tradition of the linear home where rooms increased in exclusivity the farther one travelled from the main entrance. The kitchen and other utilities, or 'offices' as they were known, such as pantry, larder and scullery, were often on the inner side of the apartment, as at Alexandra Court (1898) or St George's Terrace, where they faced into a diminutive courtyard known as a 'well-hole' that provided a little natural light and allowed all services, such as water supply and waste water, to be removed from the building without cluttering the facade. Individual rooms were connected by a warren of corridors, which in a well-planned apartment would be kept to a minimum. Servants' rooms, ideally, were separate from the main suite, forming a kind of apartment within an apartment.

One of the principal improvements to be found in the late-19th-century apartment that was rarely found in individual houses and which made it particularly attractive to the aspiring middle classes was the bathroom. The bathroom was a uniquely Victorian invention, but to suggest the Victorians hurried to develop it would be highly misleading. The bathroom was a product of so many characteristics of the 19th century – higher standards of hygiene, a greater awareness and understanding of science, prolific technological innovation, improving construction techniques and materials and changing social attitudes all played a part, but Victorian society vigorously resisted the bathroom's jostling for a position inside the modern home. Many obstacles stood in the way of the bathroom becoming an essential and entirely novel feature of the British home, unseen in Britain since the bath-houses of Roman times, but once it found its way in, no one looked back.

The modern bathroom depended on an elaborate system of plumbing that delivered hot and cold water around the house in lead pipes, but, most important of all, it depended on the invention that occurred in the 1870s of the modern lavatory, with its innovative and smell-eliminating S-bend that prevented the odours from London's newly laid sewerage system rising up out of waste pipes and causing a stench in every home in the city. The popularity of the apartment coincided with these innovations and therefore every modern apartment worthy of its name contained at least one, if not two, modern bathrooms.

Despite the functional appeal and the modern conveniences it offered, as well as the kudos it brought by providing spacious accommodation in the centre of town, the apartment never truly caught on in Britain, as it did in Europe where higher land values caused it to define great cities such as Paris, Vienna and Berlin. In London, Britain had its chance to follow the trajectory of the greatest high-rise city on earth, New York, when the Queen Anne's Mansions were built near St James's Park. Constructed in stages by the wealthy investor Henry Hankey, the first tower was a 35-metre-high 10-storey block (1873–5), followed by a 12-storey extension (1877), then an even taller extension (1880–90) containing 500 rooms that reached 50 metres. The unprecedented size of the apartment building attracted widespread reprobation, an article in the professional journal *The Builder* describing the finale extension, designed by ER Robson, as 'the loftiest and ugliest of any similar structure in the metropolis'. Referred to as 'Babel-like structures' and 'monster blocks of dwellings', Queen Anne's Mansions were very popular among prospective tenants who were generally prominent public figures. With the recent introduction of the lift, the upper floors proved especially fashionable because of the exceptional panoramic views they offered. This popularity caused the erection of the taller extensions from the late 1870s.

> A modern turn-of-the-century bathroom in a wealthy home, here at Goddards, Surrey, designed by Edwin Lutyens.

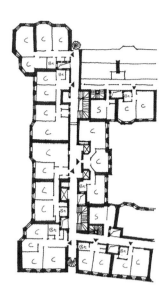

∧ Left: Ground-floor plan of Queen Anne's
Mansions (1873–90), Westminster, London.

Middle: First-floor plan of Queen Anne's
Mansions (1873–90), Westminster, London.

Right: Typical upper floor plan of
Queen Anne's Mansions (1873–90),
Westminster, London.

C: Chamber · Bt: Bathroom
WC: Water Closet · Se: Service
DR: Drawing Room · Ds: Dressing Room
S: Sitting Room · O: Office · V: Vestibule
Po: Porter

Queen Anne's Mansions offered a glimpse of the future of
housing brought about by the possibilities of modern materials
and technologies, but rather than embrace this future, Victorian
London stepped back from the brink. In 1890, in response to
the furore over Queen Anne's Mansions, Parliament passed an
Act to empower the newly established London County Council,
which had replaced the Metropolitan Board of Works two years
earlier, to impose height restrictions on new buildings of 90
feet (27 metres) excluding two storeys in the roof, followed by
the more comprehensive and stringent London Building Act
in 1894, restricting heights to 80 feet (25 metres).

In Britain, including the outskirts of London, land was
comparatively cheap and so housing spread outwards. The
economics of inexpensive land was one factor that prevented
Britain's espousal of the apartment, but, as Queen Anne's
Mansions shows, another reason was more innate. Thomas Escott
described the flat as being 'merely a house, with [the] difference
that the rooms are arranged, not on the perpendicular plan, but
on the horizontal', but to the British public the difference was
much greater. Centuries of emotional, cultural and social baggage
weighed on the British home, preventing it from making the
necessary conceptual leap from a house to an apartment. On the
Continent, wealthy families were content to occupy a part of a
large mansion, but, as Thomas Webster (1773–1844) explained
in the *The American Family Encyclopedia of Useful Knowledge*, 'this
practice is inconsistent with those views of domestic comfort
which an Englishman looks forward to at his own fireside'. Of
the horizontal arrangement, Escott wrote: 'No arrangement can
be imagined more diametrically antagonistic to the tastes with
which Englishmen are generally credited.' By the Great War,
only three per cent of dwellings in England and Wales were flats.

The economics of cheap land combined with Britain's enduring attraction to the traditional home – insular, retreating, and warmed by a hearth – precipitated another housing phenomenon unique to the Victorian age: the suburb.

THE RISE OF SUBURBIA

While a small minority of British families opted for a horizontal lifestyle in vertical blocks, the vast majority preferred a vertical lifestyle in horizontal blocks. With overcrowded cities, improving urban transport that promised a quick route to the countryside where land was cheap, the lower and middle classes flocked to the now distant urban periphery where, on virgin farmland, they could build spacious semi- or detached villas with gardens. Convinced of having the advantages of both rural quietude and urban entertainment, families of modest means created the suburb – that most Victorian and medial concept.

The 18th-century writers who bemoaned the carpeting of London's environs in brick and tiles would be aghast at what occurred a century later. The suburbs became a vast housing catalogue where, as an article in *The Builder* (1848) titled 'The Building Mania' described, you could find:

> ... aristocratic cottages, which have nothing in the world of the cottage about them except the name ... streets, squares, crescents, terraces, Albert villas, Victoria villas ... you may get a new house, of almost every conceivable pattern, and at any conceivable price ... You may take your choice, according to the length of your purse.

Homeownership was very rare in Britain, with fewer than 10 per cent of homes being owner-occupied in the 19th century. Most were rented from the landlords or builders of their homes, who retained the freehold.

The scene created by the rapid rise of London's suburbs was described by romantic theorists such as John Ruskin (1819–1900): 'What a pestilence of them [houses] and unseemly plague of builders' work – as if the bricks of Egypt had multiplied like its lice, and alighted like its locusts – has fallen on the suburbs of loathsome London!' His sentiments reverberated throughout the 19th and early 20th centuries, gaining an even greater tenor with the contribution of Ruskin's philosophical progeny and master of many arts, William Morris (1834–96), who wrote on the subject of the modern home: 'though many of us love architecture dearly, and believe that it helps the healthiness both of body and soul to live among beautiful things, we of the big towns are mostly compelled to live in houses which have become a by-word of contempt for their ugliness and inconvenience'.

Industrialisation not only meant the emergence of industrial cities from which the occupants of the suburbs were trying to escape, but also their flight caused the demise of the countryside they were running to. A farmer was better off selling his land for a harvest of housing than attempting to grow food, as this popular contemporary ditty described:

> The richest crop for any field,
> Is a crop of bricks for it to yield.
> The richest crop that it can grow,
> Is a crop of houses in a row.

The suburbs were a product of modern society, where home and work had become separate worlds in separate orbits linked by the filaments of modern transport networks, along which omnibuses and trains shuttled their travellers back and forth at unprecedented speeds. The site of work, whether in a factory or office, was represented as the cold, foreboding, soulless city, while home sweet home for the 'world-weary men' was in the warm, welcoming and utopian retreat of suburbia where, according to Congregational minister and writer James Baldwin Brown, women could 'pray, think, strive to make a home something like a bright, serene, restful, joyful nook of heaven in an unheavenly world'. The British home in Victorian suburbia was thus more of an idea than a physical dwelling.

As houses extended farther and farther into the farmland surrounding Britain's cities, the reality of what was being created by this unplanned and unrestricted dash for the countryside was increasingly questioned. Suburban homes, just like their urban cousins, were cheap and compact, since they were the product of speculative building in response to what HG Wells, in his social satire *Kipps*, described as 'the essential disaster of the nineteenth century ... that multitudinous, hasty building for the extravagant swarm of new births' that caused Britain's population to rise so sharply. The swathes of housing that defined suburbia and laid itself over Britain's countryside like a leaden blanket were described in *The Builder* as 'the most melancholy thing in existence'. 'I must confess honestly,' wrote Dorothy Peel, 'that the suburbs of any large town appear to me detestable.'

Loved or loathed, suburbia, unlike urban and rural living, was a novel setting for the British home. It was also, in the context of the late 19th century, distinct from the homes of the classes above and below for not employing an architect. Certain sections of the lower classes had their architect-designed tenements paid for by philanthropic organisations, and the upper classes could afford an architect. The advantages and disadvantages of life in these three different domestic environments precipitated a vigorous debate. Residing in a town was seen as more desirable for social intercourse and for the indulgence of artistic and

> Illustration showing the interior of a typical late-19th-century semi-detached house.

∨ A typical plan of a late-19th-century semi-detached house with integral kitchen showing ground- (left) and first-floor (right).

K: Kitchen · D: Dining Room · Lv: Living Room · B: Bedroom · WC: Water Closet
Bt: Bathroom

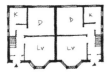

cultural institutions. A suburban home offered some of these advantages while enjoying what was considered a healthier, cheaper and less crowded environment. And the rural home had none of the advantages of the city while having pure air – a place of retirement, if not from work, then from life itself.

When suburban homes were laid out along the remote arteries of roads and railways leading to the heart of the city, it was usual for them to line these routes facing the street or with their backs to the tracks, rather than be positioned perpendicularly to them, in the manner of urban blocks of flats for the poor. Suburban houses were also largely free of the constraints imposed by building regulations in urban areas. Builders were however constrained by other factors, principally money. The result was the rule of standardisation and the suppression of individuality, as plans were cloned across former fields on which brick houses (now much cheaper since the repeal of the brick tax) were strung out along roads in 'ribbon developments' in all manner of historical styles, artlessly fashioned from predetermined moulds according to the designs published in mass-produced pattern books and trade catalogues. Much middle-class money was spent on differentiating one's home from one's neighbour's by purchasing what Sydney Perks (d 1944), the architect and author of *Residential Flats of All Classes including Artisans' Dwellings* (1905), described as 'useless ornament, hideous cornices, and plaster work that had far better be omitted'. Depending on their location, row upon row of identical houses varied in shape and size from the detached to the full-terrace, but all of them catered for hard-working, low- to moderate-income families of nascent professionals representing the middle class – bank clerks, accountants, civil servants, whose income was little, if at all, more than that of skilled workers or artisans.

The architectural story of Victorian suburban houses, if told stylistically, would fill volumes, from Gothicism to Classicism via the Queen Anne style and Arts and Crafts. The subject, though vast and fascinating, has little bearing on this exploration of the plan, which in stark contrast not only remained remarkably consistent while the adornments around it changed, but also advanced little from its 18th-century predecessors. The speculative builder had to make his profit, and to do this he

> A room designated to billiards was common in large 19th-century homes and is featured here as a later addition in Burghley House, Lincolnshire.

been lately built would contain such labour-saving appliances as lifts, buttery hatches and speaking-tubes, in addition to bathrooms, fitted wash-stands and sinks with hot and cold water on every storey.' Life for the housewife in this transitional period was difficult, since she had lost the assistance of her servants but had not yet gained the benefits of technological and architectural developments that accompanied this social and scientific transformation.

By the beginning of the 20th century, the arrangement of the suburban terraced house was well established, and it survived several more decades, but from a purely planning perspective there was no doubt that it was far from an ideal or convenient solution. 'The plan was invariably inconvenient – invariably,' wrote HG Wells in *Kipps*; 'All the houses they saw had a common quality for which she could find no word, but for which the proper word is incivility ... the Kippses, you see, thought they were looking for a reasonably simple little contemporary house, but indeed they were looking either for dreamland or 1975 AD. or thereabouts, and it hadn't come.'

THE MODERN MANSION

For those who could afford it, the ideal British home was one entirely detached from its neighbours and placed as far away from them as was possible, buffered from the outside world by the protective embrace of an expansive garden, upholding that very British desire for isolation and fuelled by the equally intrinsic trait of individualism. Stylistically, the varied but commonly Gothic-inspired character of the larger detached British country home of the mid-19th century was a dramatic departure from its Italianate predecessor. During the 'Battle of the Styles', Gothicism gained the upper hand in domestic architecture. Pointed arches, ornate tracery and medieval

∧ Goddards, Surrey, designed by Edwin
Lutyens (1898–1900 and extended
in 1910).

> The ground- (left) and first-floor (right)
plans of Goddards, Surrey, designed by
Edwin Lutyens (1898–1900 and extended
in 1910).

B: Bedroom · Bt: Bathroom · L: Library
D: Dining Room · S: Sitting Room
K: Kitchen

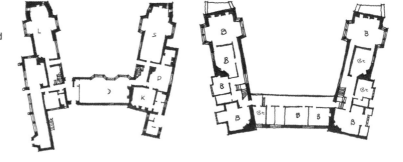

> One of the main bedrooms at Goddards, Surrey, designed by Edwin Lutyens (1898–1900 and extended in 1910).

∨ The living room at Goddards, Surrey, designed by Edwin Lutyens (1898–1900 and extended in 1910).

motifs harking back to an idealised past appeared everywhere, as Britain's architects began their quest to recover a vernacular style – a quest repeated throughout Europe around the same time in response to modernity's looming omnipresence. For the romantics, it was handy too that neo-Gothicism had oblique associations with medieval ecclesiastical buildings, for it was able to claim the moral high ground in a context that was the very font of moral values in a society, firm in the belief that, as Usher explained, 'for a family to be truly good and happy, there must exist, to some extent, a love of home'.

Despite some exemplary work by leading architects, much of the 19th century was characterised by a disoriented eclecticism. 'Some of the worst examples of domestic buildings were erected during the first decade of the 19th century,' claimed the architect Mervyn Macartney (1853–1932), 'castles having slits for windows ... turrets and impossible staircases, with keeps and moats and drawbridge ... were introduced as appropriate features in the buildings of an age especially famous for its science and mechanical inventions. Nothing could have been more absurd.' Eclecticism spread to the decor, furniture and fittings inside the home. Necessity, convenience and experience were the basis of building a home, claimed Richard Elsam. Pleasure should be the last consideration and was 'never truly obtained by whatever is immoderate'. But this tendency towards aesthetic and material profligacy was seen as repugnant by those with more discerning and artistic minds. 'I have never been in any rich man's house which would not have looked the better for having a bonfire made outside of it of nine-tenths of all that it held,' bewailed William Morris with characteristic disdain. In an age of unprecedented invention, the British home looked backwards not forwards. 'These pediments, and stylobates, and architraves never excited a single pleasurable feeling in you,' insisted John Ruskin, who despised Classicism, calling it the 'foul torrent of the renaissance'.

The bowling alley at Goddards, Surrey, designed by Edwin Lutyens (1898–1900 and extended in 1910).

The main dining room, evoking a medieval hall, at Goddards, Surrey, designed by Edwin Lutyens (1898–1900 and extended in 1910).

However, if one strips away the sentimental ornamentation, behind the facades of larger British homes throughout much of the 19th century, the plan reveals that little had truly changed. Although pitched roofs, sharp gables with elaborate bargeboards, bay windows, red brick and diminutive towers appeared far removed from the Palladian box-like villa adored by Georgian architects and builders, the double-fronted two- or three-storey Victorian houses retained the common arrangement of central entrance with four main rooms on each floor around a staircase.

Inside these larger 19th-century aristocratic homes, the distinct function of individual rooms was rigidly upheld. Every social, private or practical undertaking had its own designated space within the home. The drawing room and dining room retained their supremacy, while additional reception rooms included the living room and an enlarged hall inside the main entrance, from which access to the rest of the house was strictly controlled. Recreational rooms became popular, with smoking rooms for the men and a ladies' drawing room for the women allowing for the separation of sexes after meals. The popularity of billiards heralded an entirely new and often very large room designated to the sport and socialising. Kitchens and other utilitarian offices were at the rear of the house, the basement having been disposed of, private

> The chimney stacks that Edwin Lutyens
made a prominent architectural feature
when altering Goddards, Surrey, in 1910.

modern society was sealing their fate. America and Continental
Europe were mastering the open plan and fitting their new
homes with every type of comfort and convenience that modern
technology could provide. When visiting Britain in the early 20th
century, foreigners were horrified at its antiquated aristocratic
homes and their fusty customs, but the accomplishments overseas
had not been without their struggles. Central heating, modern
plumbing, heated bathrooms and showers, and airy, light, open-
planned interiors, all of which were largely absent in the homes
of Britain's wealthy, had been achieved at the expense of what in
Britain were long-held and vigorously defended traditions that
not only had come to define home for the British, but in Victorian
Britain had been elevated to an almost spiritual status. 'To an
Englishman the idea of a room without a fire-place is quite simply
unthinkable,' wrote the celebrated German historian Hermann
Muthesius in his seminal *Das englische Haus* (*The English House*)
(1904), as the Victorian era began its descent into memory.

None of these traditions was more symbolic and weightier than
the open fire. The demise of the open fire in the face of the sealed
stove or modern central heating was robustly resisted. 'I have not
yet seen one in England; neither, so far as I can remember, have
I seen a house warmed by a furnace. Bright coal fires, in grates
of polished steel, are as yet the lares and penates of old England,'
wrote one American author in 1854. However, for modernity's
sake, the sacrifice had to be made, irrespective of how unattractive
the future appeared without the open fire. But for Britain,
tradition was too strong. The lamentation had been deafening
when the ancient hearth began its slow retirement to the wall in
16th-century halls. The Victorians would not allow the remnant
of this transition, the fireplace, so mocked by their forebears, to be
replaced by the distant and invisible furnace or gas-fired boiler,
regardless of the fact that it delivered hot water and warmth to
every corner of the home.

The open fire was a shrine in all types of Victorian home,
from the rented room of the urban poor up to the aristocrat's
mansion. Indeed, the ancient reverence of the hearth burned
brighter and warmer in the homes of Victorian Britain than it
had done since its slow removal from the hall centuries ago. In
the home of the costermonger it was, like in centuries past, a
place for cooking, but in all homes, irrespective of wealth, the
fireside was a site of domestic union, warmth and exhibition
– from the costermonger's trinkets to the aristocrat's absurdly
elaborate mantelpiece. 'By the fireside still the light is shining, /
The children's arms round the parents twining,' whispered the
soothing words of the poet Dinah Mulock Craik, 'From love
so sweet, O, who would roam? / Be it ever so homely, home is
home.' For the Victorian, the hearth *was* home and it was not
going to be surrendered easily to the phenomenon that would
define the next century: modernity.

THE 'MODERN' HOME

THE 20TH CENTURY AND BEYOND

« A building on the Heygate Estate in Southwark, south London, designed by Tim Tinker and completed in 1974.

Having traversed five thousand years of domestic planning in this small island, the final hundred years of this journey might appear temporally insignificant, but for many reasons it has been unparalleled. It witnessed the world's first two global conflicts; a near quadrupling of the world's population; and a revolution in global communications that continues to unfold. These and many other transformations over the last century have challenged cultural, political, economic and environmental conditions around the world so profoundly that nobody's way of life or their home can claim to have been unaffected.

For the life of the British home, the last century represents a comparatively concise conclusion to this exploration, but the diminutive time span belies the scale of change that has taken place. In 1901, there were over 6 million homes in Britain with an average of 5.2 people and nearly 5 rooms per household. Ten per cent of homes were owner-occupied. By 2001, there were nearly 25 million homes in Britain with an average of 2.4 people and 5.5 rooms per household, and 70 per cent were owner-occupied. The trend over the previous century confirms Thomas Webster's observation made in mid-19th-century America that 'In England, it is generally the desire of every one whose finances can afford it, to have a house of his own,' but it also masks the reality that until very recently homeownership has been beyond the means of most. At no time before or since the coining of the phrase 'An Englishman's home is his castle' in the early 17th century has the maxim had a more universal application than in the early 21st century when the majority of the population seek dominion over their domain.

But what can be said of the character of these miniature castles? Contributions to British housing in the 20th century are often typecast by the precast concrete monuments erected by advocates of the Modern Movement since the Second World War, but Britain's penchant for tradition combined with an obsession with homeownership dwarf these prefabricated concrete towers. The most reliable account of the development of the British home over the last hundred years is not told by these conspicuous concrete structures created by Britain's Modernist architects. These are a mere drop in the broader ocean of mediocrity engendered by the town suburbs and village extensions that, having been connected to urban centres over the course of the century by greatly improved transport networks, have blanketed vast tracts of countryside with a patchwork of homes and their diminutive garden plots.

The proliferation of these privately built housing estates combined with the 1980 Housing Act that gave council tenants the right to buy their homes have offered a greater proportion of the population the dream of owning their own home than has occurred at any time in British history. Against this backdrop, the brief appearance of high-rise or high-density urban developments that typify the Modernist approach to housing appears like an aberration in the middle of the last century, which ended in much the same way as it had begun – with large comparatively low-density housing developments of detached or semi-detached homes designed by private developers or anonymous council departments and erected on the fringes of existing settlements.

The model suited British sensibilities perfectly. On its own private patch of land the British home upholds the ancient insular and individualistic psyche of an island nation. The revivalist mentality that spawned countless historical derivatives has transformed the British suburb, the native home of stockbroker Tudor, accountant's Elizabethan or pen-pusher's Palladian, into an architectural horror show. 'Four postes round my bed, / Oake beames overhead, / Olde rugges on ye floor, / No stockbroker could ask for more,' chimed early-20th-century estate agents in rural Sussex as they mocked the mock in 'mock-Tudor'.

Britain's unshakeable attachment to the traditional idea of home and its defensive garden in the 21st century continues a long relationship between a focal core and protective periphery that extends far into the mists of time: the suburban home arranged around the cul-de-sac, the Victorian terraced house and fenced garden, the Renaissance mansion and estate, the medieval manor and moat, the Norman keep and castle, the Anglo-Saxon burh and earthworks, the Iron Age fort and hill – and the nation and its sea.

THE OPEN PLAN

Much has changed in the British home over the last hundred years, but from the perspective of planning there has been no significant advance. The essential plan of the British home in the 20th and 21st centuries has changed little from that which was forged by the Victorians and continued up until the Second World War. That is not to say that progress has not been made over the last hundred years – it has – only it was not sufficiently embraced to effect a permanent change to the perception and conception of the British home. Whether detached, semi-detached, terraced or an apartment, the spatial arrangements of different types of home in the 21st century present no fundamental innovation from those which were established at least a hundred years earlier.

There is, however, one exception: the open plan. As the Modernist whirlwind swept through Europe in the first half of the 20th century, stimulated by Le Corbusier's revolutionary mantra that the home was a 'machine for living in', which huffed and puffed at the 19th century's bucolic domesticity, Britain's homes remained largely unaffected. Continental influence, as had occurred throughout the ages, was tempered as it crossed the Channel before being diluted by local interpretation. Le Corbusier (aka Charles-Édouard Jeanneret, 1887–1965) was a Swiss architect who became the architectural figurehead for the Modern Movement from the 1920s onwards. In 1915, he produced a concept for flexible housing which not only had revolutionary consequences for residential design but also set a precedent for Modernist architecture over the next century. Titled the Maison Dom-ino, Le Corbusier's design comprised rectangular concrete slabs supported by slender columns interconnected by concrete stairs at one end. Until the 20th century, the walls in virtually all modern forms of housing were structurally integral because they supported the floors above, but the potential of this novel material, reinforced concrete, liberated architects and engineers from this constraint. The skeleton frame, whose modern precedent first appeared in the iron framework of the Palm House at Kew Gardens in the 1840s, liberates the internal walls from the building's structure, offering an interior unobstructed by supporting posts or walls. The open plan had become a reality and hereafter the layout of the modern home was boundless, but in Britain few seized the opportunity (although a few talented architects, such as Charles Francis Annesley Voysey (1857–1941), made important if somewhat understated contributions in this direction). A number of notable Modernist villas that utilised the open plan and were designed in the idiom of the International Style were built before the Second World War, such as Patrick Gwynne's (1913–2003) Homewood in Surrey, but Modernism's most significant impact on the British home was made in the decades immediately after the war.

Le Corbusier's design had been inspired by the First World War and was a response to the urgent need for flexible and economical housing. Beyond the realm of architecture, the political events throughout the 1910s had caused a major shift in social attitudes in Britain. Women's rights were boosted by the lack of male labour from 1914, while the working classes paid

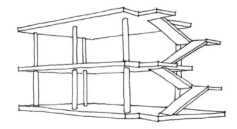

∧ Le Corbusier's Maison Dom-ino (1915), a concept for flexible housing that revolutionised planning of the home.

> An illustration of The Homewood (1938), Surrey, designed by Patrick Gwynne, showing the living quarters (foreground first floor) with office below (foreground ground floor), the central staircase (middle) and a cut-away of the huge open-plan living room with kitchen and services beyond.

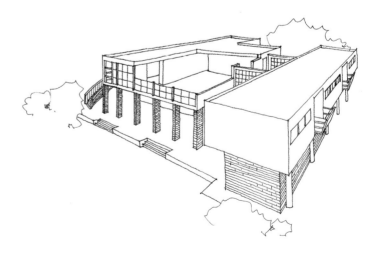

> The Homewood (1938), Surrey, designed by Patrick Gwynne after he had toured around Europe and seen the work of some of the great Modernist architects such as Le Corbusier and Mies van der Rohe, which clearly influenced this design of his own family's home.

a heavy price for their role in the war. Hundreds of thousands fought and died in the First World War and afterwards the government could no longer ignore their demands for political and social inclusion. The right to vote was a defining outcome of this fight, but the right to a decent home was another. State-sponsored housing became a priority throughout the next two decades, during which 4 million homes were constructed in Britain, most of which were in suburbs and strung out along new transport routes. The dominant type was a variant on the two-up two-down model that had been refined in the previous century, but was by now enhanced by the belated admission into virtually all homes of technological improvements offering modern sanitary standards. Bathrooms, which Victorians had been reluctant to introduce into British homes until the invention of the flushable water closet, became mandatory and lavatories began their short journey from the end of garden into closets beside sculleries on the ground floor or in first-floor extensions above the kitchen.

Throughout the 20th century, higher wages improved conditions for the working class, with considerable consequences for those who relied on their labour. The cost of maintaining let alone building mansions was increasingly prohibitive, and a surfeit from previous centuries more than satisfied any lingering demand from the dwindling ranks of Britain's aristocracy, who enjoyed their final fling in the years leading up to 1939. The wholesale changes brought about by the Second World War and amendments to inheritance law caused many large houses to fall into disrepair or forced their owners to bequeath them to charitable trusts or to the state. Enduring nostalgia and a curious interest in the affluent keeps these relics standing as their doors are opened to the paying public. Barring a few exceptions, this most extravagant housing type was consigned to history as a private home.

Middle-class homes were also affected by the overall improvement in the population's living standards. The servant problem of the late 19th century, having never been resolved, was exacerbated

by the rise in better-paid and less grinding forms of employment in the early 20th century. The small band of domestic helpers whose omnipresence in the middle-class home in the 19th century had, by the 1920s, almost entirely disbanded, left behind empty rooms in attics or rear extensions that were subsequently eliminated from the plans of new houses. The result was that the middle-class home followed two different trends: one that did away with the servants' accommodation and therefore reduced in size, and the other that retained its size either by increasing the overall dimensions of the remaining rooms or by giving different functions to former servants' areas.

In the cities, slum clearance, which had defined late-Victorian urban housing policies, continued unabated. Decaying and overcrowded tenements were replaced by modern and comparatively spacious apartment blocks that met the increasingly stringent sanitary requirements set by successive governments throughout the 1920s and 1930s. The direction of the future of modern local authority house planning (internally and collectively) in the 20th century was determined to a large extent by the recommendations in the Tudor Walters Report (1918), which drew on the earlier successes achieved by the London County Council (LCC). The committee, led by the MP, John Tudor Walters, and with architects Raymond Unwin

∧ The main entrance to one of the blocks on
the Millbank Estate (1897–1902), designed
by the London County Council.

< A housing block on the Millbank Estate
(1897–1902), designed by the London
County Council.

(1863–1940) and Aston Webb (1849–1930) among its ranks,
criticised the low standard of existing housing stock for the
poor and acknowledged that 'the general standard of
accommodation and equipment demanded in their dwellings has
been rising for some time'. Their recommendation was 'to
build dwellings which will continue to be above the accepted
minimum, at least for 60 years'. Their efforts, combined with a
general pride and belief in the public sector and dwindling
standards ever since, represent a high-water mark for state
housing, and the homes built in the inter-war years remain
among the best housing stock in the country.

On the scale of the inner-city apartment, the LCC's Georgian-
inspired Millbank Estate (1897–1902) on the site of former
Millbank Prison set the tone for successive high-density local
authority developments. On a suburban scale, spacious ranks of
standardised semi-detached housing of the two-up two-down
type were laid out along rectilinear street patterns, exemplified
by the Totterdown Fields Estate (1903–11) in Tooting, again
by the LCC, setting a high standard for later developments to
follow. On the scale of the city, Ebenezer Howard's Garden City
concept inspired the basic model that others followed. Howard's
Garden City Association aimed to provide spacious, low-
density and high-quality urban environments that succeeding

administrations used to entice a new generation of residents away from the larger cities in a bid to depopulate crowded urban centres. Letchworth Garden City (1903) in Hertfordshire, planned by Raymond Unwin and Barry Parker, was the world's first city to be designed and built according to these principles, inspiring others, like Welwyn Garden City, and in the second half of the century the New Towns. The process of de-urbanisation and improving housing stock was stimulated by the devastation wrought by the Second World War. The widespread destruction of Britain's towns and cities provided a pretext for large-scale post-war housing developments in the decades that followed.

Driven by the socially conscious ideals of post-war Britain that spawned the Welfare State, many local authority architects were inspired by the spirit of egalitarianism. Social housing was central to achieving this ideal. The earliest high-rise blocks were deliberately planted in affluent areas of cities in an attempt to encourage social integration and often enjoyed unparalleled views over open parkland. The quality of construction and planning was invariably good and for a small number of lucky residents who inhabited these new housing estates fitted with all mod cons, the future had arrived sooner than expected. However, as available land and resources quickly dried up and local opposition to such large blocks increased, local authority housing estates were pushed quietly to the urban margins – next to industrial estates, overlooking railway sidings, and buffering motorways.

On these high-density urban sites a new, brief and controversial chapter opened in the life of the British home. It had taken several decades for the radical and modern ideas emanating from the Continent and cemented by organisations like *Congrès internationaux d'architecture moderne* (International Congresses of Modern Architecture), CIAM, to influence architects and their clients in Britain. After the Second World War there

Terraced houses in the Totterdown Fields Estate (1903–11), Tooting, south London designed by the London County Council. Note the double doors in each entrance leading to a one-up one-down arrangement inside.

was both a pressing need for new housing and an increasing confidence in the lessons being preached by the leaders of the Modern Movement. New materials hastened new methods of construction, which advanced planning theories from the scale of the home up to the city. In a conceptual rebuttal of the Garden Suburb idea, Britain's new inner-city housing estates attempted to create entire communities in often poorly located sites, hemmed in by uncompromising industrial facilities and infrastructure. In some cases, planners attempted to make the estates entirely self-contained, with provision for educational, recreational, commercial and even cultural services. One of the early attempts to realise these ideas was Sheffield's Park Hill Estate (1957–61) designed by Jack Lynn and Ivor Smith for Sheffield City Council, which comprised massive concrete slabs of housing standing on a site formerly covered in run-down back-to-back tenements overlooking the city. Park Hill was constructed using a concrete frame with brick infill and employed the idea of 'streets in the sky', where access to the individual flats was provided by communal 3-metre-wide traffic-free decks elevated above the ground.

Robin Hood Gardens (1968–72), in Poplar, east London, designed by Alison and Peter Smithson.

Section through Robin Hood Gardens (1968–72), in Poplar, east London, designed by Alison and Peter Smithson, showing gallery access.

Lv: Living Room · B: Bedroom · K: Kitchen
Bt: Bathroom · G: Gallery

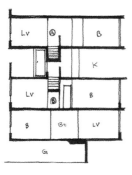

Slightly earlier than Park Hill, but offering a similarly high density of urban housing, was the City of London's Golden Lane Estate (1952–62), occupying a large area of land and former bombsite on the northern perimeter of the City. In 1951, the project to design a large-scale high-density housing estate went out to a major competition that was assessed by the architect, Donald McMorran (1904–65). He awarded the job to the young architect and lecturer at Kingston School of Art, Geoffry Powell (1920–99), later of Chamberlin, Powell & Bon, who went on to design the adjacent Barbican Estate (1963–76, with its arts centre completed in 1982). The combination of four- and six-storey horizontal blocks of two- to three-bedroom maisonettes around a central 16-storey tower of one-bedroom flats provided a series of pedestrianised and public courtyards at ground level. Golden Lane was designed to accommodate approximately 1,000 low-income residents, whereas its adjacent successor, the Barbican Estate, designed in five phases, accommodated nearly 8,000 people from a generally higher income bracket. The Barbican Estate took the concept of the self-contained community to its extreme, with pedestrian streets connecting the individual blocks and a range of educational, cultural and commercial facilities. The public galleries used at Park Hill or Golden Lane that came to be a prominent feature of post-war social housing in Britain were not used at the Barbican, and, instead, each flat was accessed

^ The 27-storey Balfron Tower in Poplar, east London, designed in 1963 by Ernö Goldfinger for the London County Council and completed in 1967.

» The Golden Lane Estate (1952–62) (foreground), designed by Geoffry Powell, who went on to design the Barbican Estate (1963–76) (background) with his firm Chamberlin, Powell & Bon.

independently. The triangular towers contained three- or four-bedroom flats arranged with three flats on each floor, each one therefore having its own full-length balcony.

Among the unsuccessful applicants for the Golden Lane competition were the architects Alison (1928–93) and Peter Smithson (1923–2003), who got their chance to realise a major housing project based on modern principles of planning and design at Robin Hood Gardens (1968–72) in Poplar, east London. Here, the Smithsons attempted to recast the notion of home and street in an intensely modern scene dominated by the motor car and in an environment defined by surrounding motorways, docks, and mixture of heavy and light industry. Their solution, overlooking a central landscaped parkland, comprised two horizontal slabs of maisonette housing, one seven storeys and the other 10 storeys, constructed in precast concrete components that allowed the free planning of each unit. These were connected by public decks in a similar manner to Park Hill and parts of Golden Lane.

Opened in 1972, Robin Hood Gardens was the product of the Smithsons' deep regard for dwelling and how to resolve the complex issues surrounding the siting of modern homes in mid-20th-century urban chaos. As construction was beginning on Robin Hood Gardens another radical housing prototype was being completed nearby at the Balfron Tower (1963–7). Unlike Robin Hood Gardens or Park Hill, this was an experiment in high-rise high-density urban housing by the Hungarian émigré architect Ernö Goldfinger (1902–87). At 27 storeys high, it was one of Europe's tallest residential buildings when completed. With Balfron Tower Goldfinger realised his experimental theories in urban housing, designing a tall block that contained flats and maisonettes accessed by public galleries every three floors. These galleries were connected to a separate service tower containing stairs and lifts that gave the whole composition its distinctive profile. Goldfinger used the scissor section to provide access to the three floors of units from one gallery level. Within the maisonettes, this use of split-level stairs recalled Richard Norman Shaw planning in Albert Hall Mansions nearly a century earlier. As with Golden Lane, Balfron Tower stood among low-rise housing blocks arranged perpendicularly to the tower so as to create pedestrian courtyards at ground level.

Balfron was Goldfinger's prototype to the 31-storey Trellick Tower (1966–72) in the London suburb of North Kensington. Here, as at Balfron, a brilliant Modernist architect provided a uniquely Modernist approach to creating the modern home. His design for Trellick replicated many features from Balfron while avoiding its faults. Homes were arranged as flats and maisonettes and all had double aspects, offering good ventilation and exceptional views over north and south London.

275   THE 'MODERN' HOME

Goldfinger was fastidious in calculating the proportions of the block so that the gallery levels, maisonettes, flats and their balconies all provide individual visual interest within a unified whole.

Time, as with all novel architectural ideas, was the true test. Despite the often very high standard of design, construction and planning, Park Hill, Robin Hood Gardens, Golden Lane, Barbican, Balfron and Trellick Towers, and many other notable examples of post-war urban housing – such as the equally distinguished Alexandra and Ainsworth council estate (1968–78) in Camden, northwest London – have had to withstand many critical storms. These have taken their toll on this unique and idealistic genre of the modern home. Most of these attempts have been disparaged, others are doomed, and some have already been demolished. Survivors or not, these large-scale high-density concrete housing prototypes have become symbols of an approach to planning and design of housing whose

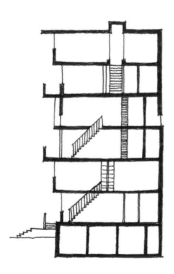

∧ Section through Trellick Tower (1966–72), North Kensington, London, designed by Ernö Goldfinger, showing gallery access.

> The Trellick Tower (1966–72), North Kensington, London, designed by Ernö Goldfinger and one of the tallest buildings in Europe when completed.

∧ The Heygate Estate in Southwark, south London, designed by Tim Tinker and completed in 1974. Despite the sound design of its flats, the estate swiftly acquired a bad image and helped bring about the end of large blocks of inner-city housing.

» The Alexandra and Ainsworth Estate, Camden, north London, designed in 1968 by Neave Brown and completed in 1978. Most of the 520 flats are arranged in terraces that fuse the old idea of the London terrace with modern design and construction principles. The northernmost block (right) is eight storeys high and protects the inner part of the estate from the railway line behind.

failure was caused by factors far beyond planning and design but which led ultimately to their rejection by the British public. It was in Britain's Brutalist housing projects of the 1960s and 1970s that the rot set in, despite every effort by many gifted architects, whose surnames read like a roll-call of the most eminent practitioners of their generation – Bon (1921–99), Brown (b 1929), Chamberlin (1919–78), Goldfinger, Powell and Smithson, as well as Lubetkin (1901–90), Powell (1921–2003) and Moya (1920–94). Poor environments and abject management stigmatised these estates and led irrepressibly to their ruin, along with the Modernist ideals that shaped them. The free planning of interiors stacked in high-rise concrete towers proved to be a relatively fleeting tryst with a utopian dream that in too many cases turned out to be a living nightmare. For the second time in a century the attempt to persuade the British public to make their homes in high-rises failed. The British home, as an ideal and a place to live, came back down to earth where it has always felt more comfortable.

THE FUTURE OF THE MODERN BRITISH HOME

The fundamental requirements of the British home have changed little over the last hundred years, but the overall space available in which to satisfy these requirements has contracted considerably. The average number of rooms might have increased slightly and the number of people per household halved, caused by contracting family sizes and families ceasing to accommodate household staff, but the volume of these rooms has reduced. Floor area and ceiling heights have decreased, leading to smaller homes with more, albeit smaller, rooms and a generally higher density of housing. This shrinking of the home has weakened the rigid delineation of functions that was characteristic of Victorian homes and, combined with the technological and material developments that facilitated the open plan, has revived a more egalitarian and communal living space. Designated social spaces, such as billiard rooms and smoking rooms, or private spaces, such as boudoirs or libraries, are not a feature of most 21st-century homes. Even entertaining rooms, such as the separate dining room, appear faintly anachronistic. In their place are new flexible or multifunctional spaces as suited to television viewing as they are to hosting formal dinners. In many respects, the 21st-century living room has a communal and multipurpose function that has not been seen in the British home since the medieval hall.

Cooking, eating, entertaining, business and relaxation are all pursuits compatible with the modern living room, whose boundaries now frequently merge with dining and kitchen areas. The modern kitchen-diner is invariably a key selling point on any estate agent's portfolio page and while it is a ubiquitous feature of new homes, in older homes it usually requires sacrificing a portion of the back garden to extend the inadequate Victorian kitchen. The kitchen-diner extension is one of many modern habits that have caused the Victorian terrace, like the Georgian equivalent before it, to be thoroughly adapted in the 20th and 21st centuries. Others include combining the living and dining rooms into an open-plan ground floor, or converting the attic into an extra suite of rooms, or even digging out extra space underground. In the modern British home people have to make better use of available space and to share this space with others, yet at the same time they are also willing to surrender this space to more modern uses. The British, who have long preferred separate bedrooms, are cultivating a fondness of en-suite bathrooms, and with nearly a third of all households owning two or more cars, many prefer to yield valuable space inside the home to their vehicles in integral garages rather than enhancing the space for the benefit of the occupants. Even the Georgians had the sense to build detached mews for their horses and carriages rather than surrender large parts of their homes to them.

^ BedZED (2000–2), south London,
designed and developed by BioRegional,
ZEDfactory and the Peabody housing
association to be Britain's first 'zero-
energy' community. Environmental
features seen here include a natural
ventilation system with idiosyncratic
outlets on the roof, rainwater recycling,
and the solar panels sandwiched
between the double-glazing on the
top-floor windows, which also shade the
highest and hottest south-facing rooms.

Modern homes have also had to contend with decreasing family
and household sizes. For centuries the size of the family and the
homes they occupy have been shrinking. Few Georgian terraced
houses have avoided the commercial process of subdivision
into separate flats. The same applies to Victorian villas, many of
which have been converted into apartments on each floor. Many
of the Victorian and Edwardian palatial apartments that offered
a new form of urban lifestyle for former upper-class urbanites
can no longer be afforded by the type of demographic for which
they were intended. Most have therefore been transformed into
commercial properties, such as hotels or offices. Even the social
housing of the late 19th and early 20th centuries was so spacious
and so well built compared with modern standards that the
21st-century middle-class family is only too willing to pay a high

> BedZED (2000–2), south London: homes are positioned on the south-facing side of the terrace, with workspaces on the north side. Almost every home has its own garden or terrace as well as the use of communal gardens on the roof, which can be accessed via pedestrian bridges on the first floor. Bedrooms are often located on the darker ground floor with living areas on the brighter first or second floor.

> Opposite: BedZED (2000–2), south London: a third bedroom on the north side of the house doubles as a study. The room is lit from a large skylight. Note the trunking to allow the easy access to and storage of electrical wiring.

price for it, while more affluent families move into former stables and pigsties just to secure their place in the smartest city-centre locations or the choicest parts of the country.

In the aftermath of the First World War, the Government commissioned a report into local authority housing. Among its many recommendations, it proposed the size of semi-detached houses should be between 80 and 120 square metres and a maximum of 30 homes to a hectare. In 2001, according to Professor Robert Home, the average British home was 76 square metres and the average density for new housing developments was 44 houses per hectare. Britain has, on average, the smallest homes in Europe and among the highest densities of housing. A small landmass cannot be blamed, since Britain's population density is 246 people per square kilometre, which compares unfavourably with the Netherlands that has 395 people per square kilometre and an average house size of 115 square metres. As our material wants and needs have increased tenfold over the 20th century, our homes that accommodate this growing mountain of stuff have steadily decreased in space and size.

Nevertheless, it should not be forgotten that when surveying the evolution of the British home, the 20th century represents its highest point of development if the interests of the entire population are taken into account. The luxurious mansions of yesteryear, sumptuous though they were, comforted only a tiny fraction of the population while the vast majority lived in relative squalor. Today, the great majority of the population enjoy a level of domestic comfort and convenience that was unimaginable even a few decades ago.

A similar improvement has been achieved in the quality of cities, not just in Britain but across the world. This trend has to continue because the 21st century has already witnessed, for the first time in human history, more people living in cities than

in the countryside. Cities have gone from being the scourge of modern industrial development in the late 19th century, to being home for the majority of humanity. The efficient and comparatively clean post-industrial city of the 21st century might yet be the lifeline the earth desperately needs. In the 21st century, London, for so long the place that presaged the future of the British home, is the site of Europe's tallest building and highest homes, just as Goldfinger's Trellick Tower was in the 1970s. The Shard (2000–12), standing over London Bridge station and designed by Renzo Piano, and many other high-rise proposals in and around London hint not only at a revival of the residential tower that dates back to Henry Hankey's Queen Anne's Mansions in the 1870s, but also a new chapter in quality high-rise and high-density living.

The greatest challenge facing a high-density or high-rise future in Britain is the nation's particular and strong desire for the idea of the country, in which the image of a detached rural abode with its adjoining garden represents a powerful and compelling vision of utopia. Britain, compared with most countries, does not favour high-density communal living, and herein lies perhaps the biggest question mark over the future life of the British home. At the beginning of the 21st century, over 80 per cent of households lived in houses, compared with less than 20 per cent in apartments (including maisonettes). The British, if allowed to pursue their primordial domestic aspiration of living independently with their own slice of the countryside as a private garden, will inevitably destroy the very ideal they seek. Over 60 million people cannot live a bucolic fantasy of isolation among rolling hills and hedgerows on this small island living out without inadvertently creating HG Wells's vision of Bromstead:

> ... a dull useless boiling-up of human activities, an immense clustering of futilities ... as unfinished as ever; the builders' roads still run out and end in mid-field in their old fashion; the various enterprises jumble in the same hopeless contradiction, if anything intensified. Pretentious villas jostle slums, and public-house and tin tabernacle glower at one another across the cat-haunted lot that intervenes. Roper's meadows are now quite frankly a slum; back doors and sculleries gape towards the railway, their yards are hung with tattered washing unashamed; and there seem to be more boards by the railway every time I pass, advertising pills and pickles, tonics and condiments, and suchlike solicitudes of a people with no natural health nor appetite left in them.

The impracticality and undesirability of this conclusion points to another predicament, one that might define the British home in the 21st century and beyond. British homes, a significant proportion of which were built long before environmental concerns were a consideration of the opportunistic builder,

> BedZED (2000–2) in south London contains a variety of different unit types from single-room apartments to whole town houses. This living room with open-plan kitchen-diner is on the first floor of a two- to three-bedroom house with two bedrooms on the ground floor. The bedrooms have access to the garden and the living room opens on to a large balcony terrace, flooding the room with natural light and warmth.

let alone the educated architect, account for a proportionally large share of the nation's carbon emissions and accommodate lifestyles that, if enjoyed by everyone, cannot be sustained by the earth. The relatively new concept of the 'eco-home' has been concerned more with materials, performance and energy use than with spatial arrangements, but with a decreasing supply of land and housing and a corresponding increase in the cost of housing and fuel, the future of the British home has to become more efficient – environmentally, spatially and functionally.

Various models of sustainable homes have been designed and built in Britain, but few are as holistic in their approach as Beddington Zero Energy Development (BedZED) (2000–2) in south London. Designed and developed as a sustainable community by BioRegional, ZEDfactory and the Peabody housing association, BedZED is the country's largest carbon neutral mixed-use development. The community comprises 2,500 square metres of business space and 82 homes arranged as apartments, maisonettes and town houses, all of which have their own patch of roof garden as well as sharing public open spaces. The design concept looks beyond bricks and mortar in achieving the zero-carbon home. The development is integrated with the local transport network (reducing car mileage by 64 per cent) and the buildings' siting and design conserve energy (reducing energy consumption for heating by 81 per cent), electricity (reducing electricity use by 45 per cent) and water (reducing water consumption by 58 per cent). At BedZED, growing your own food, recycling waste, sharing a car, or swapping furniture and other possessions is not a gimmick but part of a way of life that aims to be truly sustainable.

The sustainable home will be defined by high-density living and its urban setting, both of which have occurred for centuries but have so rarely been adequately catered for. The future of the British home will be about getting more from less, which depends on improving performance, while satisfying the age-old requirements that have tested those who have built Britain's homes over the centuries: comfort and convenience.

ENDMATTER

« The remains of the 13th-century knight's home, Old Soar (1290), Kent. The existing structure comprises a private chamber raised on a barrel-vaulted undercroft, with attached chapel and garderobe.

BIBLIOGRAPHY

STICKS AND STONES

Aristotle, *Ethics and Politics* (John Gillies trans), Strahan, Cadell & Davies, London, 1797

Richard Bradley, *Ritual and Domestic Life in Prehistoric Europe*, Routledge, London, 2005

V Gordon Childe and DV Clarke, *Skara Brae*, Her Majesty's Stationery Office, Edinburgh, 1983

DW Harding, *The Iron Age Round-House*, Oxford University Press, Oxford, 2009

Beverley Ballin Smith and Iain Banks (eds), *In the Shadow of the Brochs: the Iron Age in Scotland*, Tempus, Stroud, 2002

ROMAN HOMES AND THE NEWFANGLED RECTANGLE

Aristotle, *Ethics and Politics* (John Gillies trans), Strahan, Cadell & Davies, London, 1797

Guy de la Bédoyère, *Architecture in Roman Britain*, Shire, Princes Risborough, 2002

Guy de la Bédoyère, *Roman Towns in Britain*, Tempus, Stroud, 2003

Cassius Dio Cocceianus, *Roman History* (Herbert B Foster trans), Book 62.6.4, AD 61, Pafraets Book Co, Troy, New York, 1905

Gildas, *The Ruin of Britain*, note 24:3–4, AD 540, in Michael Winterbottom (ed), *Gildas: The Ruin of Britain and other Works*, Phillimore, London, 1978

Homer, *The Illiad of Homer* (Alexander Pope trans), Book 9, Methuen & Co, London; Yale University Press, New Haven, 1967

Horace, *The Epistles*, Book 1, Chapter Two, Macmillan & Co, London and Cambridge, 1885

Juvenal, Satire 3, *The Evils of the Big City*, lines 190–202 (Niall Rudd trans), in *Juvenal – The Satires*, Oxford World's Classics, Oxford University Press, Oxford, 2008

Dominic Perring, *The Roman House in Britain*, Routledge, London, 2002

ALF Rivet, *The Roman Villa in Britain*, Routledge & Kegan Paul, London, 1969

Cornelius Tacitus, *The Life of Agricola* (Thomas Gordon trans), Robert Urie, Glasgow, 1763

Marcus Terentius Varro, *Res Rusticae*, Book Three, Section Two, Lines 1–18, 37 BC, in Bertha Tilly (ed), *De res rusticae: Selections*, University Tutorial Press, London, 1973

WOODEN WALLS AND FLEDGLING HALLS

The Anglo-Saxon Chronicle, version referred to MJ Swanton, *The Anglo-Saxon Chronicle*, JM Dent, London 1996

Anonymous, *Beowulf*, Canto I, in John Josias Conybeare, *Illustrations of Anglo-Saxon Poetry*, Harding & Lepard, London, 1826

Anonymous, *The Wanderer*, Folio 76f, Exeter Manuscript, translated by N Kershaw in *Anglo-Saxon and Norse Poems*, Cambridge University Press, Cambridge, 1922

King Alfred's Version of St Augustine's Soliloquies, 12th century AD (Henry Lee Hargrove trans), in Albert S Cook (ed), *Yale Studies in English*, Henry Holt & Co, New York, 1904

Asser, *Life of King Alfred*, AD 893, verse 83, in *Asser's Life of King Alfred* (translated from the text of Stevenson's Edition by Albert Cook), Ginn & Co, Boston, 1906

The Venerable Bede, *Historia Ecclesiastica Gentis Anglorum*, Book 1, Chapter 25, c AD 731 (Thomas Stapleton trans), Scolar Press, Menston, 1973

SJ Crawford, *Byrhtferth's Manual (A.D. 1011)*, Oxford University Press, Oxford, 1929

Eric Fernie, *The Architecture of the Anglo-Saxons*, Batsford, London, 1983

Ernest Arthur Fisher, *An Introduction to Anglo-Saxon Architecture and Sculpture*, Faber & Faber, London, 1959

Gildas, *The Ruin of Britain*, note 26:2, AD 540, in Michael Winterbottom (ed), *Gildas: The Ruin of Britain and Other Works*, Phillimore, London, 1978

J Haslam, *Anglo-Saxon Towns*, Phillimore, Chichester, 1984

Llywarch Hen, *An Elegy of the Death of Urien of Rheged*, in *Red Book of Hergest XII*, 6th century AD

Tacitus, *Germany*, 16, in Moses Hadas (ed), *Complete Works of Tacitus*, Library College Editions, McGraw-Hill, New York, 1942

THE HEARTH AND HALL

Calendar of Liberate Rolls, Henry III, Volume 1–4, AD 1226–55, Her Majesty's Stationery Office, London, 1916–59

Geoffrey Chaucer, *The Nun's Priest's Tale*, Line 12, 14th century, in George H Cowling (ed), *The Prologue and Three Tales*, Ginn & Co, London, 1934

Geoffrey Chaucer, *The Book of the Duchess*, c 1369–72

Chrétien de Troyes, *Perceval: The Story of the Grail*, 12th century, Lines 1785–7 (Burton Raffel trans), Yale University Press, New Haven, 1999

Coroners' Roll, Number 164, 1273, in RF Hunnisett (ed), *Bedfordshire Coroners' Rolls*, Society at Streatley, Luton, 1961

Jordanus Fantasma's Chronicle, 1174, line 580, in RC Johnston, *Jordan Fantosme's Chronicle*, Clarendon Press, Oxford, 1981

Fitz-Aylewin's Assize of Buildings, Richard I, Folio 47b, 1189, in Henry Thomas Riley (trans), *Chronicles of the Mayors and Sheriffs of London, A.D. 1188 to A.D. 1274*, Trübner & Co, London, 1863

Ranulphi de Glanvilla, *Tractatus de Legibus Anglie etc.*, 1183, British Library MS 14252, 129b

William Harrison, *A Description of England or a briefe rehersall of the nature and qualities of the people of England*, London, 1577, in Frederick Furnivall, *Harrison's Description of England in Shakspere's* [sic] *Youth*, N Trübner & Co, London, 1877

William Langland, *Piers Plowman*, Passus X: 96–101, late 14th century, in Donald and Rachel Attwater (trans), *The Book concerning Piers the Plowman*, Dent, London, 1907

Orderic Vitalis, *Historia Ecclesiastica*, Book IV, ii.166, early 12th century, in Marjorie Chibnall, *The Ecclesiastical History of Orderic Vitalis*, Clarendon Press, Oxford, 1983

Marcus Vitruvius Pollio, *The Ten Books of Architecture*, 2:1:2, in J Gwilt (trans), *The Architecture of Marcus Vitruvius Pollio in Ten Books*, London, 1826

Leslie Weston, *Sir Gawain and the Green Knight*, David Nutt, London, 1898

Margaret Wood, *Norman Domestic Architecture*, Royal Archaeological Institute, London, 1974

ARCHITECTURE AND AVARICE

Anonymous, *Cyvile and Uncyvile Life*, Richard Jones, London, 1579

Roger Ascham, *The Scholemaster*, John Daye, London, 1570

Francis Bacon, *Of Building*, 1623, in David Mallet, *The Life of Francis Bacon*, A Millar, London, 1740

Andrew Borde, *The boke for to Lerne a man to be wyse in buyldyng of his howse for the helth of his soule, and body, etc.*, Robert Wyer, London, c 1540

Richard Brathwaite, *The English Gentleman: Containing Sundry excellent Rules or exquisite Observations, tending to Direction of every Gentleman, of selecter ranke and qualitie; How to demeane or accommodate himself in the manage of publike or private affaires*, John Haviland, London, 1630

Nicholas Breton, *In Praise of Queen Elizabeth*, British Museum, MS 6207, fols

James Cleland, *The Institution of a Young Noble Man*, Joseph Barnes, Oxford, 1607

Howard Colvin and John Newman (eds), *Of Building – Roger North's Writing on Architecture*, Clarendon Press, Oxford, 1981

Nicholas Cooper, *Houses of the Gentry*, 1480–1680, Yale University Press, New Haven and London, 1999

William Cornwallis, *Essayes*, Essay 9, 'Of Entertainment', Edmund Mattes, London, 1600

John Dee, 'Mathematicall Præface', in Henry Billingsley, *The Elements of Geometrie of the Most Auncient Philosopher Euclide of Megara*, John Daye, London, 1570, d.iiij recto-verso

Thomas Dekker, *A Strange Horse-Race*, Joseph Hunt, London, 1613

Letter from John Evelyn to Lord Cornbury, 20 January 1666, in William Bray (ed), *Memoirs, Illustrative of the Life and Writings of John Evelyn, ESQ. F.R.S.*, Nichols, Son, & Bentley, London, 1818

Frederick, Duke of Wirtemberg, 1592 (translated from the German), in William Brenchley Rye, *England as Seen by Foreigners in the Days of Elizabeth and James the First*, John Russell Smith, London, 1865

Mark Girouard, *Robert Smythson and the Elizabethan Country House*, Yale University Press, New Haven and London, 1983

Robert Greene, *A Quip for an Upstart Courtier*, John Wolfe, London, 1592

RT Gunther (ed), *The Architecture of Roger Pratt*, Oxford University Press, Oxford, 1928

Joseph Hall, *Virgidemiarum, Six Bookes*, Lib 5, Satire II, Thomas Creed for Robert Dexter, London, 1597

William Harrison, *A Description of England or a briefe rehersall of the nature and qualities of the people of England*, London, 1577, in Frederick Furnivall, *Harrison's Description of England in Shakspere's* [sic] *Youth*, N Trübner & Co, London, 1877

Paul Hentzner, 'Travels in England', 1598, in William Brenchley Rye, *England as Seen by Foreigners in the Days of Elizabeth and James the First*, John Russell Smith, London, 1865

William Horman, *Vulgaria*, R Pynson, London, 1519

Maurice Howard, *The Building of Elizabethan and Jacobean England*, Yale University Press, New Haven and London, 2007

Maurice Howard, *The Early Tudor Country House*, George Philip, London, 1987

Benjamin Jonson, *The Devil is an Asse*, Act V, Scene IV, lines 18–20, 1616, in *The Workes of Benjamin Jonson*, facsimile reprint of 1st folio edition, William Stansby, London, 1616, Scolar Press, London, 1976

Benjamin Jonson, *The Satyr* (or *The Entertainment at Althorp*), 1603

Benjamin Jonson, *To Penshurst*, 1616, in *The Workes of Benjamin Jonson*, facsimile reprint of 1st folio edition, William Stansby, London, 1616, Scolar Press, London, 1976

King's Proclamations, Robert Barker, London, 1603–15

King's Proclamations, Bonham Norton and John Bill, London, 1625–6

Richard Lassels, *The Voyage of Italy: or a Compleat Journey through Italy in Two Parts*, Vincent du Moutier, Paris, 1670

Levine Lemnie, *The Touchstone of Complexions* (Thomas Newton trans), Thomas Marsh, London, 1576

Donald Lupton, *London and the Countrey Carbonadoed and Quartred into Severall Characters*, Nicholas Okes, London, 1632

Gervase Markham, *The English Husbandman*, Henry Taunton, London, 1635

Gervase Markham, *A Health to the Gentlemanly Profession of Servingmen*, WW, London, 1598

William A McClung, *The Country House in English Renaissance Poetry*, University of California Press, Berkeley and London, 1977

Draft letter from Henry Oxinden to his brother, James Oxinden, 1636, in Dorothy Gardiner (ed), *The Oxinden Letters 1607–1642*, Constable & Co, London 1933

Andrea Palladio, *Quattro libri dell'architettura*, Venice, 1570

Henry Peacham, *The Compleat Gentleman, Fashioning him absolute in the most necessary & commendable Qualities concerning Minde or Bodie, that may be required in a Noble Gentleman*, Francis Constable, London, 1622

Katherine Philips, *A Country Life*, in *The Female Poets of Great Britain*, Frederic Rowton, Longman, Brown, Green, & Longmans, London, 1848

Colin Platt, *The Great Rebuildings of Tudor and Stuart England*, UCL Press, London, 1994

Roger Pratt, 'Certain Short Notes Concerning Architecture', 1660, in *The Architecture of Sir Roger Pratt*, Oxford University Press, Oxford, 1928

Queen's Proclamation, *By the Queen, A Proclamation concerning new Buildings and Inmates, in or about the Citie of London*, Robert Barker, London, 22 June 1602

William Shakespeare, *Richard II*, Act III, Scene I, 1595

William Shakespeare, *The Two Gentlemen of Verona*, Act III, Scene I, *c* 1591

John Shute, *The First and Chief Groundes of Architecture used in all the auncient and famous monymentes: with a further & more ample discouse uppon the same, than hitherto hath been set out by any other*, Thomas Marshe, London, 1563

John Skelton, *Colyn Clout*, John Wallye, London, 1550

[James Stuart], *Critical Observations on the Buildings and Improvements of London*, 2nd edition, 1771

Philip Stubbes, *The Anatomie of Abuses*, Richard Jones, London, 1584

Emanuel Van Meteren, 1558–1612 (translated from the Dutch), in William Brenchley Rye, *England as Seen by Foreigners in the Days of Elizabeth and James the First*, John Russell Smith, London, 1865

William Vaughan, 'Of Hospitality', Chapter 24, in *The Golden-Grove, Moralized in Three Bookes*, Simon Stafford, London, 1608

William Vaughan, 'Why housekeeping nowadaies is decayed', Chapter 26, in *The Golden-Grove, Moralized in Three Bookes*, Simon Stafford, London, 1608

Letter from the Hon Horace Walpole to George Montagu, 1 September 1760, in *Letters from the Hon. Horace Walpole to George Montagu from the year 1736 to the year 1770*, Rodwell and Martin, London, 1818

George Whetstone, *An Heptameron of Civill Discourses*, Richard Jones, London, 1582

Henry Wotton, *The Elements of Architecture*, John Bill, London, 1624

THE COMPACT COMMODITY

Robert Adam and James Adam, *The Works in Architecture of Robert and James Adam*, London, 1773

Joseph Addison, *The Spectator*, Number 403, Thursday 12 June 1712, p 42

Anonymous, *Hell-on-Earth; or the Town in an Uproar, Occasioned by the late horrible Scenes of Forgery, Perjury, Street-Robbery, Murder, Sodomy, and other Shocking Impieties*, J Roberts, London, 1729

Johann Wilhelm von Archenholz, *A Picture of England*, Volume 1, Edward Jeffery, London, 1789

Dana Arnold, *The Georgian Country House: Architecture, Landscape and Society*, Sutton, Stroud, 1998

Nicholas Barbon, *A Discourse Concerning Coining the New Money Lighter, in Answer to Mr. Lock's Considerations About Raising the Value of Money*, Richard Chiswell, London, 1696

William Blake, *Jerusalem*, 1804

James Boswell, *The Life of Samuel Johnson*, Charles Dilly, London, 1791

James Bramston, *The Man of Taste*, 1733, in *A Collection of Poems by Several Hands in Three Volumes*, R Dodsley, London, 1748

Edmund Burke, *A Philosophical Enquiry into the Origin of our Ideas of the Sublime and Beautiful*, R & J Dodsley, London, 1757

Colen Campbell, *Vitruvius Britannicus, or The British Architect*, London, 1717–25

George Chalmers, *An Estimate of the Comparative Strength of Great Britain*, John Stockdale, London, 1794

William Chambers, *A Treatise on Civil Architecture*, London, 1759

Howard Colvin and John Newman (eds), *Of Building – Roger North's Writing on Architecture*, Clarendon Press, Oxford, 1981

Dan Cruickshank and Neil Burton, *Life in the Georgian City*, Viking, London, 1990

Daniel Defoe, *The Life and Surprising Adventures of Robinson Crusoe of York, Mariner*, Blackie & Son, London, 1719

Roger L'Estrange, *The Art of Fair Building: Represented in the Figures of Several uprights of houses, with their Ground plots, fitting for persons of several Qualities*, Robert Pricke, London, 1670

Thomas Fairchild, *The City Gardener*, London, 1722

Harry Forrester, *The Smaller Queen Anne and Georgian House, 1700 to 1840*, Tindal Press, Chelmsford, 1964

David Garrick, Prologue to *A Trip to Scarborough, as performed at the Theatre Royal in Drury Lane. Altered from Vanbrugh's Relapse; or, Virtue in Danger. By Richard Brinsley Sheridan spoken by Mr King*, R Marchbank, Dublin, 1781

Peter Guillery, *The Small House in Eighteenth-century London: A Social and Architectural History*, Yale University Press, New Haven and London, 2004

RT Gunther (ed), *The Architecture of Sir Roger Pratt*, Oxford University Press, Oxford, 1928

Sir W Hillary, 'Improvements, and Extension of the Metropolis', in *The Pamphleteer*, Volume 25, AJ Valpy, London, 1825

William Hogarth, *The Analysis of Beauty*, J Reeves, London, 1753

William Hutton, *An History of Birmingham*, Pearson & Rollason, Birmingham, 1781

Batty Langley, *Gothic Architecture Improved by Rules and Proportions*, John Millan, London, 1747

London Building Act, 1667

John [Claudius] Loudon, *A treatise on forming, improving, and managing country residences*, London, 1806

James Malton, *An Essay on British Cottage Architecture*, London, 1798

Charles Middleton, *Picturesque and Architectural Views for Cottages, Farm Houses, and Country Villas*, Edward Jeffery, London, 1793

Alexander Pope, *Of False Taste: An Epistle to the Right Honourable Richard Earl of Burlington*, 3rd edition, L Gulliver, London, 1731

John Pouncy, *Dorsetshire Photographically Illustrated*, Bland & Long, London, 1857

Stephen Primatt, *The City and Country Purchaser and Builder*, London, 1667

Augustus Welby Northmore Pugin, *Contrasts, or, A Parallel Between the Noble Edifices of the Fourteenth and Fifteenth Centuries and Similar Buildings of the Present Day; Shewing the Present Decay of Taste*, London, 1836

Albert Edward Richardson, *An Introduction to Georgian Architecture*, Art & Technics, London, 1949

Thomas Shadwell, *Lancashire Witches and Tegue O Divelly the Irish Priest: A Comedy acted at the Duke's Theater*, Act III, John Starkey, London, 1682

Louis Simond, *Journal of a Tour and Residence in Great Britain during the Years 1810 and 1811, by a French traveller*, A Constable & Co, Edinburgh, 1815

Louis Simond, 'Travels in England', in *North American Review*, Volume 2, Number 4, Wells & Lilly, Boston, 1816

Rachel Stewart, *The Town House in Georgian London*, Yale University Press, New Haven and London, 2009

James Stuart, *Critical Observations on the Buildings and Improvements of London*, J Dodsley, London, 1771

John Summerson, *Georgian London*, Pimlico, London, 1991

Horace Walpole and George Vertue, *Anecdotes of Painting in England*, J Dodsley, London, 1782

Isaac Ware, *A Complete Body of Architecture*, T Osborne and J Shipton, London, 1756

Isaac Ware, *The Four Books of Andrea Palladio's Architecture*, London, 1738

John Wood, 'An Essay Towards the Description of Bath', 1742, in *A Description of Bath*, W Bathoe, London, 1765

HOME SWEET HOME?

Anonymous, 'The Building Mania', in *The Builder*, 14 October 1848

Anonymous, 'Extension at Queen Anne's Mansions', in *The Builder*, 18 February 1888

Anonymous, 'Flats for the Middle Classes', in *The Building News*, 15 May 1868

Anonymous, *Homes of the People*, Hull, 1884

Anonymous, leading article on housing, in *The Times*, 2 March 1861

Anonymous, *The Iron Age; or, the Dandy Moralist*, in *Universal Songster; or Museum of Mirth*, Jones & Co, London, 1827

Anonymous, 'The Plough, the Loom, and the Anvil', in *American Farmers' Magazine*, Volume 7, Number 7, January 1855

Anonymous poem in Edward Lance Tarbuck, *Handbook of House Property*, Lockwood & Co, London, 1875

Anonymous, 'Queen Anne's Mansions and Milton's Garden', in *The Builder*, 2 June 1877

Samuel Bamford, *Walks in South Lancashire and on Its Borders*, Blackley, 1844

H Barrett and J Phillips, *Suburban Style – The British Home*, Macdonald, London, 1987

John Birch, *Examples of Labourers' Cottages, with Plans for Improving the Dwellings of the Poor in Large Towns*, Edward Stanford, London, 1871

Hugh Stowell Brown, *Lectures to the Men of Liverpool*, Gabriel Thomson, Liverpool, 1860

James Baldwin Brown, *Young Men and Maidens, a Pastoral for the Times*, Hodder & Stoughton, London, 1871

The Builder, 3 December 1853

John Burnett, *A Social History of Housing*, 1815–1970, David & Charles, Newton Abbot, 1978

Jenni Calder, *The Victorian Home*, Batsford, London, 1977

Henry Clarke, *Dwellings for the Poor*, WH & L Collingridge, London, 1884

CJ Harold Cooper, 'The Home and its Bedrooms', in W Shaw Sparrow (ed), *The British Home of Today: A Book of Modern Domestic Architecture & the Applied Arts*, London, 1904

Dinah Mulock Craik, in John Halifax, *Thirty Years, Being Poems New and Old*, MacMillan & Co, London, 1880

MJ Daunton, *House and Home in the Victorian City: Working-class Housing 1850–1914*, Edward Arnold, London, 1983

Richard Elsam, *An Essay on Rural Architecture*, The Philanthropic Society, London, 1803

Thomas Hay Sweet Escott, *England: Its People, Polity and Pursuits*, Cassell, Petter, Galpin & Co, London, 1879

First Report of Her Majesty's Commissioners for Inquiring into the Housing of the Working Classes, Eyre & Spottiswoode, London, 1885

William Gilbert, 'The Dwellings of the London Poor', in Norman Macleod (ed), *Good Words for 1872*, Strahan & Co, London, 1872

Mark Girouard, *The Victorian Country House*, Clarendon Press, Oxford, 1971

George Godwin, *London Shadows: A Glance at the 'Homes' of the Thousands*, George Routledge, London, 1854

George Haw, *No Room to Live – The plaint of overcrowded London ...With introduction by Sir W. Besant (Reprinted from 'The Daily News')*, Wells, Gardner & Co, London, 1900

AGE Heine, *Dwellings of the Poor – Some Suggestions on this Great Question of the Day: For Christmas 1866*, Henry Vickers, London, 1866

HJ Jennings, *Our Homes and How to Beautify Them*, Harrison & Sons, London, 1902

CC Knowles and PH Pitt, *The History of Building Regulation in London 1189–1972*, Architectural Press, London, 1972

The Liverpool Health of Towns' Advocate, Number 1, Monday 1 September 1845

The Liverpool Health of Towns' Advocate, Number 2, Wednesday 1 October 1845

John Claudius Loudon, *The Suburban Gardener, and Villa Companion*, Longman, Orme, Brown, Green & Longmans, London, 1838

Mervyn Macartney, *The Home and its Halls*, in W Shaw Sparrow (ed), *The British Home of Today, A Book of Modern Domestic Architecture & the Applied Arts*, London, 1904

Henry Mayhew, *London Labour and the London Poor*, George Woodfall & Son, London, 1851

Andrew Mearns, *The Bitter Cry of Outcast London: An Inquiry into the Condition of the Abject Poor*, James Clarke & Co, London, 1883

William Morris, *The Art of the People*, lecture for the Birmingham Society of Arts and School of Design, in *Hopes and Fears for Art*, Ellis & White, London, 1882

Hermann Muthesius, *The English House*, Francis Lincoln, London, 2007

John Howard Payne, *Clari, The Maid of Milan*, London, 1823

Dorothy Peel, *The New Home*, Archibald Constable & Co, London, 1898

Sydney Perks, *Residential Flats of All Classes including Artisans' Dwellings*, BT Batsford, London, 1905

JR, 'Domestic Arrangements of the Working Classes', in *The London and Westminster Review*, Volume 27, 1836

John Ruskin, Fors Clavigera, Letter 29, *La Douce Amie*, 1873, in ET Cook and Alexander Wedderburn (eds), *Library Edition of the Works of John Ruskin*, Volume XXVII, Oxford, 1907

John Ruskin, *Lecture 1*, delivered in Edinburgh in November 1853, in *Lectures on Architecture and Painting*, Smith, Elder & Co, London, 1854

Gavin Stamp, *The English House 1860–1914: The Flowering of English Domestic Architecture*, Faber & Faber, London, 1986

Harriet Beecher Stowe, *Sunny Memories of Foreign Lands*, Phillips, Sampson & Co, Boston, 1854

Rufus Usher, 'Cottages of the Rural Poor', in *Essays on the Dwellings of the Poor and Other Subjects*, Wyman & Sons, London, 1877

Frank Verity, Edwin T Hall, Gerald C Horsley and W Shaw Sparrow (eds), *Flats, Urban Houses and Cottage Homes, a Companion Volume to the British Home of Today*, Hodder & Stoughton, London, 1906

Max Weber, *The Protestant Ethic and the Spirit of Capitalism*, 1905 (Talcott Parsons trans), Charles Scribner's Sons, New York, 1958

Thomas Webster and Frances Parkes, *The American Family Encyclopedia of Useful Knowledge*, JC Derby, New York, 1856

Deborah EB Weiner, *Architecture and Social Reform in Late-Victorian London*, Manchester University Press, Manchester, 1994

HG Wells, *Kipps, The Story of a Simple Soul*, in *The Pall Mall Magazine*, Editorial and Publishing Offices, London, Volume 2, July–December 1905

Crawford Wilson, *Adventures of Benjamin Bobbin the Bagman*, in *Bentley's Miscellany*, Richard Bentley, London, Volume 38, 1855

Anthony S Wohl, *The Eternal Slum: Housing and Social Policy in Victorian London*, Edward Arnold, London, 1977

THE 'MODERN' HOME

Eileen Balderson, *Backstairs Life in a Country House*, David & Charles, Newton Abbot, 1982

Ian Colquhoun, *Housing Design: An International Perspective*, Batsford, London, 1991

Colin Davies, *The Prefabricated Home*, Reaktion, London, 2005

M Glendinning and S Muthesius, *Tower Block: Modern Public Housing in England, Scotland, Wales*, Yale University Press, New Haven, 1994

Greater London Council, Department of Architecture and Civic Design, *Home sweet home: Housing Designed by the London County Council and Greater London Council Architects, 1888–1975*, Academy Editions for the Greater London Council, London, 1976

Robert Home, 'Land ownership in the United Kingdom: Trends, preferences and future challenges', in *Land Use Policy*, Elsevier, 26S, 2009, S104

Osbert Lancaster, *Homes Sweet Homes*, J Murray, London, 1948

Roger Sherwood, *Modern Housing Prototypes*, Harvard University Press, Cambridge, Massachusetts and London, 1978

Thomas Webster and Frances Parkes, *The American Family Encyclopedia of Useful Knowledge*, JC Derby, New York, 1856

HG Wells, *The New Machiavelli*, John Lane, London, 1911

GENERAL READING

MW Barley, *The English Farmhouse and Cottage*, Sutton, Gloucester, 1987

Helena Barrett and John Phillips, *Suburban Style: The British Home, 1840–1960*, Macdonald, London, 1987

Hugh Braun, *The Story of the English House*, BT Batsford, London, 1940

Wendy Davies (ed), *From the Vikings to the Normans*, Oxford University Press, Oxford and New York, 2003

Mark Girouard, *Life in the English Country House: A Social and Architectural History*, Yale University Press, New Haven and London, 1978

Andor Gomme, Michael Jenner and Bryan Little, *Bristol: An Architectural History*, Lund Humphries, London, 1979

J Alfred Gotch, *The Growth of the English House: From Early Feudal to the Close of the Eighteenth Century*, Batsford, London, 1928

Barbara A Hanawalt, *The Ties That Bound: Peasant Families in Medieval England*, Oxford University Press, New York and Oxford, 1986

P Hembry, *The English Spa, 1560–1815*, Athlone Press, London, 1990

David Herlihy, *Medieval Households*, Harvard University Press, Cambridge, Massachusetts and London, 1985

CC Knowles and PH Pitt, *The History of Building Regulation in London: 1189–1972*, Architectural Press, London, 1972

Nathaniel Lloyd, *A History of the English House from Primitive Times to the Victorian Period*, Architectural Press, London, 1975

Michael Mennim, *Hall Houses*, William Sessions, York, 2005

Hermann Muthesius, *The English House*, BSP Professional Books, London, 1987

Stefan Muthesius, *The English Terraced House*, Yale University Press, New Haven and London, 1982

Anthony Quiney, *Town Houses of Medieval Britain*, Yale University Press, New Haven and London, 2003

Ross Samson (ed), *The Social Archaeology of Houses*, Edinburgh University Press, Edinburgh, 1990

JT Smith, PA Faulkner and A Emery, *Studies in Medieval Domestic Architecture*, Royal Archaeological Institute, London, 1975

Michael Thompson, *The Medieval Hall: the Basis of Secular Domestic Life, 600–1600 AD*, Scolar Press, Aldershot, 1995

Thomas Hudson Turner, *Some Account of Domestic Architecture in England*, Parker, Oxford, 1851

John K Walton, *The English Seaside Resort, 1750–1914*, Leicester University Press, Leicester, 1983

Margaret Wood, *The English Medieval House*, Phoenix House, London, 1965

INDEX

FEATURED SITES

Aston Hall, Trinity Road, Aston, Birmingham, B6 6JD, Tel: 0121 675 4722, www.bmag.org.uk/aston-hall

Apsley House, 149 Piccadilly, Hyde Park Corner, London, W1J 7NT, Tel: 020 7499 5676, www.english-heritage.org.uk

Audley End House and Gardens, Off London Road, Saffron Walden, Essex, CB11 4JF, Tel: 01799 522842, www.english-heritage.org.uk

Beddington Zero Energy Development (bedZED), BioRegional, 24 Helios Road, Wallington, SM6 7BZ, Tel: 020 8404 4880, www.bioregional.com

Bignor Roman Villa, Bignor, nr Pulborough, West Sussex, RH20 1PH, UK, Tel/Fax: 01798 869259, www.bignorromanvilla.co.uk

Burghley House, Stamford, Lincolnshire, PE9 3JY, Tel: 01780 752 451, www.burghley.co.uk

Burlington House, Piccadilly, London, W1J 0BD, Tel: 020 7300 5614, www.burlingtonhouse.org

Butser Ancient Farm, Chalton Lane, Chalton, Waterlooville, Hants, PO8 0BG, Tel/Fax: 023 92 598838, www.butserancientfarm.co.uk

Chiswick House, Burlington Lane, Chiswick, London, W4 2RP, Tel: 020 8995 0508, www.english-heritage.org.uk

Clifton Hill House, University of Bristol, Clifton Hill House, Lower Clifton Hill, Bristol, BS8 1BX, Tel: 0117 903 5190, www.bristol.ac.uk/cliftonhillhouse

Cowdray Heritage Trust, Visitor Centre, River Ground Stables, Cowdray Park, Midhurst, West Sussex GU29 9AL, Tel: 01730 810781, www.cowdray.org.uk

Cressing Temple, Witham Road, Cressing, Braintree, Essex, CM77 8PD, Tel: 01376 584903, www.cressingtemple.org.uk

Fishbourne Roman Palace, Salthill Road, Fishbourne, Chichester, West Sussex, PO19 3QR, Tel: 01243 789829, www.sussexpast.co.uk

Gainsborough Old Hall, Parnell Street, Gainsborough, Lincolnshire, DN21 2NB, Tel: 01427 612669, Fax: 01427612779, www.gainsborougholdhall.co.uk

Goddards, Abinger Common, Dorking, Surrey RH5 6JH, Tel: 01628 825920, www.landmarktrust.org.uk

Herstmonceux Castle, Hailsham, East Sussex, BN27 1RN, Tel: 01323 833816, Fax: 01323 834499, www.herstmonceux-castle.com

Jarlshof, Shetland, ZE3 9JN, www.historic-scotland.gov.uk

Jorvik Viking Centre, Coppergate, York, YO1 9WT, Tel: 01904 615505, www.jorvik-viking-centre.co.uk

Kenwood House, Hampstead, London, NW3 7JR, Tel: 020 8348 1286, www.english-heritage.org.uk

Knap of Howar, Papa Westray, Orkney, Tel: 01856 872 044, www.historic-scotland.gov.uk

Layer Marney Tower, Layer Marney, nr Colchester, Essex, C05 9US, Tel: 01206 330 784, www.layermarneytower.co.uk

Longleat House, The Estate office, Longleat, Warminster, Wiltshire, BA12 7NW, Tel: 01985 844400, www.longleat.co.uk

Medieval Merchant's House, 58 French Street, Southampton, Hampshire, SO1 0AT, Tel: 02380 221503, www.english-heritage.org.uk

Moor Park Golf Club, Rickmansworth, Hertfordshire, WD3 1QN, Tel: 01923 773146, Fax: 01923 777109, http://www.moorparkgc.co.uk

Mousa Broch, Shetland, Tel: 01856 841815, www.historic-scotland.gov.uk

Moyse's Hall, Cornhill, Bury St Edmunds, IP33 1DX, Tel: 01284 757160, www.stedmundsbury.gov.uk

Norwich Castle, 1 Bank Plain, Norwich, Norfolk, NR2 4SF, Tel: 01603 493 625, www.museums.norfolk.gov.uk

Old Soar Manor, Old Soar Road, Kent, TN15 0QX, Tel: 01732 810378, www.english-heritage.org.uk

Parham House and Gardens, Storrington,
nr Pulborough, West Sussex, RH20 4HS,
Tel: 01903 742021, www.parhaminsussex.co.uk

Penshurst Hall, The Estate Office, Penshurst
Place, Penshurst, Tonbridge, Kent TN11 8DG,
Tel: 01892 870307, www.penshurstplace.com

Prince Consort Lodge, Kennington Park, Kennington
Park Place, Lambeth, SE11 4AS, www.lambeth.gov.uk

Royal Pavilion, Brighton, West Sussex, BN1 1EE,
Tel: 03000 290900, Fax: 03000 290908,
www.brighton-hove-rpml.org.uk/RoyalPavilion

Skara Brae, Orkney, KW16 3LR,
Tel: 01856 841815,
www.historic-scotland.gov.uk

Stokesay Castle, nr Craven Arms, Ludlow,
Shropshire, SY7 9AH, Tel: 01588 672544,
www.english-heritage.org.uk

Strangers' Hall, Charing Cross, Norwich, Norfolk,
NR2 4AL, Tel: 01603 667229,
www.museums.norfolk.gov.uk

Tudor House and Garden, Bugle Street, Southampton,
Hampshire, SO14 2AD, Tel: 023 8083 4242,
www.tudorhouseandgarden.com

The Weald & Downland Open Air Museum, Singleton,
Chichester, Sussex, PO18 0EU, Tel: 01243 811363,
www.wealddown.co.uk

West Stow Anglo-Saxon Village, The Visitor Centre,
Icklingham Road, West Stow, Bury St Edmunds,
Suffolk, IP28 6HG, Tel: 01284 728718,
www.stedmundsbury.gov.uk

Wilmington Priory, The Street, Long Man,
nr Eastbourne, East Sussex, BN26 5SW,
Tel: 01628 825920, www.landmarktrust.org.uk

Winchester Great Hall, Castle Ave, Winchester,
Hampshire, SO23 8PJ, Tel: 01962 846476,
www.hants.gov.uk/greathall

Wollaton Hall, Wollaton, Nottinghamshire,
Nottingham, NG8 2AE, Tel: 0115 915 3900,
www.nottinghamcity.gov.uk

ZEDfactory, Beddington Zero Energy Development
(bedZED), 24 Helios Road, Wallington, SM6 7BZ,
Tel: 0208 404 1380, Fax: 0208 404 2039,
www.zedfactory.com

PICTURE CREDITS

COVER IMAGE
Popular Cottage (mid-17th century) © Edward Denison, photographed with the permission of The Weald and Downland Museum

BACK COVER IMAGES LEFT TO RIGHT
Burghley House © Edward Denison, photographed with the permission of Burghley House; Albert Terrace (1820), Norwich © Edward Denison; The Alexandra and Ainsworth Estate, Camden, north London © Edward Denison

PHOTOGRAPHS OF PROPERTIES
Aston Hall pp 141, 142 (t & b), 143, 144, 149 © Edward Denison, photographed with the permission of Aston Hall; Apsley House p 189 © Edward Denison, photographed with the permission of English Heritage; Audley End pp 106-7, 114, 117, 138, 139, 145 (b), 147, 163, 182 © Edward Denison, photographed with the permission of English Heritage; Bignor Roman Villa, pp 30-1, 34-5, 43, 44 © Edward Denison, photographed with the permission of Bignor Roman Villa; Burghley House, pp 132-3, 136, 137, 145 (t), 148 (b), 150, 151, 169, 186, 256 © Edward Denison, photographed with the permission of Burghley House; Burlington House, p 173 (b) © Edward Denison, photographed with the permission of the Royal Academy of Arts; Butser Ancient Farm pp 12-13, 22-3, 24, 25, 26, 27, 28, 40, 41 © Edward Denison, photographed with the permission of Butser Ancient Farm; Chiswick House p 173 (t) © Edward Denison; Clifton Hill House pp 174, 175 © Edward Denison, photographed with the permission of Clifton Hill House; Cowdray Heritage Trust pp 127, 129, 130, 131 (t & b) © Edward Denison, photographed with the permission of Cowdray Heritage Trust; Cressing Temple pp 78, 79 © Edward Denison, photographed with the permission of Essex County Council; Fishbourne Roman Palace pp 46, 47, photo Edward Denison, photographed with the permission of Sussex Archaeological Society, © Fishbourne Roman Palace; Gainsborough Old Hall pp 94, 95 (t & b) © Rich@Hines-Images; Goddards pp 249, 257, 258 (t & b), 259 (t & b), 260, 263 © Edward Denison, photographed with the permission of The Landmark Trust; Herstmonceux Castle pp 120-1 © Edward Denison, photographed with the permission of Herstomonceux Castle; Kenwood House p 188 © Edward Denison, photographed with the permission of English Heritage; Layer Marney Tower pp 156-7 © Edward Denison, photographed with the permission of Layer Marney; Longleat House pp 109, 116, 134 © Edward Denison, photographed with the permission of Longleat; Medieval Merchant's House p 103 © Edward Denison, photographed with the permission of English Heritage; Moor Park Golf Club pp 177, 184 (t & b), 185 © Edward Denison, photographed with the permission of Moor Park Golf Club; Moyse's Hall p 75 © Edward Denison, photographed with the permission of Moyse's Hall Museum; Norwich Castle, p 70 (t & b) © Edward Denison, photographed with the permission of Norwich Museums; Old Soar Manor pp 82, 83 (t), 288-9 © Edward Denison, photographed with the permission of English Heritage; Parham House and Gardens p 148 (t) © Edward Denison, photographed with the permission of Parham House; Penshurst Hall p 84 © Edward Denison, photographed with the permission of Penshurst Place; Prince Consort Lodge p 235 © Edward Denison, photographed with the permission of Lambeth Council; p 60 Musée de la Tapisserie de Bayeux © Edward Denison, photographed with the permission of Reading Museum; Royal Pavilion pp 180-1 © Edward Denison; Stokesay Castle pp 85, 86-7, 88, 89 (t & b), 90, 91 © Edward Denison, photographed with the permission of English Heritage; Strangers' Hall pp 153 (t & b), 154, 179 © Edward Denison, photographed with the permission of Norfolk Museums & Archaeology Service; Tudor House and Garden p 161 © Edward Denison, photographed with the permission of Southampton City Council; The Weald & Downland Open Air Museum pp 80, 96, 97, 98, 99, 101, 102, 155 (l & r) © Edward Denison, photographed with the permission of The Weald and Downland Museum; West Stow Anglo- Saxon Village pp 2, 48-9, 53, 54-5 © Edward Denison, photographed with the permission of West Stow Anglo Saxon Village; Wilmington Priory p 83 (b) © Edward Denison, photographed with the permission of The Landmark Trust; Winchester Great Hall p 76 © Edward Denison, photographed with the permission of Hampshire County Council; Wollaton Hall pp 8-9, 140, 146 © Edward Denison, photographed with the permission of Wollaton Hall; BedZED pp 283, 284, 285, 287 © Edward Denison, photographed with the permission of BioRegional.

NEW HAND-DRAWN ILLUSTRATIONS AND PLANS BY GUANG YU REN
pp 6, 7, 15, 16, 17, 19, 21, 24, 26, 42, 45, 52, 61, 74, 77, 78, 80, 81, 82, 84, 90, 93, 94, 96, 118, 123, 124, 126 , 128, 134, 135, 136, 139, 140, 141, 143, 154, 161, 167, 170, 171, 175, 182, 194, 195, 196, 210, 213, 215, 232, 233, 235, 238, 240, 242, 243, 244, 245, 246, 247, 248, 250, 253, 254, 255, 257, 268, 269, 274, 275, 278 © Guang Yu Ren, 2011

STREET-VIEW PHOTOGRAPHS OF PROPERTIES TAKEN BY EDWARD DENISON
pp 105 (t & b), 164-5, 193, 194, 197, 199, 200, 201, 203, 204, 205, 206, 207, 208-209, 210, 211, 212, 213, 214, 215, 216, 217, 219, 220-221, 224, 225, 227, 231, 237, 238, 242, 243, 244, 245, 246, 247, 266-265, 270, 271, 272, 273, 274, 276-7, 278, 279, 280-1 © Edward Denison

HISTORICAL EVENT

Date	Event
1642	Start of the English Civil War
1662	Birth of Nicholas Hawksmoor
1664	Birth of John Vanbrugh
1666	Great Fire of London
1685	Birth of William Kent
1688	The Glorious Revolution
1707	Act of Union (between England and Scotland)
1711	Completion of St Paul's Cathedral
1723	Birth of William Chambers
1728	Birth of Robert Adam
1732	Birth of James Adam
1752	Birth of John Nash
1753	Birth of John Soane
1781	Completion of Ironbridge, Shropshire
1790	Act of Union (between the Kingdom of

TYPE OF HOME

1635	Completion of Aston Hall, Warwickshire
1638	Completion of Broome Park, Kent
1638	Completion of Swakeleys, London
mid-1600s	First terrace houses in London
1662	Completion of Coleshill, Warwickshire
1707	Completion of Chatsworth House, Derbyshire
1712	Completion of Castle Howard, Yorkshire
1718	Completion of Burlington House, London
1720	Reconfiguration of Moor Park, Hertfordshire
1724	Completion of Blenheim Palace, Oxfordshire
1725	Completion of Wentworth Woodhouse, Yorkshire
1728	Completion of Seaton Delaval Hall, Northumberland
1729	Completion of Chiswick House, London
1729	Completion of Marble Hill, London
1730s	Completion of Houghton Hall, Norfolk
1736	Completion of Queen Square, Bath
1750	Completion of Clifton Hill House, Bristol
1754	Completion of Wrotham Park, Hertfordshire
1764	Completion of Holkham Hall, Norfolk
1766	Completion of Danson House, London
1766	James Craig wins competition to design Edinburgh New Town
1767	Completion of King's Circus, Bath
1775	Completion of The Royal Crescent, Bath
1776	Completion of Strawberry Hill, London
1778	Completion of Apsley House, London
1779	Completion of Kenwood House, London
1781	Completion of Berrington Hall, Herefordshire
1783	Completion of north side of Bedford Square, London
1790	Completion of the Crescent, Buxton, Derbyshire

1724 Blenheim Palace, Oxfordshire

1775 The Royal Crescent, Bath

1635 Aston Hall, Warwickshire

1729 Chiswick House, London

1778 Apsley House, London